Out of Hand in a Foreign Land

Stephen Koral

Stephen Koral
Out of Hand in a Foreign Land
© 2020, Stephen Koral
Self-published

ISBN: 9798697716540

Thanks to Mel, Mum & Dad, Robbie Birchall, Jen Hulse & Richard Lees, for their help on putting this book together.

Thanks to Chris Burrows for the cover design.

Thanks to Asbjørn Vedsted, Mark Candey, Jason Seaton-Stewart & all the travellers I've met on the road who kept me going.

Dedicated to Samuel John Percival. Rest in peace Grandad.

AUTHOR'S NOTE

Everyone has a book in them, as the old adage goes. I've been travel writing for well over a decade now, crimping out online blogs as I slowly complete my target of visiting one hundred countries before I kick the bucket. Putting a book together felt like the next step, especially after the wild ride that started in 2013, leaving me with a story I thought was worth telling. I've had a lot of fun writing this, but at the very least, I am hoping it inspires others to get out there, beyond the usual holiday destinations, and see the brilliant world we live in (hopefully doing it better than I did here!).

The book is split into two distinct halves; it starts off with my carefree time backpacking around Asia, and then my frightening experiences with Indonesia's law, corruption and prisons from chapter eight onwards. I know liberties are sometimes taken when writing accounts like this for ease of storytelling, but I decided to keep this as true to life as possible, using the actual timeline, and whenever possible I kept the names of those I encountered on the road. The people mentioned in the prison later in the book, notorious or otherwise, have kept their real names, giving you the option to further read into the interesting stories that crossed paths with mine. Some names and other details have had to change, mainly to avoid any potential legal issues down the road.

'If you think adventure is dangerous, try routine. It is lethal.''

– Paulo Coelho

Chapter One

Try not to get stabbed

New Delhi, India – Midnight, 25th January 2013

Getting into a car with a stranger on your own at night, in a foreign country, is something I would usually advise against, but desperate times called for desperate measures. I'd only met this particular stranger, a middle-aged Indian man, a few minutes ago at New Delhi's international airport. His English was pretty good, not to mention he was smartly dressed, but trying to gauge his trustworthiness off these was not much to go off. A couple of days ago, I managed to upset a group of men who were currently on the way to the airport to kick the shit out of me. Arriving eighteen hours before my flight, I'd banked on being able to get through airport security and run the clock out by the gate – crying in a corner, of course – but safe. Much to my dismay, I'd only just learned that you aren't even allowed to enter the building if you arrive too early for your flight at New Delhi international. Overhearing my frustration with the security guards at the airport entrance who wouldn't let me through, the stranger seemingly approached from nowhere and introduced himself as Ayaan, and said I could stay at his place for a few hours, returning me here in the morning. He claimed he had just dropped his uncle off at departures and was about to head home. Panicked, and with no other apparent options other than hiding in a bush I noticed by the airport entrance, I reluctantly agreed. I loaded my backpack into the boot and got onto the car's back seat.

"I look forward to hosting you tonight, sir," Ayaan began and asked what my name was and what I was doing in the country. I explained I had come here for a ten-day holiday with my friend to experience India for the first time and to see the Taj Mahal. Thinking it was for the best, I left out the part where there was a group of men currently hunting me down. I suspected he knew something was up by my nervous demeanour, but he didn't question it. He did ask where my friend had gone, and I said he was now on a flight out of here and heading to a different country.

The car drove through the airport grounds, but instead of taking the exit, Ayaan pulled up around the rear of the airport, and to my surprise, several other Indian men jumped into the car either side of me, wedging me into the rear seat. Had I known there would be other strangers joining us on this ride, I would have politely declined Ayaan's offer and taken my chances waiting at the airport. Who are these chaps, then? They began to talk to each other in Hindi, apart from learning 'thank you' a few days back, I didn't understand a word of what they were saying. They could have been talking about what they had for dinner tonight, or perhaps where they were taking their new lanky hostage. We drove away from the airport, four Indian men and me, crammed into an old *Hindustan Contessa*. I could just about see the lights of the airport getting smaller and smaller in the rear-view mirror. I was heading into New Delhi, *back* to the place I was trying to get away from.

None of Ayaan's buddies addressed me, and after the initial conversation passed between themselves, we all sat in silence. The potential severity of this situation had begun to hit me. India had a rough edge to it compared to other developing countries I had visited previously. Sure, it wasn't like it was Somalia here, and no harm had come to me. Yet. But there were little events throughout my time here that had cropped up, reminding me just to be that extra bit careful. These events had included people appearing out of bushes suddenly and walking closely alongside as a possible mugging attempt, and later having a man pull a knife out and unsettlingly stare at me from across the street. Even the monkeys in the street weren't beyond banging the doors to try and get into my apartment. I had been warned to avoid the streets after dark and hadn't been to many places with that kind of stark instruction before. It was pitch black outside right now.

I weighed up my options, and they had boiled down to two. One: Ride this out and see where they take me, hoping this a genuine offer of somewhere to stay with this group of weirdly quiet Indian lads. Or Two: Assume that I might now be in the process of being abducted, therefore need to roll over the guy on my left, throw a punch if necessary, bail out of the car, run as fast as my legs would allow, and forget about my backpack. Then, probably walk back and hide in that bush by the airport entrance I mentioned earlier. Thinking about it, my passport may have been in the boot with my backpack. Okay – so if I go with Option Two, I could be stuck here without a passport. My heart began pounding, playing out in my head what I would do if things started to go badly, worrying that I can't really throw a proper punch either. Fifteen minutes passed, and the silence continued as the car rolled into a residential area. I could have been anywhere in Delhi now. We crawled to an unlit dirt road, and then down into an alleyway. An alleyway! This is it; I'm definitely being abducted! My fists clenched and adrenaline pumped, not that it would be much good for anything – I'd sort of decided in my head already that I'd be taking Option One, just for being too much of a fanny to start a fight to escape from the car.

There were hardly any people out in the streets, which in itself was a cause for alarm. I had grown accustomed to seeing at least some people around at all hours, so this quiet part of the city they were taking me to seemed out of the way. The car pulled into the driveway of a small white building, which stood in good condition compared to the state of the neighbours' dilapidated houses. Abducting foreigners clearly brought in some money for these guys. I glanced around to see if there were any notable landmarks in case I needed it for my escape route later, but there was nothing other than more houses, plus it was hard to see much in the night anyway. The men spoke Hindi among themselves, breaking the silence, then got out of the car, walked to the boot, and began shuffling stuff around inside. A rope and a gag for me, no doubt! I sat there not sure what to do with myself whilst Ayaan opened his glove box and began fumbling around. I then saw Ayaan's mates walk away, which I thought was a weird thing to do in an abduction. Ayaan got out of the car, took my backpack out of the boot and asked me to follow him into the white building.

A small child ran out of the door and hugged Ayaan as we approached. I anxiously continued inside the building with him, and to my relief, a small family was sat there in a proper house, round a television and a fire stove. Relief came as I began to realise that this probably wasn't an abduction, and likely those guys were only getting a lift into the city. I started to feel guilty for doubting the kindness of someone who gave me help when I needed it. He still asked me to pay £10 in the equivalent Rupees to sit in his living room for a few hours, but that's beside the point. I was safe. I sat myself down on a chair whilst Ayaan's kids played by my feet, and for a moment felt relieved I had evaded the wrath of the men out to get me, for now at least. I still had to make it to the airport and through to the true safety point past the security checks in a few hours, but if even I didn't know where I was, there was no chance anyone else would find me. I looked at my phone, and there were sixty-two missed calls, all from the pursuers. I switched it off to try and get some peace, and possibly even some sleep.

All this trouble had only begun a couple of days ago. Prior to this, it had been a fun little trip, away with my friend Liggy, having decided on a ten-day trip to see India's capital together. I had known Liggy for several years, meeting him in the heady days of college, doing absolutely no work in favour of skiving off to get drunk. Travelling with him is always advantageous – we'd sometimes egg each other on and end up getting into trouble, but quite frankly, he's built like a tank, and his size had pulled us out of trouble more than once. Above all though he's always a great laugh to go away with. He had grown bored with his life in England, so he had saved up over the past couple of years and bought a one-way ticket to Asia. His plan being to have months of doing whatever he liked, and when finances started to get low, he was going to settle down in Australia and look for a job. I had only just come out of a five-year relationship, so I was looking for something different, and with nothing else better to do decided to join him for a few days. Whether I wanted to make a big trip like his was still up in the air. I had already been lucky enough to go backpacking in 2008, so I had arguably fulfilled my travelling quota for one lifetime, and I would be leaving a good job this time if I left to do it again. Ten days with him in India was effectively my time to decide if I was going to join him in the near future. If I decided to travel, after I returned home, I was going to quit my job, tie up loose ends and then buy myself a one-way ticket, too.

After a bit of consideration where the short trip together would be, we settled on India, and it was my personal choice for a few reasons. It was a completely new country for us both, which always has an appeal. Then, there's the item on most people's bucket list: Seeing the Taj Mahal, one of the most famous buildings in the entire world. Another tick for India was I knew a local who was currently living in New Delhi, a girl named Riya, and I swear by seeing a place with someone from there makes all the difference. Finally, Indian food. My all-time favourite. A chance to eat the real thing was more than reason enough. For me, it was a no brainer. Liggy on the other hand, ever the cultured traveller who just wanted to get the beaches of Thailand, was slightly apprehensive about India for reasons he never really elaborated on other than "It will probably stink of shit there", and he needed a bit of persuasion to visit the country.

We touched down early morning in New Delhi with a mix of excitement and drunkenness, having quaffed whiskey the entire flight. As I had nipped to the toilet during the flight, Liggy had taken the opportunity to deface my filled-out immigration card with a crude drawing of a jizzing penis. To my horror, I only realised this just as I handed the card to the immigration officer and I had to go through an awkward moment explaining it was a crass joke, which he didn't find amusing. Riya was waiting for us at arrivals clearly dressed up to impress. It had been almost five years since we saw each other last and as we'd only spoke occasionally online, there was a brief awkwardness seeing each other in person again. We hugged, and I introduced her to Liggy and told her about the dick on my landing card. She thought it was great. I don't think I could ever truly be friends with anyone who wouldn't find an immature prank like that funny. I had initially met her out in Thailand on my first backpacking stint. She was my age, and a native from India's far east state of Manipur but had relocated to New Delhi to go to university there. Manipur being over a thousand miles away from where we were now, Riya herself in her own words said she looked more Chinese than the stereotypical Indian (This often made her a subject of prejudice, locals from New Delhi sometimes attach a certain stigma to the Chinese). English was her primary language as it's prominent in Manipur, but additionally, she spoke Hindi and a few other local dialects. She'd gone the extra mile and organised a place for us to stay in New Delhi's trendy Haus Khaz district.

The brilliant thing about travelling – for me at least – is what would be considered mundane for the locals is interesting for me because it's an entirely different take on the way people live their lives. Not long even after leaving the airport the fun started; winding little alleyways crammed with people carrying stuff on their heads - some wearing humble rags; masses of rickshaws and bikes; whole thick nests of electrical wiring above signposts in a language I had never seen before. But, being in India, there are the outright weird things which appeared unique to the country, which are probably still mundane to the locals. I had soon seen an old man with no pants on openly urinating in the middle of the street who was causing a huge traffic jam on one side of the road, and at the same time in the other lane, a man was riding a decorated elephant. There appeared to be a significant number of loose cattle just rummaging around unhindered through the endless mounds of litter (Cows are protected in the country's widespread Hindu beliefs that they're sacred. Beef is hard to come by, *McDonald's* doesn't even sell it, and there are even groups of "cow vigilantes" that go around beating anyone up that hurts, or eats cows!). It didn't matter that I'd missed a night of sleep or drank half a bottle of whiskey on the flight over, tiredness could take a back seat as I looked on at all the bustling activity outside.

"You guys look tired" began Riya. "If you want, we can stock up on alcohol for tonight and then get you guys checked into your place. Oh, by the way, you're staying at my friend's place that he usually rents out. His name is Niraj, super cool guy".

"Wait, we're drinking tonight?" I wanted to be certain.

"Sure, why not?" Alcohol had been mentioned at seven in the morning, it sounded like it was going to be a fun trip. I forgot Riya enjoyed a drink or ten.

Hauz Khas is a curious part of south New Delhi. Considered an affluent district that caters to the city's hipsters, there lies a multitude of apartments and restaurants, trendy cafes and art-shops. The buildings are up to three stories high and compacted together, in a series of alleyways bridged by thick electrical cabling overhead. Roughly an entire third of Hauz Khas belongs to a vast historic park, and within that, a lake and several ancient red-brick structures, along with a colossal fortress style wall which lay across some of the park's border. Whilst this is still just a public park, seeing all these exotic structures with monkeys running around was a reminder that I was now thousands of miles away from home. The balcony of our apartment bordered this park, and the overlooking view was incredible. There was an early morning haze across the horizon, and even though it was pretty chilly, as New Delhi gets a little cold in January, students were sat on the grass enjoying the crisp morning.

As well as an outstanding view of the park, the apartment was of a decent enough standard inside to keep Liggy and me happy, including a proper Western-style toilet (not one where we had to squat) and a comfy bed. The only real downside was there was only one bed that I had to share with Liggy, I was well aware that he doesn't like to sleep with clothes on. Some might call me a prude, I honestly wouldn't mind were it not for the considerable morning erections he has, either enough to jab my leg or create a single-pole tent out of the bedsheets. We sat for a morning coffee on our balcony with Niraj who gave us a rundown on the dos and don'ts of India. Riya looked a little sad as we were *her* guests, and Niraj was doing her job with the induction. The main rules were: Avoid the streets after dark (even in this relatively safer part of the city), it's imperative to keep your wits about you even in the daylight and avoid drinking the tap water.

It was good to see Riya and Liggy clicked immediately. To their credit though, they are both the sort of people who have bags of charisma. Over coffee we formed a rough plan, which was to have a little mooch around to get a feel for the immediate area, maybe get some food, and as the afternoon rolled on, head to Riya's. There we'd have a couple of whiskeys and then have an early night, ready to hit India head-on tomorrow. Riya's place was about five minutes on foot from our room, which she led the way on after we'd said bye to Niraj. I hadn't been to Asia for a few years and was thoroughly loving walking around the foreign environment again. I couldn't help noticing the use swastikas above several doorways which looked striking to see at first – the symbol originated from this part of the world, and the meaning here is of peace and divinity. The Nazis stole it and used it as a symbol for their atrocities. I have seen petitions back home from people who wish to "reclaim" the symbol for its original meaning, but coming from my European perspective seeing the symbol here, I think it's unlikely it'll ever be able to break the links that it has today.

We turned down several dusty alleyways, each getting increasingly narrower to the point it blocked most of the sun out, almost making it cold. Stopping at a large metal gate tucked away, we could see through it a small indoor car park with stairs leading up to Riya's apartment. At the bottom of the stairs, I noticed there was what I assumed was a family; mum holding a baby, dad, and a young boy. They sat there with a few cooking utensils across the floor and clothes hanging out to dry. They appeared shy but still managed a little smile for us as we passed them. They were actual tenants of the car park. Riya said they essentially pay rent by guarding the cars at night, and in return, they get to live with relative shelter under the staircase. From what I'd seen so far in terms of poverty in the city, I guess it wasn't too bad of a setup. I'd already seen many homeless people sleeping rough on the streets without a pot to piss in.

Riya's apartment was basic, but apart from the classic Asian squat toilet and traditional tribal Manipuri decor, it could have been a cheap apartment anywhere in England. I did, however, notice a huge crack along the wall in the living room, and as ever inquisitive as I am, learned from Riya that this third floor used to be the top floor of the building. Apparently, planning permission isn't really a thing here, so one day the landlord decided they were going to get another two floors above them. That was fine until there was an earthquake in the city some months ago, then these huge cracks started to appear along the walls.

"Is it sturdy?" I said with some alarm as knowing my luck there would be some record-breaking earthquake on my visit.

"I guess not" she replied as the seal of a bottle of *Johnnie Walker* cracked "but I reckon it's got another good couple of earthquakes left in it yet. It'll hold out for your visit, don't worry". *Johnnie Walker,* and by extent all whiskey is loved here, as much as I can say from my experience at least. I read that India consumes more whiskey than any other country, three times more than second place, and is one of the biggest importers of Scotch whiskey. They love it. I love it too, so upon learning this, it felt kind of apt that we'd been downing large amounts on the plane over. It was some time near midnight as I realised we were about to open our third bottle, as the three of us stayed up chatting shit, having a great time. So much for this early night. I hadn't slept in two days, and with all the whiskey floating around in my system, I was completely off my tits.

I woke up late morning, finding myself on a sofa bed next to Riya. My head was spinning. I was still tired, yet jet lag was over-riding my need for sleep, forcing me awake. I wasn't really sure what had gone on towards the end of the night. I was pretty sure me and Riya had slept together at least once though but couldn't remember what had happened to Liggy whilst this was going on. I sat on the end of the bed for a moment to gather my thoughts and noticed she was still asleep. Careful not to wake her up as I got up, I tiptoed through the empty bottles and pizza boxes from a few hours ago. We'd had a drunk kiss sometime before bed, and then more later, and wondered if it was going to be awkward when she woke up. I couldn't see Liggy anywhere in the apartment, which was a little alarming. Maybe he had gone home at some point in the night, but I'd be surprised if he managed to navigate home in the drunken state we were all in. I left the apartment and said a 'Hello' to the car park family cooking food on a little stove. I was slightly dazed walking through the winding alleyways of Hauz Khas and even more so once I got onto the main street. The sun, although not particularly hot again today, was still bright enough to amplify my hangover to the point I recoiled like some sort of vampiric creature once I stepped out into it. Through the busy streets, I just about managed to find my route back to the apartment, only to see Liggy asleep in a foetal position by the front door using his shoes as a pillow. I had the key to our apartment in my pocket.

Liggy, Riya and myself enjoyed the following days together, visiting the main tourist spots of the city, eating at little restaurants or just walking around seeing stuff that wasn't necessarily on the tourist "to do" list. We left the plans entirely up to Riya who fit right in with Liggy and me. It was like the three of us had been friends for years – mainly because she was always keen for a drink. We didn't directly address the first night on her sofa bed, but as drunk as she was, she definitely remembered the spot of goosing we'd done before we slept, and it had fired up some ongoing flirting between each other.

Riya's parents had flown over from Manipur on a connecting flight out of New Delhi and were staying for a few days at Riya's place. We were invited over for dinner in the evening, me and Liggy arrived at 7 PM promptly, ready for a feed. We had purposely not eaten much throughout the day, so we'd be up for eating lots of the traditional food from Manipur that they were cooking up for us. There was particular excitement because the Naga chilli comes from their region, and we both love spicy food. Entering Riya's apartment, I could see the food was already prepared, little pots on the table covered in cling-film. I couldn't quite work out what was there underneath all of the plastic, but I was hungry and couldn't wait to find out. Her parents were already sat down in the living room waiting for us, both well dressed and in their late fifties. I was a little anxious, I suppose, as I'd never really spent any significant length of time with someone of their age who weren't from my part of the world. I didn't know what to expect. Would we have little common ground? Would they be a bit uptight? Would the culture difference be too much? Worst of all, would we have to be on our best behaviour for the whole night? Everybody shook hands and introduced themselves, Riya almost acting like an intermediary between the two parties. The parents having only arrived an hour before us had left an open suitcase in the middle of the living room, filled with goods that they had brought over from Manipur. I watched with curiosity as her dad put on washing-up gloves to begin unpacking some of the contents of the suitcase. As he rummaged around, I glanced at her mum, and she smiled at me and nodded. He first pulled out two bottles of *Johnnie Walker* and put them to the side, then continued to bring out a parcel that had been wrapped in newspaper, and after some struggle getting the elastic bands around it removed, he pulled out several bright red Naga chillies that just looked like they'd be crazily hot to eat. I reckon if we turned the lights off, they would have glowed in the dark.

"These, gentlemen" he began "are the final piece of tonight's dinner!" Then he scurried off into the kitchen and came back with five glasses. "I hope you like whiskey!"

An interesting fact about Indian culture that I didn't know, which sits in stark contrast to when we have guests over in England, is out here they eat as a way to signal to guests that after the meal it's time for you to leave. In England, when we have guests over for dinner, say at 7 PM, you'd maybe eat at 7.30, continuing with drinks once the food has gone, and guests would leave any time thereafter. Well, as it ended up being such a good night with the five of us, and Riya's parents were actually quite amusing, we ended up eating at 2 AM. I didn't realise all this until a few days later, but at the time I was just sat there watching the food go cold, feeling my stomach digest itself. By midnight, I'd kind of lost my appetite as I'd filled up on alcohol. It's a polite way to tell your guests that you want them to leave, but when we ended up eating cold food that had been sat there for hours, I think I much prefer how we do it in England (it was the first time I'd eaten bamboo as well, which had an aroma of dog breath – avoid!). Her parents were interested in us, and what we were doing out here, they were fairly Westernised in their outlook in life. Ultimately, I was surprised by how well we all got on. The Naga chilli was brutal as well, half a single chilli was hot enough for a meal of five.

Riya was due to meet her sister from the far north-west state of Punjab, and escort her back to Delhi with a hired taxi driver. Her folks were here on such a long layover in Delhi before their onward flight because they were all planning a family reunion the following day. Riya asked Liggy and me if we wanted to join picking her up, warning us it would take a full day to make the trip, the state being so far away that it bordered Pakistan. We were lost without Riya who had organised our entire itinerary, so it seemed joining her would be a bit of an adventure compared to wasting the day in Delhi. Delhi was perhaps a little on the dusty side, so getting into the countryside came as a welcome break from the dust and traffic pollution. As frenzied as the city was, it was worse in the countryside. I got out of the car for a quick wee and was chased down the road by a gang of monkeys; they were either threatened by me being in their territory or wanted some of that tiny white banana popping out of my shorts. The rest stops in poor rural villages always became a small drama too, as we were swamped by locals who simply don't see white tourists around these remote parts. We were mostly greeted by curious natives of said villages, which would quickly form into crowds of hundreds of people, escalating into unsettling events. Riya kept her cool and would yank us out of the rabble when it got too much. Whilst I am always keen on meeting the locals, I prefer doing so with no more than a handful a time; otherwise, it starts to get too overwhelming, so these mass crowds pushing towards us here wasn't my cup of tea. I wasn't aware that some of the rural Indians believe touching white skin gives them good luck, which explained the old men that kept reaching out to rub my arms from behind. It was harmless, I guess, but unsettling and weird. One young lad was so keen to talk to us he came bouncing over and wanted to practice his English. I would have been fine having a chat with him under normal circumstances; however his gums were bleeding so severely that his teeth were red, and as he spoke, little flecks of blood came out, not quite reaching us but landing by our feet.

"I'm putting my sunglasses on to stop it getting in my eyes if we're talking to this guy", Liggy muttered to me, "I'm not being the first guy in the world who caught AIDS from a conversation".

I half expected to be caught out by needing the toilet on the journey, because if it's going to strike, sod's law says it'll be when you're on a road trip with no toilet around. We were two thirds into the holiday, and among the various stories I'd heard prior to my visit, the one that people were always sure to mention was the unavoidable super-diarrhoea. I had so far eluded *Delhi belly* by ensuring to wash my hands thoroughly and being careful about what I ate.

During our second road trip the following day, now en route to the Taj Mahal and still feeling fine inside, I was smugly confident I would avoid the squits entirely. Whilst the toilet worries were on the back burner, India, on the whole, had been fun, but ultimately exhausting. The relentless traffic, thick air pollution, wild animals wandering around, and having to be extra careful of the dodgy people on the streets were constant concerns. New Delhi in particular isn't somewhere I'd recommend for a relaxing getaway. Liggy was feeling it a bit as well, manifesting in him being uncharacteristically quiet. I couldn't complain as I'd come here for a different experience, but just being in such a frenetic country had zapped my energy. Admiring the early morning sunrise on the route to the Taj Mahal, feeling a bit tired and shitty, I looked around and without the large crowds of people at this time in the morning, for a moment the city caught me out. I was thinking maybe it's not so bad here after all, sat admiring the beauty of the sunrise out of the window of our taxi – only to have the view ruined by seeing an elderly man squatting in the middle of a street filled with litter, having a massive runny shit. The Taj Mahal was our chance for a break from the streets at least, to have a bit of peace and to experience one of the *Seven Wonders of the World*. Riya had never visited it before either, which I thought peculiar as she had lived in New Delhi for some time now. That said, there's plenty of places in my own country that I haven't been to. I guess people are more inclined to see a bit of the world if they can, and not necessarily what's in their own back yard.

And there it was. Sudden gurgling cramps in my stomach. The urgent need for a shite. *Delhi Belly* decided to strike mid-way through to the Taj Mahal, which is a three hour journey to get there, passing through mostly rural areas without anywhere to go. I asked Riya to please inform the taxi driver he needs to take us to a 'Western toilet' as I had never used a squat toilet before and didn't think right now was the time to start. The driver spoke back in Hindi, and Riya translated that there weren't toilets nearby except for an upcoming restaurant he knew of. I said it'll do. Liggy started saying he needed the bathroom as well; It dawned on Riya it was probably the questionable tea we'd been given by a street vendor in the Punjab yesterday that she insisted we try. It was a delicious chai red tea, but had most likely been brewed with tap water. Tap water is borderline lethal for those that haven't developed a tolerance to germs here, with travel advice putting emphasis on ensuring you don't even get any in your mouth whilst showering. At least I wasn't struggling alone, although Riya was fine, Liggy was in the same boat.

The urgency increased by the second, this was forming into top tier bum squirts. The taxi pulled up by a small whitewashed concrete building in what felt like the middle of nowhere, I was out of the car before it even entirely stopped, armed with my trusty roll of toilet paper that on all trips out of the apartment had either been taken as the whole thing or a few sheets in my back pocket 'just in case'. I ran into the restaurant, consisting of nothing more than a single room with a small stove in one corner, and dotted around with a few tables and chairs made from pallets. The restaurant staff informed me in broken English that there was no toilet inside the building, but there was through the doorway leading to outside at the back. I continued through, and to my horror, a tiny wooden outhouse sat by itself without a door, in a vast dusty expanse. Upon closer inspection, it was the loosest definition of the word 'toilet' I had ever seen. It was literally a hole in the dirt, filled with shit. I weighed it up for a few seconds, bog roll in hand, stomach gurgling away, sweat forming on my forehead. I may have attempted using it, but as there was no door, it left me exposed to three guys stood at the back of the restaurant who had purposely left the building to watch me with grins on their faces. I decided I could give it another five minutes so waddled back over to the car and the search continued. I don't believe in miracles, but suddenly seeing a hotel further along the road, which also offered a proper sit-down toilet to use was indeed one. It seemed out of place for a rather large hotel (I initially thought it was a mirage brought on from feverishly needing a shit). There was nothing else around for miles, but there it was, a beautiful hotel in the sticks with proper toilets. I could hear Liggy in pain in the next cubicle as I struggled away myself. It was a pretty bad start to the day. Anyway – enough shit talk, for now at least, let's get onto the Taj Mahal.

The Taj Mahal sits in the northern Indian city of Agra, and whilst noticeably smaller on the map than New Delhi, it was just as full-on there. A mass of rickshaws, motorbikes, people, all moving underneath the same thick electrical wiring and heavily polluted air. It left me a little disappointed as I was hoping for a break, not more of the same. I picked up on a police car tailing us for several streets upon entering downtown Agra. They pulled our car over not long after, stating there was an issue which they were vague about. We sat at the side of the road for twenty minutes before an agreement was reached where we had to pay around £2 in Rupees for the problem to go away. Riya said it was likely the police had spotted two white guys in a car and saw a bribe opportunity, which I thought was mental that they were allowed to do that. India ramped up its intensity once in the car park to the Taj Mahal entrance. There were hundreds of people pushing around, sellers trying to sell their wares. Noise, music, smoke - even the monkeys who were usually everywhere on the pavements had decided they were better off up in the trees rather than being down here. The sellers were primed and shot up from the floor once they saw Liggy and me approaching the entrance on foot. They started shoving things like carved wooden elephants in our faces or tried putting large necklaces on us. We pushed through the crowds, taking all our energy to get through it all, and finally to the entrance. I will admit, with everything that had gone on today, my first ever experience of corrupt police, the bad stomach and even the stress of getting here from the car park, I wasn't in the best of moods. But once we entered the premises and saw the Taj Majal, the tranquillity washed over me. It truly was peaceful. It was hard to imagine literally over a wall was the everyday hectic of India, whilst we were here in these serene grounds looking through the haze at a massive iconic building. It was honestly impressive, it had such a calm aurora about it, although this could be because anything is calmer compared to directly outside the grounds here. I've been to calmer drum and bass raves than what was going on over that wall.

I could just about overhear from a nearby guide of a tour group that the structure itself was built in 1632 by an emperor called Shah Jahan as a gesture of love to one woman, his third wife (I bet the first and second were jealous!) and it took ten years to build whilst nearly bankrupting the ruling empire at the time. These days, it's not in a good way due to lack of maintenance and investment, and as the nearby Yamuna river it sits on depletes through human overuse, the building itself is slowly sinking into the mud. It might not be here in a few decades if things continue the way they do! For the present, though, it was nice to appreciate and enjoy.

Whilst I was having a moment in awe of the building, Riya, possibly deciding that being here was the optimal time of romance, grabbed my hand and said she wanted to take things further between us. Then she followed it with a sentence of utter madness. She told me that just before my arrival, she was already contemplating a split with her boyfriend, and so she decided to end it over a phone call last night. To really get at him for pissing her off over the years, she told him she was in love with an English guy she'd met, about the shenanigans from my first night here and that I was still here in India. I didn't really know what to say, apart from utter the word 'What'. I fancied her a bit, and the flirting I'd been doing was intentional, but even if I did think there was any way things could continuing after this trip, this was not the way to go about it.

Things started to unravel when we got back to Delhi. I learned from her that the boyfriend was understandably upset, and was coming to find us both with a few of his mates for "a talk". Luckily, he was currently in Mumbai, as the two cities are far apart it would take him a day or so to get up here. I searched for his name on *Facebook*, and he looked like a massive dirty great meathead who took martial arts as a hobby. Worse still, he had Riya's old phone with my number saved on it, which I've had for years – from when I first met Riya in Thailand. He started to call me repetitively. I was miffed that Riya's attitude had changed, she'd done all that flirting, and we'd goosed on my first night, but now it seemed like I was increasingly being used to get at her ex-fella. By the last full day, I had managed to evade him, even though he was now in Haus Khas with several lads, but Riya said they were just getting more annoyed by not finding me, warning that the lads knew Niraj and were more than likely aware I was at the apartment. I read a couple of the text messages I received from various numbers, general threats and intimidation. "We are coming for you!". I texted one of the numbers back saying I didn't know Riya was seeing someone, but that just increased the abuse. The trip had started to get a bit weird and scary, Liggy said he thought the whole situation was really funny.

Liggy had his onward flight to Thailand, which was eighteen hours before my flight back home. This meant I'd have to wait alone in the apartment overnight, which didn't appeal to me at all. We decided to go to the airport at the same time, and although I would be waiting for ages for my flight, preferably at the safety there than in the city by myself. When we realised I wasn't getting through security at the airport, I said to Liggy not to miss his flight because of this stupid situation I had gotten myself into, and he should go off ahead of me. He took no convincing to go, and his parting words were: "Try not to get stabbed".

So that, my friends, is how I ended up in this situation. Frightened and alone, and a bit hungry as well, with a group of angry lads after me in a foreign country.

My only friend around being a 45-year-old Indian man which I had only known for an hour, half the time of which was spent thinking he was abducting me. I'd been in some situations over the years abroad, but this was something else. Ayaan came into the room and asked if I wanted a cup of tea. Hearing his voice startled me a little, I realised I must have been in a light sleep. I switched my phone on and saw what time it was, 5 AM! I could risk getting into the airport now with the bit of darkness we still had left. Stuff your tea mate, get me out of here! Apart from the darkness, another thing working in my favour was that New Delhi's airport has three terminals. I wasn't flying directly back to Manchester either, but connecting via Helsinki, which would definitely throw anyone who was looking for a direct flight to England. The irate Indians knew I was leaving this morning again thanks to Riya who appeared to be set on making my escape as difficult as possible, but other than that it was a lot of area to cover and they would have to get lucky to spot me. Telling myself this didn't do much for my nerves, though.

There was minimal traffic at this time of the morning, and the drive back to the airport didn't take long. I was mildly amused to see the spot of road that on the way here a few hours ago I had made my decision not to punch Ayaan's mate's head in and run away from the car. As we pulled up outside departures, I thanked Ayaan profusely and slipped him the last few rupees I had in my pocket. He offered me a bed the next time I came back to Delhi, and as nice as his gesture was, I knew it would be a long time, if ever, before I visited again. The same security guys from earlier were still at the door. They inspected my papers with some scrutiny. They knew something was up with me. Everything was in order though, yet they almost appeared reluctant to let me pass. I entered the terminal and made my way to the check-in desk. The whole room was lit up and had huge windows running along the car drop-off point outside. I felt quite exposed, mostly as there wasn't many other people around in these early hours. The lady at the counter couldn't initially find my booking on the system, wasting more time as she messed around with her computer, which of course was bloody typical. Whilst she typed my details, I kept my eyes glued to the window, trying to see which cars were pulling up and who was getting out.

"Here is your boarding card. You are at gate 23 sir, have a nice flight". I will mate, don't you worry. My last checkpoint was passing through security, and then finally, I would be able to take a bit of a breather from the madness. Coming up to the security point ready to leave this area forever, I happened to turn round back to the main entrance, and to my utter disbelief, I could see a group of Indian lads trying to get into the building. I obviously couldn't say for sure it was them, but considering it was relatively quiet at the airport and there was suddenly a gang of agitated lads here, it seemed too much to be a coincidence. I had either missed their car pulling up, or they had possibly been prowling the airport grounds on foot. The front door security men that had stopped me passing through earlier had now become my heroes, as they wouldn't let the group of angry pricks past. Luckily, I was able to slip beyond the doors into the security checking area seconds after they spotted me. As I was getting away, I was tempted to give a middle finger out to them for all the grief the ex-boyfriend had given me over the past few days, but decided as I'd already shagged his missus, not to push my luck.

Only after I had passed through security and immigration did I genuinely feel like I had escaped. The relief was overwhelming. I crashed out on an electric massage chair in the terminal, I had no money to operate it so just lay on it exhausted. I was so glad to be out of the whole situation, it had gone from being a great trip to an absolute nightmare. If these ten days had been to decide whether I was going to travel or not, then after this little experience, I'd be happy to stay at home with my nine to five job and get on with life. What was I doing out here anyway? It's horrible here. Take me home, back to the pub with my mates and mum's Sunday roast dinners. Thanks for the perspective, India!

I think it took my first day of being bored back at home for me to change my mind, and I booked a flight back out to Asia. Did I really want to do a nine to five until I retire? No. I'm only 27, there was plenty of time to settle down. I wanted a bit more adventure in my life before I did. I would just have to think things through a little better this time, and definitely keep my dick in my pants. Plus, it's pretty easy for most travellers to avoid getting into these situations. I had been unlucky in India, there's no way I'd have to flee a country again…!

I was very, very wrong on that one.

Chapter Two

Billy no mates

Monday 8th April 2013

Handing your work's notice in is a good feeling, handing it in and knowing that shortly you are off around the world is even better. I had spent the time after my return from India thinking about the other places I could go. South America maybe, after a brief stint in Asia? What's Africa like? I genuinely couldn't decide. I thought best, for now, would be to get out to Asia with Liggy and make my decision sat on a tropical beach. Either way, it was a good problem to have. I spent the entirety of my last few days in England partying with friends and family to say goodbye and had a massive send off in my local pub. Monday morning soon rolled around, and instead of clocking on, I was waving to my family as I boarded a one-way flight to Thailand. Even as the plane was taking off, it hadn't actually sunk in yet that this was it. I had savings close to six grand and was armed with an Australian working holiday visa too, I could potentially be away for years. I was off and embarking on the adventure of a lifetime... once again.

My plan was to meet up with Liggy who had wound up on the Thai island of Koh Phangan, living in a fully furnished rented apartment on the south coast, enjoying the beach-bum lifestyle. At forty-eight square miles of tropical island in the Gulf of Thailand, Koh Phangan is famous for the infamous *Full Moon*

Party, and it's a classic, well-trodden destination for backpackers in the region. The island does offer some hidden delights for those willing to spend a little more time there beyond a full moon; epic sunsets, hidden beaches, luxury resorts, and street parties. Stay longer, and you'll see drugs, gangs and lady-boys having fistfights. Outside of the main tourist spots, the towns are only small, and mostly found along the coast, with only a handful of people in each area. There was an "everyone knows everyone" vibe going for it, and after you've been around for a few weeks, you begin to make friends having your face seen around a bit. I made a few local mates over my time there, mostly Thais, but also a few European expatriates who were either running small businesses or staying beyond their visa's expiry date, drinking their days away in the pokey little bars found around the island. My favourite thing to do on an evening would be catching the sunset on the pier, watching the fishermen hauling all sorts out of the sea, meanwhile having a few frosty beers with Liggy and our new mates. Time flies when you're having fun. Before I knew it, seven weeks had passed, and I began to realise I was losing sight of what I came out here to do – see the world. I was falling into a trap somewhat and could have easily pissed all my money away here, having fun but hovering around the same area, seeing and doing nothing new. It was when Liggy and I were getting months of rent together to carry us here until August that I decided that I shouldn't be doing this, and would make a break for something else. Liggy was committed to staying and was even looking at buying a bar to run, so we would be parting ways once I left.

I began to scribble a few ideas down about where I could go. Liggy recommended somewhere he'd been on a visa run from Thailand to Malaysia last month. He told me of Tioman, a small tropical island with *Finding Nemo* reefs with an even more laid-back lifestyle than Koh Phangan. Sounded great. From there I would try to see some orangutans for my birthday at the end of June in Borneo. It was a loose plan, but it was enough to get me going. I had my last couple of days of partying with Liggy and my new local mates, and that was that. I was on the ferry leaving the island. For the first time in my life, I was on the road by myself with no one waiting for me at the other end. I sat at the top deck of the ferry and saw Koh Phangan fading through the haze on the horizon. It had been an incredible drunk blur. I was sad to be leaving, and not knowing if I would ever return.

The ferry took me to the Thai mainland and into the city of Surat Thani, landing on a gloomy day with the rain absolutely tipping it down, setting the tone for the glum mood I was in. I waited at a bus depot for a ride further into the city, the depot itself nothing more than an expanse of mud with a few wooden sheds to the side. Dogs chased chickens around, offering the only amusement to pass the time as I waited for a bus in the rain. I had a moment stood getting wet where I wondered if I should turn back and go to the life I had grown to love in Koh Phangan. What was I doing? I'm here in a wet car park by myself already missing my friends. I was anxious about travelling alone – all the worries that could possibly come as solo traveller started to run through my mind. What if I get lost, or abducted, who has got my back out here? What do I do if I lose my wallet, will anyone lend me money until I sort myself out? Did I really want to do this without any mates with me? Travelling alone wasn't really something I had properly considered back in England. I guess I was lucky a taxi didn't show, if one was already there, I might have just gone straight back to the ferry port. Luckily, I had some time to think, and I convinced myself I was doing the right thing by moving on.

Kuala Lumpur, Malaysia – 5th June 2013

I am unsure if it's just my bad luck, but I find short-haul flights in the tropics are usually turbulent affairs. I have absolutely no scientific knowledge to back me up on this, but I put it down to all the warm, humid air moving around that interferes with the plane. Coming down through the clouds for landing, I experienced the worst turbulence I'd ever been in. The aircraft would drop so violently as to actually make me need to use the toilet, accompanied by rough rocking from side to side, enough to occasionally cause people's items to fall about the carriage. An adult woman behind me started crying and screaming, whilst sat nearby in contrast, a young kid was laughing and cheering away at the violent shaking. They were both like looking into a mirror at various stages of my life; when I was a kid, I used to love turbulence, nothing could go wrong because I was always with good old mum and dad. Now I could hear the woman screaming "OH MY GOD, ARE WE CRASHING?", which were thoughts shared by myself. I think understanding more about how a plane works as I got older, and the fact it's in an unnatural forty-five-ton flying metal tube had set me off down a path of fear of flying. It's great that kids don't care.

Through a cursory look online of a map of the city before I set off, I knew my hostel was somewhere in Kuala Lumpur's huge Chinatown district. I regretted not making more effort to find the exact location when I had the chance, as I walked through the rain with no access to a map, backpack getting soaked, realising how big the Chinatown was when there in person. Kuala Lumpur is one of the wealthier cities in South-East Asia, which shows in the upkeep. The streets were clean, and it seemed there were no expanses of shanty-towns like in the neighbouring country's cities. It is also the country's capital, hosting 1.6 million people, small compared to other capitals, yet by miles the biggest in Malaysia. I'd briefly passed through once before whist backpacking in 2008, but from what I remembered, none of it helped me now.

I was unsure about getting a hostel again. For all the backpacking I had done previously, it was with my ex-girlfriend who would push for beds placed more on the luxury side of things. I'm not really sure we could have called it true backpacking at times to be honest, especially when hopping from resorts to four-star hotels. I naively let her take the lead, burning through our savings in a mere few months. I had stayed in a hostel only once before, on the Australian leg of the same trip, just because of how expensive Sydney is – hotels were not an option for those on a relative budget. It was a horrific experience. There was almost certainly dried semen on the floor, the bedsheets left me with a rash and the reception had a PA system with a speaker hooked up into every room which they would use to make loud announcements. Drunk people would grab the microphone at all hours when presumably left unguarded by the reception. Waking up covered in a rash to drunk girls singing *Hit me baby one more time* at 3 AM over the tannoy just firmed up my ex's argument that hostels were hell on Earth. I pressed on in the rain, and eventually found my second ever hostel, and I was relieved to find it looked clean and calm, with a great rooftop area on the top for socialising. The only criticism I had was the continent chosen for the *Continental Breakfast* could have well been Africa, because breakfast consisted entirely of slices of dry bread and a bowl of peanuts. I got into my double bunk bed dormitory, and it appeared I was in a dorm with three others who weren't currently there. For the first time ever, I found I was judging people solely by their possessions as opposed to them. They were extremely untidy. I think one of them was, let's say a large person, because their underwear would fit three good-sized watermelons in it. Don't want me judging your arse size based on watermelons? Don't leave your dirty fucking underwear lying around.

I got up early on my first full day in the city, looking to get my laptop and phone fixed. Both didn't work from being dropped at some point in Koh Phangan. I'm usually pretty good with looking after electronics on holiday, cautious they're not left direct sunlight, for example, continually fussing my phone is not accidentally baking away somewhere on a sunbed. Somehow, I had destroyed the lot in the reckless, drunken states I had managed to get myself in. For the past few weeks, I'd had a sort of 'digital detox' imposed on me. It got to the point in Koh Phangan that if I needed to know the time, I would just guess based on where the sun was in the sky. It wasn't like I ever needed to be somewhere at a specific time, so it didn't matter if I was wrong, but still, having that complete disconnect from gadgets was great. I enjoyed not having *Facebook* notifications vibrating away in my pocket, nor reaching for my phone when bored just to scroll through mindless photos of people's dinners or cat memes. It would have been nice to have carried on with this mindset, however, now back on the road, maps and alarms on demand were needed, so I didn't miss flights or end up lost. Plus, you can't beat *Skype* for keeping in touch with your family. After realising both my laptop and phone were broken beyond repair, limited by finances, I had the tough choice between a new replacement for only one. Weighing up the pros and cons, I decided on a laptop, offering the benefit to catch up on TV (the new season of *Game of Thrones* was out, after all).

With my brand-new laptop stored safely in my bag, I took an aimless walk around some of Kuala Lumpur. I came across an Irish pub shortly after and attracted like a moth to a light I wandered in, sat down and had my first pint of *Guinness* in over two months. I swear I got goosebumps as the first drop hit my tongue; that's either genuine appreciation for something, or the signs of a borderline alcoholic. I couldn't shake the feeling of being by myself though, supping my black pint in solitude. It was weird. I was literally sat here in a country without knowing a single other person. Now would be a good time to go out and meet people then I suppose? Nah. Armed now with my laptop and therefore the option to watch telly for the first time in weeks, the first couple of days in the city were a weird mix of catching up with TV, intense sleeping, and only leaving the room to eat. Watermelon arse and the rest of my room-mates must have thought I was some sort of creature, stirring only for food, giving a grunt as means of a greeting and then hibernating for the rest of the day. I had heard hostels were great places to meet other travellers, but it wasn't the case at all for these couple of days, I probably went the whole time without any real human interaction, and honestly, it was brilliant. This all changed when two Irish girls moved into the dorm, fresh from their flight to start a year or so of travelling. Whilst unpacking their stuff, we exchanged the usual pleasantries, and like dedicated Irish people, within twenty minutes of dumping their bags, they already had plans to hit the city's bars. They asked if I wanted to join. I needed to get out there properly and start acting like a normal person again, so thought why not?

I know Ireland is a different country to England, but our cultures are pretty similar, and one of the many things we have in common is we both love nothing more than a good piss-up. During my travels over the years and more recently in Koh Phangan, I had met many people from around the world, as you naturally would on these sorts of things. Almost all loved a drink, but none drank quite like the Brits or Irish. I'm always excited to meet either of them on the road, and these two Irish girls were not only a good laugh but utter drinking machines. A small group of like-minded heavy drinkers formed in hostel over the days, with me and the Irish girls as prime members. I was chuffed I was making friends by myself, content my social skills were adequate enough, which had been a bit of worry before I'd left Koh Phangan. It's easier to meet new people if you've already got other friends around you. Previously, me and Liggy would be a duo, chatting shit to whichever lost backpacker we'd bump into in the bars. He was often the more charismatic one of the two of us, so it was easy to meet people with him around. When you're by yourself though, it's intimidating meeting new people, and the thought of just walking up into a hostel and having to chat with a group of absolute strangers put knots in my stomach. But if I didn't make the effort eventually, I'd be alone for the whole trip. I think most people would surprise themselves once put into this situation though, plus I realised all backpackers are in the same position— they're often by themselves too, and *they're* keen to make *you* as a friend. It was a worry ticked off my list anyway, although alcohol and been a huge friendship catalyst. Either way, I was enjoying my new friends, so much in fact that I realised that if I wasn't careful, I'd end up falling into the same trap that I did in Koh Phangan - staying here having fun but not actually seeing anything other than inside a bar. I decided to have one last day in the city sightseeing with the Irish girls and then make a break for Tioman island.

The Irish girls had planned to travel to the far north of the city to see the Batu caves, formed out of old limestone hills, these days turned into a sizeable Hindu shrine. Apparently, it's on the city's tourist tick list. I'd never heard of them. During the journey, a young little Malay fella got on and sat directly in front of my seat. He seemed excited to be sat near me for some reason, he said 'Hello' at least three times whilst continually smiling. I could tell he wanted to talk to me but appeared nervous.

"I have photo... you?" he asked. I nodded slowly, I didn't really know how to respond, it caught me off guard that a complete stranger wanted a photo with me.

"When we're off the bus you mean, or now?" I replied, confused. He smiled back, clearly not understanding a word I said, and shifted closer. He fumbled around, then pulled his phone from out of his pocket, lifted it up and took one of me by myself looking unprepared for the photo. He bowed, said "Thank you" and turned round in his seat. What the hell was that? I looked over his shoulder as he played with his phone, wondering what he was doing with my picture – I couldn't process what I saw at first as it was so odd: He set the picture of me looking startled as the background of his phone. I could see my gormless face partially covered amidst the icons for various apps on his homescreen. I wanted clarification on what was going on, and I very nearly tapped his shoulder and asked him to delete it, but it was all too weird, and I thought this lad's next step would be taking the actual skin from my face. I was best just leaving it alone.

The Batu caves were a treat, but you certainly needed to be fit to enjoy your time there, the two hundred and seventy steep steps to reach the entrance were hard work in the tropical heat. Massive recesses cut through the side of a cliff face, showcasing a plethora of tropical plants and wildlife up near and around them. They were deep enough to spend some time walking around in, and to our relief, the air was a little bit cooler once inside. I'm sure there were all sorts of cultural Hindu stuff there to appreciate – I was more interested in the large group of naughty resident monkeys that were bothering tourists. I saw one eat a *Cornetto* like a human that it had snatched from a small child, and it was probably the highlight of the entire trip so far. It was nice this, spending time with new friends, sightseeing and drinking in the evenings. A little tame on the adventure side maybe, but the trip on my own was at least going well.

The Road to Mersing, Malaysia, 12th June 2013

There are two types of people that travel. There's those that treat any impending hefty travel days with respect and rest early in preparation for it, mainly so they're not late for that plane or train, and not suffering from something lethal like a hangover whilst in transport. Then, there are the idiots like me that pull an all-nighter on a giant bender because they're having fun at the time, with the mindset of "I'll deal with it tomorrow". It was now tomorrow, I felt horrendous and was running late for my journey to Tioman island. I had woken up on the floor of our dorm with the Irish girls and a Dutch guy called Jeroen, who I'd met over the past couple of days. The four of us had bounced around the city's clubs until sunrise, and I could briefly recall us stealing a security guy's shoes and getting a legger back to the hostel. It was a fun night, but I was annoyed with myself for both putting myself in this hungover situation and not being able to find one of my shoes as I frantically packed my backpack. Karma for the security guy, I guess. I hadn't really learned my lesson from when I first arrived in Kuala Lumpur either; I hadn't done adequate research about my next stop. I didn't have an excuse as I had my new laptop which I could have easily spent some time looking into my onward travel plans. Five minutes on *Google* would have done. Jeroen was also leaving, so the pair of left us a quickly scribbled goodbye note written on an inside out cigarette packet for the sleeping Irish girls and left for the bus terminal. I swapped details with him as there was a chance we'd meet again, both of us had plans to be in Borneo in a couple of weeks. I said bye and then for the first time in nearly a week, I was by myself again. I was sad, sat there with my hangover feeling sorry for myself, alone again in an unfamiliar place. I realised I had arrived far too early; I had rushed here for no reason. I sat on the floor in a quiet little corner of the bus depot, away from the crowds.

When I'd bought my bus ticket at the counter, I was told I had a four-hour bus journey to Mersing, a little coastal town in the south of the Malaysian peninsular. So, leaving at 6 PM tonight, I would get to Mersing by 10 PM. This bus was making two stops, so I only had to get off the right one, which should be easy, or it risked a 50% chance of failure, depending on how you look at it. From Mersing the next morning, I would be able to take the ferry to my ultimate destination, Tioman island. Armed with a big bag of paprika crisps and water from the shop, I entered the bus and asked which of the two stops would I have to get off at. The ticket inspector tried his best to convey in broken English that it was the first one I needed. Great. I still had no idea if I would find somewhere to sleep once I got to Mersing but noticed one other Westerner climb on board, so if everything went tits up, I decided I would just cling to her and become her new friend. The seating inside the bus was surprisingly comfy considering it looked like rusting heap from the outside. The seats reclined almost like beds. A young local lad sat next to me, I nodded and said "hello", which was met with a blank stare. I wondered if he was going to ask for a photo of me like that bell-wipe did the other day, but he fell asleep straight away. I ate my paprika crisps within minutes and didn't really have much else to do. I was tired from my recent session, but I couldn't sleep. I was still feeling the nerves of doing this by myself.

The bus set off and night quickly drew in, which was a little disappointing as I realised my first time of being out in the Malaysian countryside would be in the dark, unable to see it. It nice enough in what little dusk there was, but we were soon moving through the darkness, with nothing but the glow of the headlights giving occasional glimpses of what was out there. I tried to sleep again, but some guy was playing some sort of computer game on his phone, there were a lot of beeps and noises coming from the front of the bus. This went on for about an hour with me just getting increasingly frustrated. No-one else seemed bothered though, so I let out a few loud sighs to indicate my disapproval and just had to lump it. 10 PM rolled on by, the four hours that this journey was supposed to take had passed, and judging from what little I could see outside, we were still in the country. It couldn't be long now, though, could it? An hour later, the bus stopped outside a small metal arch over the road with a single light dangling from it, and other than that it was still pitch black through the windows. I assumed we were still in the country. It certainly couldn't be a supposed large town like Mersing, could it? Where were all the lights? I swear the driver shouted "Mertan" or something and opened the doors, and no one budged from their seats, so he continued to drive. I had a moment's thought, which quickly turned to panic. Did he just say "Mersing" then and did I hear wrong? I asked the guy next to me what was that stop for, who only gave a blank expression again. Either he didn't speak English, or he was deaf as a post. This was bad, I had no idea where this bus was taking me. Didn't the ticket inspector say it was the first stop anyway? Panicked, I legged it the length of the bus to the driver.

"Excuse me mate, was that Mersing then?" He laughed and carried on driving. I continued "No seriously, that stop then, was that Mersing? I need to go to Mersing". He looked positively bemused and said, once again struggling with English,

"No, Mersing" which could have been interpreted in a few ways. No, Mersing is coming up. Or no, the next stop isn't Mersing. Or even you're not on the right fucking bus for Mersing. Either way, he wasn't stopping for me to get off so if that was Mersing back then, I could kiss goodbye to it tonight. I went back to my seat and felt like sobbing. Fucking Mersing.

Midnight. Oh God, that had to be the stop for Mersing. I've been on this bus for six hours now, so where the hell was it taking me? Would there be a hotel there? If not, would it be safe to sleep in a doorway for the night? What if it rains? Then I remembered there was that Westerner sat at the front, she had been asleep whilst I was talking to the driver earlier, but I could see her head bobbing away with her headphones on now. I rushed over to her seat. I was beginning to cause a few looks from the other people on the bus, I mean, no one likes to see a flustered foreigner running up and down on public transport do they? After a brief chat to her, she turned out to be a really nice girl from California, who not only knew where the bus was heading but lived in the area and knew it like the back of her hand. She told me not to worry and that Mersing was the last stop. Also, we had another hour to go. Another hour? I must have been given incorrect information at the start, or my hungover brain misheard something. Whatever – I'm not lost, and that's all that matters. I got to Mersing just after 1 AM, kissed the ground, grabbed my bags and went straight to find a hotel. Panic over!

The town of Mersing felt weird terms of layout and left me feeling slightly underwhelmed. Everything was really spaced out away from each other, and wasted scrubland lay between buildings. The town was mostly dead, which was to be expected given the time of night. There were however small pockets of light, with people underneath eating at a few of the open-air diners, which I was surprised were still open. I found a hotel near the bus depot, which offered the absolute basics – four walls and a slightly dirty mattress on the floor and run by a chain-smoking local who had converted the reception into his living room. He didn't budge from his settee and instructed me from his horizontal position that I had to get my own key, find the book to log my own name in, and even get the correct change from the till.

I went for a little wander for some food after dropping my bags off, shortly coming to a large restaurant. I would have eaten anything at this point and did spot open trays of food as part of a buffet at the front of the restaurant by the street, but it looked like it has been sat there for a while. Luckily there was an option to have chicken and fried rice prepared fresh from the menu. I took a seat and quietly observed others eating.

As I waited for my food, a stray cat came wandering into the restaurant from off the street. Poor thing had half of its arse hanging out, like some sort of mega piles, dragging along the floor as it moved about which gathered dirt as it did. The cat looked around, made eye contact with me, and must have realised I was the only person here amongst the handful of patrons that had noticed it. It decided I was far enough away, looked around again, and jumped up onto the buffet counter and began to sniff around. A stray from the street walking around pre-cooked food was bad enough, but the turbo piles were also being dragged around the food trays as the cat searched around for the best stuff. It spotted the chicken wings and went straight for it, leaving its arse-dangler to hang in a tray of something that resembled beef curry. Just at this moment, a waiter came out to drop my food off. He clocked the cat chowing down, seeing it quickly angered him to the point where I wondered if this prolapsed puss might be a regular here. He sneaked up behind it, and once close enough, used the back of his hand to whack the piles, and shouted something in Malay. The cat ran off with a chicken wing in its mouth and left a streak of food as the curried piles dragged along the floor. I instantly lost my appetite. I realised it was enough Asia for one day and was best off going to bed.

I checked out of the hotel the next morning by resting the room key on the chest of the settee guy who was now asleep. I assumed he must get up every now and then, but I was yet to witness it. I was pretty hungry after being put off from most of my food last night. Unfortunately, on my way to the docks, only *Cat's-arse cafe* was open, so I gave it a miss and went straight to the ferry hoping I could eat something there.

Tioman island, Malaysia – 12th June 2013

My retention of pointless knowledge knows no bounds. I still remember my bike's padlock number from when I was fifteen. *5773.* Apparently, in Switzerland, it's illegal to mow your front lawn dressed as Elvis. I have no idea if that's even true, but it's stuck in my brain. And, for some reason, I'll never forget the name of the fictional island from *Jurassic Park,* which incidentally is *Isla Nublar,* and that's what I thought as soon as I could see Tioman through the steamy ferry window. For a moment I wondered if it was the same island where the movies were filmed; I was expecting to see a little flat tropical island, so was stunned to see huge hills in the middle of the island, punching through the clouds. I stared at it for a while with my mouth open, two-thirds impressed to one-third tiredness. It had taken a few days longer to get here than anticipated after dithering in Kuala Lumpur, but I had finally made it: A speck in the South China Sea, no more than thirteen miles long and three across. There are *loads* of islands off the coast of Malaysia. Many backpackers I met would often recall the epic beach fires, partying and scuba on Langkawi, Perhentians or elsewhere, claiming them far more superior than Tioman. They came at the cost of more tourists. I liked the idea of Tioman more, it was quiet and remote. My intention now was just to chill out for a few days, enjoying the beautiful beaches, clear waters and a jungle interior. Faithfully tracing Liggy's journey here earlier in the year, I disembarked on the part of the island weirdly known as *ABC,* on the west coast. My first impressions of *ABC* certainly caused me to think "wow" because after coming from an island like Koh Phangan where everything had large pockets of built-up areas, and insane partying, here I saw only a few huts along the coastline. It made me question whether I would eventually end up bored with the lack of things to do. I'm supposed to be spending at least a week here – Going to be a bit quiet, isn't it? I had brought a good book to get stuck into anyway, so at least I had that. I had visited remote islands in Fiji on previous travels though, and they were similar, sparsely populated settlements along beaches with palm trees. I'd enjoyed myself there, so probably would here to be fair.

One could walk along the entire "main road" of *ABC,* and it would take about five minutes. The road itself being nothing more than a slightly wide footpath – mopeds and people, as well as a whole host of occasional animals – cats, monkeys and monitor lizards, all have to share it. The path runs along the coast, so you have the sea a couple of metres away to one side, and a variety of huts that are either accommodation, shops, dive shops and the occasional bar on the other. There must be only sixty buildings in the whole of *ABC*, most of which being chalets for tourists. It is so quiet. And yet, days into my stay, it got under my skin. I loved it. My room was virtually on the beach. I loved waking up in the morning to the sound of the waves crashing a stone's throw away from my bed. It was still lively at night, relatively speaking, and there were a couple of bars that put on small bonfires and music once the sun set. The sea – crystal clear, and like Liggy promised, complete with his "*Finding Nemo* reefs". The food – outstanding, I think freshly caught fish that was grilled on the beach was one of the best meals I had ever eaten in my life. It was seasoned to perfection, and the flames from the BBQ gave it that extra bit of taste. What have I been eating all my life because it tastes like shit in comparison to this!

The pace on the island did take some getting used to. I didn't see people stressed out and rushing. Whilst the islanders were generally friendly, there's an odd way about one or two of them. I guess being part of a small island community without much new DNA being pumped in will do that though. The guy who worked at the chalet I stayed at was often foul-tempered, who guarded his Wi-Fi password with a fury I had not seen before in a person. One evening whilst reading on my porch, I noticed some backpackers who had checked out the previous day sneak up to the premises again to use the Wi-Fi. They sat behind a tree which conveniently blocked his view from reception. They didn't anticipate him sweeping up around the property though, and when he caught them sat on their laptops, I watched him shout so much at them that foam had started to form around the side of his mouth. I am not sure why I am telling you this now. Anyway, locals aside, I had met some superb travellers, most of them at my 'local bar', and the gang of friends ranged from teenager to late fifties. The bars weren't open in the day, so I'd sometimes spend my time at a dive shop whenever I wanted something to do, and through this became particularly friendly with a teenage girl from New York, Mo, and a young Kiwi called Clive, and we'd just sit around all day talking shit. My days were busy spent doing nothing with these guys, and I loved it.

It saddens me when I think about the wildlife back on Koh Phangan because the growing development and mass of tourists that descend monthly for the *Full Moon Party* and the other massive raves they host must have caused wildlife numbers to plummet over the years. The authorities were clearing large parts of the northern jungle to make room for an airport, wiping out acres of natural habitat just to save everyone an hour's ferry over from the neighbouring island which already has a place you can fly into. Most locals were happy about it, it meant bringing in extra tourists and ultimately revenue. For me, I liked the quiet charm on parts of the island when you needed a break from the partying. I hadn't really thought about the wildlife numbers there before I came to Tioman, and it's on a completely different scale. Tioman teemed with wildlife, precisely because there are fewer people here. I had numerous mad little ferrets regularly running around the top of a palm tree outside my gaff. Monitor lizards here are big and plentiful, one bugger I saw was nearly two metres long. Koh Phangan would have been similar years back, as it now slowly turns into another bland tourist destination in the tropics. Animals are rare and you don't see much in the immediate waters around the island. I wondered if the fate of Tioman island would have it heading the same way, as it too develops to accommodate more tourists. Word in the bars here was that they were planning to destroy large parts of coral reef to create a new ferry port for tourists and industries in raw materials. I shudder to think about it. In the meantime at least, I was one of a handful of tourists here, and I enjoyed the lack of impact people had on the environment (although it wasn't lost on me that my actual being here made me part of the problem I had just been complaining about).

One thing that could do with a bit of a culling though is the Macaque monkeys, if not a culling then a least a slap to let them know who's boss. Initially, a bit of a joy to see at first, they have now become nothing more than a pest to me; emptying bins near my room looking for food, shitting on my porch and generally being a bit intimidating. If there's a 'gang' of them on the *ABC* road, then I hate having to walk past them. It's like being back in school and having to walk through a gang of bullies loitering in a corridor. They stare you out as you approach and you wonder if you're going to be able to walk through without incident, or if one of them has had a bad day and feels like not only tormenting you a bit but getting his mates in on it too. Some of the braver ones show their teeth and charge at you, and the worst thing you can do is show you're scared, as I found out one afternoon running to the dive shop like a big girl with several of the horrors chasing me. The following day my new tactic was running at them and making a bit of a noise which I found usually works. Nothing starts your day like shouting and charging at a ruck of primates on your way to breakfast. Their favourite time to cause havoc is at dawn, just to disturb any lie-in you might want. I watched *Aliens* before bed one night and on occasion after watching something with disturbing scenes in it, it will play on my mind, and I'll sometimes dream about it. Around 6 AM the following morning, I heard scuttling on the roof which woke me up, and I thought it was a load of those *Facehuggers* in the movie out to get me. Genuinely startled at first, I peeked out of the window and noticed a group of monkeys on my porch. Brilliantly, one was sat playing with his cock, which made me laugh, and I was no longer annoyed about being woken up early.

Whilst the monkeys in and around *ABC* are a pain in the arse, their jungle-dwelling cousins that are sometimes spotted whilst out trekking are not so used to humans, so keep away, usually right up in the jungle canopy. I had done the jungle trek to the town of Juara across the island twice, with two different groups, and spotted many of them. Juara is merely a handful of restaurants and rooms to stay in, making *ABC* look like a city. The beach is decent though, arguably better than our side of the island, with some of the clearest waters going. The trek itself is mostly doable, although I consider myself relatively fit when it comes to walking as my friends and I attempt endurance walks back in England. We have, however, the benefit of doing it in a temperate climate – along nice, flat canal tow-paths. I noticed some bits here were physically hard going in comparison. The path would occasionally disappear into rocks, which continue to go up-hill, whilst your battling with the tropical humidity and the water you need to carry. Although short compared to many of the jungle treks around South East Asia, it's still a satisfying one to complete at 7km. With the centre peak being around 600 meters high, which gives the island that *Jurassic Park* vibe, you're rewarded by some cracking jungle scenery once you reach the top. Plus there's a picturesque waterfall and lagoon you can swim in on the route. You can't beat being able to have a complete body wash to get all the sweat and dirt off you during a walk like that. There's probably some skin eating worm or some other parasite in there, but at the time all I cared about is freshening up!

Should the abundance of land creatures on the island not be enough, you're only moments away from the coral reef, again teeming with wildlife. I found hours of entertainment just hovering in the water with a snorkel on, surrounded by thousands of fish. I honestly can't name the species, except for the 'classics' like angelfish, clownfish, barracudas and reef sharks. The nighttime brought out the best of the sea, there's a strange bioluminescent phytoplankton which responds to any forceful movement in the water by glowing bright blue. Me and my new crew would often sit in the sea at night with only the moonlight shining down on us, moving our arms in the water whilst the phytoplankton glowed like stars around us.

Swimming with another Brit one afternoon I had met, he had to leave me alone in the sea as his ferry back to Mersing was due. I was having such a good time I thought I could do another half hour or so by myself and swam further out to see if it offered anything else. I was alone for some time, marvelling at the sheer sight of what was underneath me. A black and white striped sea snake shot out from the reef, only a short distance in front of me. I had never seen one before, so for the first few seconds, the wow-factor was off the scale. The thrill quickly became panic as I recognised this could be a problem, mainly because water is not my preferred medium to be in when I need to quickly get away from a potentially dangerous animal. I popped my head out of the water. "Where the fuck's the shore?" The snake was between me and land. I put my head back under the water and was utterly horrified to see it swimming towards my direction at some speed. I tried the flapping and noise-making technique used on the monkeys. In hindsight, this could have possibly aggravated the snake more, and seeing it still coming at me, I swam away as fast as I could, never before realising I was such a fast swimmer! People I had spoken to since seemed to have taken pleasure in telling me about the toxicity of the venom sea snakes possesses – which is a lot. Ten times the potency of a king cobra if the tales around the fire that evening were to be believed. There was no anti-venom on the island others told me. It's rare for them to go for people, but it does happen, so who knows? Maybe I had a lucky escape there? I think I'll just stick to my land snakes from now on, they're easier to kick away.

I had really bonded with Clive and Mo in such a short amount of time, as well as the others on the island. I was having as much fun here as anywhere and wondered if I could stay another day or so, but I was already cutting it fine. I had to leave; otherwise, I wouldn't make my flight to Borneo in time. The journey to my next destination was going to take three days in total; a ferry to Mersing and stay the night there, then at least two buses the next day to Kuala Lumpur airport, and then on the third day fly out to the city of Kuching early morning. It was going to be a grueller. I spent my last morning with the guys from the dive shop, waiting for the ferry, and said my goodbyes. Twice now as a solo traveller on this trip, I began to realise I was saying bye to the great people I had met, leaving me by myself, and it genuinely pained me. It wasn't being by myself that was so much the issue, it was just when would I see these great guys again? Most of them were all staying on the island at least another month, and I was the first one of the gang to leave. I was sad to get onto the ferry.

I had to start taking anti-malaria tablets to get firmly into my system well before entering a malaria area, its standard use of them. I was informed it's rife in parts of Borneo. In case you didn't know, there's a whole host of malaria tablets you can take. They range from the type of malaria resistance in the area you're going to, whether you can drink alcohol on them, cost, side effects and duration you have to take them either side of your stay. For me, the winner was the price, and most importantly, I got mine for free from that guy Jeroen I'd met back in Kuala Lumpur. *Mefloquine* has mixed reviews depending on where you look online. It's supposed to be effective, and you only need to take one once a week, but it's one with the most side effects. I dropped one and it was massive for a tablet that a human is expected to take. I wondered if it was genuine for a moment due to its size and wondered if I had been given something like an equine worming tablet as a joke. I felt it scrape its way down my throat, and that was that. On to the ferry!

2 PM. The ferry was crammed. *ABC* being the last stop of about five places along the island, by the time I got on there was nowhere to sit, except for the deck floor outside at the rear of the ferry. I attempted to read a book for ten minutes but was overcome with a weird feeling in my stomach, and then my head. Was it the malaria tablet kicking in, or was my body punishing me for that bottle of duty-free vodka I polished off with everyone last night? I was sat right above the ferry's engines which were unbearably hot, loud and smoky. I attempted to sleep. Everything went really strange, and I started hearing weird music in my head in time with the repetitiveness of the engines churning, my entire body vibrating along with it. I couldn't sit there for the duration of the trip and got up into the cabin hoping I had somehow missed a seat. As I got up to go inside, I noticed the outline of Tioman in some strange fog that had been plaguing the island for the past few days, but looking just as impressive as when I first arrived.

After upsetting people who had already fallen asleep as I scuttled through the walkway, I managed to find somewhere to sit. At the very front of the cabin, there was a step leading to an emergency exit. It wasn't much, but it would do me fine! I couldn't believe no one had thought it was worth sitting on. I sat there and had the unique view of seeing all of the passengers on the ferry face on. Everyone looked miserable, probably because they all knew we were leaving this nice tropical island, and the next stop was the grim collection of buildings known as Mersing. We were due to hit land around 4 PM. I'd have the rest of the day there, so thought to myself I would at least give the town a chance this time, not being very impressed as I passed through last week. Suddenly, Mick Hucknall! What the hell?! One of the faces I spotted from the seats facing towards me was Mick Hucknall from the mid 80's soul band *Simply Red*. Or was it? I couldn't tell you for certain. It really looked like him though. Famous in England, womanising gingers, have to go on holiday somewhere, don't they? Why not Tioman? This has been the only time on my trip I really wished I had a working phone so I could have *Googled* Mick Hucknall just to hold up next to this guy to determine if it really was him. I'd have to go for a photo with him as well, imagine seeing someone famous on a boat to fucking Mersing of all places! Hucknall kept clocking me looking at him, and it began to get a bit weird, so I decided the best thing to do was just to close my eyes and leave the ginger singer to his business.

The air-con on the craft fired up. The ferries back and to from Tioman have to be the coldest place in Asia. Everyone comments on how cold it gets on them, you see people wrapped in blankets, shivering. The weird outside fog had really begun to engulf the boat, and coupled with the military-grade air-conditioning, looking out of the window you could have been forgiven for thinking we were off the coast of the Faroe Islands, not in the tropics. We arrived, and the humid air busted through the opening doors. The first thing I noticed was the dirty sea, as compared to Tioman's crystal blue waters. I looked up and sighed. I was back in Mersing.

I had a little walk around Mersing, past *Cat's-Arse Cafe*, and tried to find something to do for a while. Hucknall appeared again! He ran past with his luggage and shouted,

"Excuse me, which way is the bus station?!" He had an English accent as well! I pointed in the direction, but it was pointless him asking me really because he barely waited around for my reply. I don't think it was him to be fair, surely someone as loaded as Hucknall wouldn't be running through a tiny Asian town looking to get a cheap bus, although I knew how he felt if he just wanted to get out as soon as possible. It was a pretty grim day in a grim town. As the fog became denser, I noticed it was actually smog, partly because most of the locals were wearing breathing masks. It was making me feel a little bit queasy being out in it. The smog, I would later learn a few days later, was caused by people burning a large area of jungle, clearing it for palm oil plantations. This was happening in the neighbouring Indonesian island of Sumatra – the whole Malaysian peninsular and Singapore was currently experiencing record high pollution. The moon had turned red several days ago in Tioman, and this explained why. With no other real knowledge of where to go Mersing, I headed back to the hotel I stayed in on my first night in the town. I even ended up with the same bed, and was pretty sure it was the same bedsheets from ten nights ago – at £5 a night, who am I to complain?

I clocked myself in a mirror outside of my room, noticing I was in dire need of some proper grooming. Not that I can grow any sort of beard, just a patchy goatee at best, but it was looking a right mess. I had mop hair, and I had run out of virtually all my toiletries. My intention was to spend a load on grooming products and have a haircut on my first day in Borneo and get myself feeling human again, but I had some time to kill here in Mersing, so decided to get all this sorted today instead. It's mad, off-the-cuff decisions like that you make all the time whilst travelling! The first barber I found wasn't too far from my room and guessed it was as good as anywhere. Whilst inside the barbers had the appearance of being a wide-open room, it still managed to be incredibly hot and stuffy. A radio was on in the background, but the oscillation from the colossal ceiling fan in the centre of the room made the most noise. I have a mild fear of getting my hair cut abroad. My fear is mainly that my request for a short back and sides being lost in translation and ending up with a reverse mohawk or something. Three locals were sat being idle; two young barbers slouching on their seats were looking bored, and an older bloke gestured to me with his hand to sit down the moment I walked in. Here we go..! Getting your haircut abroad is an experience. Every hairdresser is obviously different anyway, but I find each country has it's quirks about the whole thing too. For example, the ones I had been to in Thailand had caked me in talcum powder before they started. Here, the haircut took only minutes (and looked just as good as one from home), and it also ended in an unexpected fifteen-minute back massage whilst sat in the barber's chair. Perhaps I was lost in the moment of the wonderful massage, but I even decided on a shave, something I've never had done at a barber's before. There's that crazy traveller decision making again! Brilliantly, it was all for the equivalent of £3! I looked at myself in the mirror just as the guy was finishing the sides off, and thought I looked so much better after a haircut. It's a cruel paradox for me – I think I look better with short hair, but growing my hair is going to be the only way to cover my increasingly receding hairline in the future. Thanks for the shite genes, dad! Still, for now, I felt great. I got back to the hotel, washed with all the new toiletries I bought, and whilst in the mood even contemplated starting on my overgrown gorilla pubes with some travel scissors, but decided I could save that excitement for another day.

My sleep was awful. The malaria tablet threw up plenty of side effects, the most noticeable was involuntary leg spasms, kicking the wall several times in the night. I had a couple of intense dreams of being cornered by Macaque monkeys and falling off a cliff. Another significant side effect was needing to poo – badly – at 3 AM. I woke with an intense cramp in my belly. I shot up, ran to the toilet down the corridor and was horrified to see one of the classic Asian squat toilets. I have a combined time of nearly six months in Asia so far, and I have managed to avoid these lavatorial nightmares entirely. I hesitated about using it, but the cramp returned, and after checking the other nearby rooms in the hotel, there was no other option. I honestly don't get why these bloody foreigners insist on using toilets like this when they've seen you can actually have a proper sit-down shit like in the Western world. Now I can say I've used both, a Western toilet certainly makes taking a crap enjoyable. I like to bring something to read with me and make it a good twenty-minute affair. Even if I forget a magazine, I'll read the ingredients on the back of a nearby bottle of shampoo or bleach to draw it out a little. But here, the only thing my hands were being used for was stability on the slimy floor. I can't even imagine being old and having to use these toilets, my legs were aching after a minute. Horrified to find there was no toilet paper either, I washed my rusty sheriff's badge with a combination of my bare hand and a hose pipe. Asia had finally cracked me. A rough night indeed.

The smog had lifted somewhat from ground level by early morning but was clearly still in the sky above. The sun had an eerie neon glow to it, trying its best to break through the smog, and the streets were weirdly quiet. I could well have stepped into *Silent Hill* for all I knew. I found a little open restaurant and like many of the eateries around here, found the breakfast menu unappealing. Fried rice, spicy noodles, chicken wings. I could have smashed this for dinner no problem, especially with a couple of pints of ale already inside me, but I just wanted something simple like toast or porridge at this time of the day. I struggled to eat my noodles and a weird crab cake thing. Feeling a bit off from my greasy breakfast, I grabbed my gear and took a walk to the bus station. I passed the same blokes at the barber's from yesterday, and they smiled and waved at me, probably admiring their work.

The bus took hours, passing through the countryside. Most of it seemed like endless palm oil plantations, the frequency of buildings slowly increasing as we got closer to Kuala Lumpur. Killing time, I watched the whole first series of Ricky Gervais' *Derek*, and if you've seen the last episode, you'll know it's a proper tearjerker. With an extended version of *Fix you* by *Coldplay* playing in the background, the lead character Derek is reunited with his dad after living most of his life without him. Genuinely trying not to cry on public transport, I kept telling myself it was just another side effect from the malaria tablet.

I got to my hotel and lay on the bed exhausted, wanting to just get tomorrow's early flight to Borneo over and done with. I noticed Jeroen had messaged, who I had last seen at the bus terminal on my way to Mersing. He had made it to my next destination and wanted to know if I was keen to meet up. I'd had enough of my own company and was frankly still disgusted with myself after having touched my own arsehole last night, so I was entirely up for meeting someone I already knew.

Chapter Three

Jungles, cities & man-titties

Borneo, Malaysia – 23rd June 2013

The country of Malaysia consists of two parts major parts. The peninsular side hangs from the bottom of Thailand, and then across a narrow strip of sea to the east on the neighbouring island of Borneo lies some of Malaysia as well. This huge island is shared with both Indonesia and the smaller country of Brunei. The time had come to leave the Malaysian peninsular and push onwards to Borneo. For the past few days, there had been an increasingly thickening smog being pumped from Sumatra, and it wasn't at all pleasant being out in it. Even for the first hour of the flight, the dirty air surrounded the plane, and I couldn't see anything out of the window other than the strange neon orange glow of the sun through the surrounding grey. Landing in the city of Kuching (the name translates simply as "Cat" in English), it was great that we were clear from it all and I could have clean air in my lungs once again. The sun was bright in the sky, meaning it was a nice day in an even nicer city. Okay, first things first, Kuching is a visually attractive, not just by Asian standards, but rivalling places I'd been to across the world. Sitting north-west of coastal Borneo in the state of Sarawak, the locals clearly take pride in their city, and it's easy to see why. I was stunned to see well-manicured lawns, trimmed hedges, and flower beds alongside the road. The streets showcasing numerous expensive residential estates would continue to surpass the last one I had just passed. I was caught a little off guard because in my complete ignorance before coming, I naively imagined Borneo to mostly tribal villages and rainforests. There's all that here undoubtedly, but seeing these wealthy, clean and built-up areas which I was currently passing through now on my taxi from the airport took me by surprise to learn. I really need to do more reading online about these places before I arrive, instead of just booking a flight to a place arbitrarily!

I was to see Jeroen again this evening who'd arranged to meet me with his local friend and some other backpackers for dinner. I was impressed he had only arrived yesterday but had already managed to amass a small group of friends. I later learned he had achieved it via a website called *CouchSurfing*. People I had met on the road had nothing but positive things to say about it. From what I could gather, you could arrange to meet up with people – quite often locals of a destination – and can even in some instances stay at their place for free. It sounded pretty good. I had a few hours to myself to explore the city and thought a wander around would kill some time. Much like Mersing, there wasn't many people around, although I assumed that with it being a Sunday was perhaps the reason why it was so quiet on the streets today. It was almost eerie.

Without any real direction, I soon found myself having a pleasant stroll along the waterfront; it's hard to miss the large river cuts right through the city. On my side of the river, it had been converted into a modern promenade, complete with red brick paving and black painted handrails to stop you falling into the water. Some street performers were playing traditional music in the native Borneo tribal dress wherever the promenade would open its path slightly. Across the river lay some impressive structures, most notably a large temple that stole the tourists' attention away from the street performers. Not that there were many other tourists around today either. There were a few ice-cream stalls too, but with no one buying. Possibly not racking up much in sales today with it being quiet, the ice cream sellers would get excited when they saw me walk past, shouting me over, trying to entice me in with their frozen produce. Sorry lads, as nice as one would have gone down in this hot weather, I'm not interested! I had eaten tons crap lately, never mind the daily gallons of beer. I really had piled on the pounds since leaving home, and I didn't really leave there in great shape either. Right now, I needed a bra more than ice cream and wanted to opt for something more healthy. I had heard of stories of people returning from their travels with their clothes hanging off them, budgeting on everything including food, and burning it all off with jungle treks and scuba diving. The opposite had been happening for me. My shirts were getting a little tight, I often wondered how strong the sewing was on the buttons, and whether there was a risk of them pinging off and taking someone's eye out.

On the walk home, I noticed my chance to be healthy, and at a fruit, stall stopped in for three apples and an orange. It came to the equivalent of about £1.50.

"That's even more than what I'd pay in England", I said to the woman, startled at the cost.

"Go to England to buy them then!" She snapped. Fair enough. I looked at my fruit at the bottom of the paper bag. It seemed pathetic sat there considering all of the beer and fried rice I'd consumed since getting out here. It was going to take more than just a few bits of fruit to get myself into shape. I hoped it was at least a start.

The evening had rolled in and Jeroen pulled up outside my hostel in the passenger seat of a car with a guy called Jack, a Malay of Chinese descent who was in his early twenties. I'd only spent a couple of days with Jeroen on heavy nights out, and that was weeks ago. I didn't really know him well; Still, he was a face I recognised which was good enough for me. He was a few years older than myself and had bags of confidence, complete with his long wavy hair. His new mate Jack seemed really friendly, perhaps a touch on the quiet side, either because he was focusing on driving, but most likely because Jeroen was leading the conversation for all three of us. We drove to another hostel to pick up even more backpackers. All wedged into the car, our next stop was a huge local food market lead by Jack, somewhere in a residential area of Kuching. There were multiple rows of stalls, selling all sorts of things I had never even considered as food before. I always swear that you can't beat travelling with a local, and again tonight was no exception. From an affluent part of Kuching, Jack lived for both seeing the world and hosting backpackers, helping to give them a good insight into the way of life here. He was a great host and had clearly done this before. I assumed many tourists didn't come to this part of town – this market wasn't in the *Lonely Planet* guides that the well-planned backpackers always seem to carry around with them – and this was reflected in the food available. The highlight of complete craziness for me was *Chicken Dessert,* which was a long piece of soft bread, cooked slightly. On top of that, there was mayonnaise, dried chicken and cinnamon powder. It did taste a bit like dessert I suppose but was tough to get my head around.

After going through Jack's suggestions, we went off again individually, ordered our own plates, sat down together and shared the weird delights we had found at the stalls. It was fun to try, and if the food wasn't all great, it was at least memorable. Sat around a plate of fried cow lung and stingray, Jeroen told me about a place called Bako national park; effectively a jungle with a lodge in it, where you can stay overnight with a few of the amenities you're used to, but getting to still spend some time in a wild area. He was going tomorrow and said I should join. It sounded great and precisely the sort of thing I had come to Borneo for. Who needs to plan around a *Lonely Planet* book when you have a random chance instead?

Early the next morning, I sat down for breakfast at the hostel, having already packed ready to meet Jeroen before our trip to Baku. *DIY breakfast,* said the sign which appeared to have been prepared by a maniac as they provided raw eggs with no visible way to cook them, and toast with "Jem". "Jem" annoyed me a bit. Why spell it differently? Malays were introduced to the Latin Alphabet when the European settlers came over. Yet, they have also taken something as profoundly English as jam and then decided to spell it differently to be awkward. There is plenty of English words that have their own Malaysian touch to them. Teksi (taxi), Bas (bus), Buku (book), Garaj, (garage), Kaunter (counter). All completely pointless variants of normal already existing words as far as I'm concerned. And I gave up with these sodding breakfast eggs as I couldn't find any "Mikrowave" to cook them in. Jeroen met me at my hostel, leading the way; A bus ride took us out of the city and to a pier on a river, just on the outskirts of a jungle. In no time we were on a small longboat with an outboard motor driven by a native guide and a couple of other tourists. We chugged along a muddy river with dense jungle either side of it. I had no idea what to expect, having once again done no pre-planning, but was really excited for whatever was in store. The smog from Sumatra had begun to catch up with Borneo by this point, so the visibility had been somewhat reduced, I could just about make out mountains covered in jungle foliage further through the haze. Just for some scale here, I believe Sumatra is over a thousand kilometres away from Borneo, and yet smoke was still reaching us here. That must be one hell of a fire to make that much smoke. What are we doing to our planet?

The longboat pulled up alongside a shabby wooden dock in the river, which didn't look like it could hold more than ten people at a time. It was nothing more than a small platform, slightly rotted, sticking out into a mangrove swamp. The mangrove trees were without leaves, like they'd all be plucked, looking like massive twigs sticking out of the thick mud. As I waited for the other passengers to disembark, I noticed there was a sign indicating that the brackish water was not safe to swim in because of jellyfish. I looked at the muddy brown water and twigs, and I could not imagine anyone thinking swimming there would ever be a good idea. We grabbed our bags and carried on down a concrete path after the dock, carving right through the dense jungle foliage. Within moments we could see the Proboscis monkey, a weird primate with what looks like – as something maybe Attenborough would say to describe it– a big dick for a nose that droops over his mouth. They're fascinating creatures to watch and can fly around the tops of trees like acrobats. These are one of the highlights of the park and spotting them moments into our arrival had me eager to see what else we'd find here. As I checked us in at reception, Jeroen started to read through the comments book left by the previous guest, reading them out loud as I was trying to concentrate on filling out our forms. He was a funny guy and reading out the complaints in his Dutch accent was making me laugh.

"French fries in the canteen are too cold", he says quoting one of the comments, "Why would you bother complaining about that? Why don't you just fuck off back home if you're going to come out here to a jungle to complain about the fries?!" It was a good point to be fair. The fact that there's an established settlement with beds, running water, and food, whilst being miles away from proper civilisation and you're taking the time to write a complaint about cold chips? Some people, hey?

We took one of the minor jungle trekking routes in the area after we located our simple sleeping lodge. There were treks on offer to the other side of the park, taking a whopping eight hours. We decided an hour's route would be enough for today. As mentioned earlier about the jungle walks in Tioman, the trouble with trekking here is the tropical humid, so you have to carry a lot of water with you to replenish what you lose from sweat, especially if you're planning a lengthy one. There's usually no proper path either, so stomping around uneven terrain or climbing over fallen trees can be challenging. All that said though, it's still nice to be inside a jungle. Coming from northern England and being here in this amazing alien environment with strange tropical plants, underneath the tree canopy with vines hanging down – and the bonus chance of spotting exotic animals – it's an exhilarating experience. We decided to do a night trek also some hours later, which sounded to me like it would have had an almost dangerous edge to it with it being dark, but it wasn't too bad. Jeroen and I decided to get drunk beforehand to make it even more of a surreal experience. The wildlife we saw though was pretty impressive and really came out at night; a whole host of snakes and spiders, and the absolute treat of the nocturnal flying lemurs moving from tree to tree.

That night a massive electrical storm struck the area. I can only compare the lightning to when you flick a fluorescent tube lamp on, and it initially flickers before coming on fully. The lighting continued like that for hours, with the thunder constantly rattling on, some of it so loud it would cause the thin walls of our wooden lodge to vibrate. I was lying there listening to it in complete darkness as the power generator for the camp had been turned off, combined with the rain thudding down on the roof, and for a moment I truly appreciated how isolated from the rest of the world we currently were. Some of the evil macaque monkeys – who seem to be everywhere in Asia – had moved under our porch for shelter and instead of trying to sleep, decided now was the time to tit about, wanking and play fighting. The same floorboards the monkeys were on went under the wall and were supporting my bed, so when the monkeys moved about, it would cause my bed to move slightly and wake me up. Then, the roof started to leak, the heavier the rain, the more the water would leak through. I think this was what initially woke me up because I remember thinking a dog was licking my elbow in a dream. One side of the mattress was soaking and made me worry in case wise-cracking Jeroen saw it in the morning and thought I pissed the bed, and to top it off my pillow stunk of melted cheese. So, take heed, 'cold fries complaining guy', I had a lot worse than cold slices of potato and still didn't make a fuss about it. Write a mediocre travel book and moan about all of it there!

Gulping down the coffee the next morning at breakfast after my shit night's sleep, there was a young couple from Sri Lanka who sat at our table with Jeroen and me, and we struck up a conversation with them. They asked if I had ever been to Sri Lanka before. I said no. They said why don't I go then? I said I don't know if I could and joked it off with them. When I got back to my room that night, I had a think. Why don't I go? What's stopping me? I had Indonesia planned next, and then had to be back in Thailand mid-July to meet a few friends who were coming out for a two-week holiday. Why don't I go after that? Is there actually anything stopping me? I checked the flight situation, and there was one direct from Bangkok the day my friends were due to leave, for a reasonable price. Fuck it, why not? I booked the flight!

Return to Kuching, Malaysia - 28th June 2013

My birthday was here, and I had surprised myself that I had reached it to the age of 28 without dying. For the first time ever, I wasn't sat in a pub at home and was in fact in a far-flung country preparing to see orangutans, which in itself is a cause for a celebration. I'm a wildlife lover and a bit of a conservationist at heart, and the only thing I knew I wanted to do on this whole trip was to see something iconic like orangutans in the jungle. Having since parted ways with Jeroen, I was back in Kuching and excited like a kid on Christmas, I shot up, showered, ate some toast and *jem*, and jumped in the taxi with some new friends I had met in the hostel. The orangutan park, named Semengoh, is a fantastic concept. There's a lot of illegal logging that goes on around these parts, not to mention burning down of the jungle, like what they were currently doing over in Sumatra. The orangutans are always the victims in mankind's reckless endeavours. Instead of placing all of these rescued and displaced orangutans into zoos, acres upon acres of the jungle have been declared a national park, so the orangutans have freedom in a protected area. Of course, they're only semi-wild, but as an unorganised backpacker, this was the most comfortable choice for me to see them. It was either this, or spend £350 doing a seven-day trek in the jungle getting attacked by mozzies and leeches, and then with only a remote chance of seeing them. Arriving far too early as there wasn't a soul around other than the ticket booth operator, we bought our tickets and made our way into the thick jungle, and to the waiting area. The waiting area was a large wooden platform that was stationed on top of a large dip on the jungle floor.

Being the only people there at first was great, initially thinking we may even have the place to ourselves for this viewing. To my great annoyance, as time went on the waiting area *totally* filled. Within half an hour it was more like a crowd waiting at a festival for a band to come on rather than an endangered primate. With a lot of people comes a lot of noise. The park ranger repeatedly asked the group to be quiet but there's always going to be some knob-head that has to talk, and trying to quiet down over a hundred people, with the likes of Americans in the crowd was always going to be difficult. At the one side of the clearing, there was a large bamboo platform where one of the rangers stood with a bucket of bananas. He again told everyone to be quiet and begun to do a call that only the rangers can accurately perform to call the orangutans to the area. The call echoed through the jungle.

Certain types of people always have to take a phone call, be they driving, in the cinema or in this instance waiting for an endangered jungle primate to show up for breakfast. Some guy's phone near me begins to ring, and instead of turning it off, he picks it up and starts having a full-blown conversation. I couldn't believe it. We had been warned about the dangers of the primates earlier by the ranger: If they approach and become annoyed – you run. Serious advice. So the last thing you'd want to do is bring a baby, right? This American woman had brought her baby in, which I thought might not have been the best idea, but when it started crying loudly, it was enough to even get the guy on his phone turning around looking annoyed. Why on earth bring it here? This is not the place! Whilst I'm on the subject, if you're at a wedding or a funeral if your baby starts crying or your toddler won't shut up, wait outside with it. I've seen so many weddings mildly spoiled by kids or babies crying away in the background, ruining people's special moment. Yes, they are young, but they're making a racket, you are an idiot for not getting a sitter and it's not nice for everyone else. Toddlers will be barred from my funeral, and I will haunt anyone who tries to bring them in. Ten minutes had passed, and there was no sign of the orangutans. The ranger shouted across that there was always a chance we wouldn't see anything – if they're not hungry because they've found food elsewhere in the jungle, then they're not going to make the trip for food here. I really wanted to see them and told myself I would come back tomorrow if they didn't show. Another five minutes passed, and the ranger kept calling. It wasn't looking good.

Suddenly, there was a promising rustle in the canopy of the trees for a minute or so. The top of a couple of trees swayed. Finally! A strikingly ginger arm popped out from underneath the canopy. At first, I thought Mick Hucknall had followed me from Tioman. It hung there for a few seconds, and then the rest of the creature swung out into the full view of the audience. It was the only brief moment everyone actually shut the fuck up aside from the few faint "oohs" and "aahs" from those clearly amazed. To be fair, I maybe let out a little gasp myself, it was impressive watching it swing across the branches, and we were fortunate to see a bonus baby holding onto its belly fur. The orangutan was in no rush and took its time from the initial entry, then down to the bamboo platform. Once there, it walked over to the ranger on two legs. Orangutan translates as *Jungle People* or something in the local language, and you could see why. Seeing this great ape move around, it shared many human traits despite the longer arms. People who don't believe we share a common ancestor with these creatures need to come and see one of these things. It was magnificent. For some reason, I thought of them being smaller and was surprised to see it was the same size as the ranger handing it a banana. Once well stocked with a feed, the mother climbed back into the tree canopy. Using an arm and leg to hang from the tree, the other foot was used to hold a few bananas and the free hand to feed herself and the baby. The baby was pretty cute, popping its head out from its mother's fur every now and then to look at us gawping mouth breathers on the floor, sometimes taking a gob of banana, but never really moving from the tight clutch it had on his mother. We were expecting to see more of them, but she came and went, and that was that. The idiot crowd dispersed to probably go and make some unwanted noise elsewhere that they shouldn't, like a library or a neonatal intensive care unit.

Continuing with my birthday celebrations, we headed onwards to the *Rainforest World Music Festival* on the outskirts of town. This is apparently a massive event around these parts – entirely news to me until only a day ago, but came as a nice coincidence. *Glastonbury* had been on back at home, so this was the perfect antidote for missing out – you can keep your big-name bands, this is in a rainforest, so therefore, it's a lot better! Like any festival, the prices were extortionate for not only for entry but for anything else once inside. Unlike festivals back home though, the mountainous rainforest backdrop was thoroughly impressive, as were the traditional wooden long-houses used as trinket or alcohol shops around the arena. I did wonder a little how much this noise was disrupting the wildlife, the whole area rattled as someone set up a bass guitar for one of the acts. The bass by itself it was loud enough, never mind the entire band due to play soon along with it. The bands were pretty good, featuring artists from right across the globe, not just from Malaysia. Right. It's my birthday, let's get those beers in! And I could really afford to party now because I'd had those healthy apples when I first got into Kuching. I kept bumping into people I had met from my time in Malaysia. People from Kuala Lumpur, Tioman and Borneo all here for the festival, aptly rounding off my time here in the country. It was a fantastic birthday that beat sitting in the boozer at home!

Early morning the following day, I noticed my head was burning a little more than a usual hangover, not recalling how I had managed to get home from the festival. I saw a lot of my chums were packing up and leaving for other places, but I didn't have anywhere to be today so thought I'd get sleep off my hangover a bit more. Throughout the day, my head became increasingly worse, leading up to a point where I don't think I've ever been so ill in my life. The underlying fear of getting sick in the tropics is that you've gone and got one of the big life-threatening diseases like dengue fever or malaria, both received from mosquito bites. A couple of weeks before I got out to Koh Phangan, Liggy had told me about a Brit he met there who had been doing a stint across the whole of south-east Asia and caught dengue. For most people, dengue fever will give you a good kicking, but you will eventually recover. This poor chap had the disease develop into the rare dengue haemorrhagic fever, which amongst the many things that happen to your body, perhaps the most severe is that your organs begin to leak blood. He soon fell into a coma and had to be airlifted to the Thai mainland, and the last that Liggy heard he'd then been airlifted back to England. He was just a regular backpacker that was extremely unlucky, although we didn't know his route before Phangan, he might have spent extensive time in some remote jungle somewhere perhaps, where the risk is higher. That said, Mosquito-borne disease is across the continent and is an underlying threat that you just have to put at the back of your mind. Most people, when they first get out here, take all the precautions, long sleeve shirts and insect repellent. But months into the trip, you start getting sloppy or can't be bothered. It'll get too hot for long sleeves, or you'll accidentally leave the repellent at home. This had been me over the past few weeks. I felt the itch of a beefy mosquito bite on the back of my arm and wondered if this was the beginning of a rough few weeks.

By the following day all of my buddies had moved on, leaving me in my dorm by myself and the illness now had all the symptoms of dengue, high fever being one of them, sweating more than a blind lesbian at a fish market. The worst perhaps was not being able to hold down food or drink. I was too sick to get my planned flight to Indonesia and only just managed to peel myself out of bed to go to the doctor.

The doctor's waiting room was particularly grim, a series of sick people coughing and spluttering in a sweltering room, next to a sign apologising for the air conditioning not working. The doctor was great with me though, and in fluent English, assured me that whilst I did have a pretty bad fever, it was only a standard fever, and not dengue. He told me fever is common around these parts, so not to worry, and to go to bed and keep on top of my fluid intake.

Missing my flight gave me a couple of extra days in Malaysia. With time to kill, I had a go at meeting someone on *CouchSurfing*, and they were going to show me around for my time in Jakarta for when I was finally made it there. Incidentally, this new *CouchSurfing* friend couldn't offer me a free place to stay but offered to be a free guide for my time there and could organise almost suspiciously cheap accommodation, which was good enough for me. I got a panicked message from Mo who I'd met in Tioman. I didn't quite get her full story, but somehow, she had gotten on the wrong flight and had ended up in Jakarta. I'm not sure how that's even possible, but she was only 18, out here by herself, so I cut her some slack. She was worried she had nowhere to go and didn't know what to do whilst stuck at Jakarta's international airport, so I got her in touch with my new *CouchSurfing* friend to see what she could do for her. Luckily, they were able to help her out.

CHAPTER THREE

Jakarta, Indonesia – 4th July 2013

Even though I'd been to new cities, towns and islands on this trip, Indonesia was the first truly new country. It should have been pretty exciting. A new language, currency, traditions, way of life... Plus my *CouchSurfing* friend had parties, clubbing and even an invitation as a wedding guest lined up for me. But before leaving, I couldn't get into the mood for it. Fever had broken out in the city of Kuching, and locals and travellers alike were getting ill. I couldn't even remember the last time I've had a fever, or even if I'd ever had one at all. All I knew was it had wiped out. I'd have rather remained the sweaty mess I was out of sight of people instead of struggling my best to be charming, desperately wanting to make a good impression on this new friend who was hosting me.

I'd rebooked my flight for a couple of days later thinking I would have recovered by then, but I hadn't improved much. I fully expected a little tropical short-haul turbulence and hoped for a smooth ride, as my tolerance for it had pretty much been reset to zero with the illness. Standing on the ground at the departure gate was tough enough, never mind all the rocking that kicked off whilst in a flying can up in the air. "Hold it in", I thought to myself, desperate to keep what little food I'd managed inside me, "It's only a short flight". Luckily the seat between me and the aisle was free, so I sprawled myself across it and tried to sleep. The turbulence continued. After a while, the air stewards said the usual "Return to your seats and stow away your tray tables" as we approached descent, so I had to lose my extra seat. Moments after sitting upright, a small Asian guy comes running up the aisle holding his mouth, his other hand stabilising him on the seats as he staggered toward us. This little whopper clearly needed to be sick and was making a bolt for the toilet. A stewardess shot up from the back shouting something foreign – presumably, something like "You need to sit down sir!" and shoved him into the only available seat – which was next to me. She threw a sick bag at his lap, forcibly put his seat-belt on him, and she scuttled off back to the rear of the plane. The turbulence picked up intensity as we descended into the clouds and caused us to drop for a full two seconds of the sky. This pushed my new buddy too far; he buried his face into his sick bag and let out an ungodly noise of him retching to multiple wet slaps. It was an assault on the senses, the smell was appalling. I threw up in my mouth and with nowhere to dispose of it as the stewardess had given him *my* sickbag, it took everything I had to swallow it again and keep it down, some managing to dribble out and down onto my clothes. I felt an absolute mess. I rinsed my mouth out at the first chance I had at the airport toilets, frantically scrubbing my clothes too, hoping to wash the smell away enough not to repulse my new friend Kim from *Couchsurfing*. The flight had arrived sooner than expected, and it was still early morning. Fortunately, Kim was early too. She was instantly recognisable from her photos, an Indonesian in her late twenties. We greeted, hugged, and I tried to avoid breathing near her so she couldn't smell my breath.

The money in Indonesia takes some time to get your head around. At the time of writing, £1 equates to 19,600 Indonesia Rupiah, and the natives must all be math geniuses working with all these numbers every day. I withdrew 3,000,000 from the airport ATM and was horrified at the number of paper notes that came flying out of the machine. Some of it was as low denomination as 10,000 and wouldn't fit into my wallet properly once all together. I bought a much-needed chewing gum at a kiosk for 6500 and for a moment was struggling to work out if was good value or not, rooting through all the new notes in my wallet looking for something closest to 6500. It's a nightmare, and I was dreading when I actually went out to a bar or somewhere, trying to work out how much a round of beer costs in British pounds, as I fumble through as much paper as a copy of *War and Peace*.

New Delhi has since been the benchmark of a crazy city that I now compare other cities to. Although Jakarta appeared nowhere near as bad, it did share many of the hectic city traits. On our taxi ride to the apartment, I could see long expanses of shanty-towns hugging miles of the roadside into the city. The roads were in a pretty good state, but the pavements which ran alongside were uneven or had large gaps leading to the sewers underneath, and bits of the kerbs had broken off into the road. You'd be screwed for getting around if you were in a wheelchair. The traffic was almost on par Delhi save for the loose buffalo and elephants. Multiple mopeds weaved between the cars, some folk were pulling food carts on wheels; all making an attempt to cross the road look like a game of *Frogger*. Kim had primed me about the city's terrible traffic before I'd even arrived. After a mere ten minutes from the airport, the car slowed in a traffic jam, and the remainder of the journey was made roughly at walking speed. It was undoubtedly all go here, and despite the bustling city vibe, I was left a little underwhelmed. There are thousands of islands in Indonesia. Jakarta sits on one of the bigger ones called Java, which is a third of the size of the British Isles, yet still has a population of 140 million living on it– which is more than most of the world's countries have! Jakarta is by far the largest city in the whole country. On first impressions, it was an overpopulated, hot, dirty, built-up metropolis.

We talked about the city, and what we'd be getting up to over my ten days in more detail. Kim elaborated more on Saturday's wedding. It was at a posh venue with hundreds of people there. The bride– her friend, knows a few Indonesian celebrities and TV personalities, so they were going to be at the wedding as well. Considering it was our first face to face meet up, it wasn't at all awkward, and conversation was easy. Kim's English was pretty good, and she asked what other languages I spoke. Only English, I was sad to say. She spoke three. Much like Jack does in Borneo with his free time, she often met up with travellers to show them around the city. It astounded me that there must be an army of people out there just taking time out of their lives just to make sure strangers are having a good time in their hometowns. It's admirable. The rain began to come down hard, bouncing off the country's iconic bright blue *Bluebird* taxis, which often makes up half of the city's traffic jams. The city hosts 9 million people - larger than London – but without the transport infrastructure to help everyone get around. We eventually turned off into a residential area and then to a cul-de-sac somewhere in central Jakarta. This area was noticeably quieter, I found it somewhat of a relief to see the city did have places where the traffic could move quicker than walking speed. The road carried us over a waterway clotted thick with litter, close to busting due to the hard rain.

The taxi pulled up outside of an apartment block, a small building comprising of three floors. It was a lot less than I was expecting – very basic downstairs, and my room on the second floor almost looked like it had been abandoned. I had a bare mattress on the concrete floor and no real cover for the windows, so outside vegetation had crept through, along with the mosquitoes. Both taps broke whilst I tried to wash my face resulting in them being permanently on. The lock on the door wouldn't work, or rather it worked too well, as once in the locked position it wouldn't open again, so Kim had to call the landlady over to let us out. Mould grew up one of the walls, and there were droppings from small mammals in the shower. Still, only £4 a night in the centre of a capital city, I can't complain. One of Kim's friends lived downstairs, so after we managed to prise the door open, we went for a visit. There were two of Kim's friends there, both local girls in their early twenties, plus to my initial surprise, Mo. Mo ran over for a hug.

"Hey Steve, you wanker! I'm staying in your room with you!" I had taught her the word 'wanker' in Tioman, and she loved using it, mainly as a name for me. It was great she was around, but I wasn't sure how my single mattress would comfortably accommodate both of us. Still, at least if the lock jammed again, there would be the strength of two of us to try and open it now. I was introduced to Kim's two friends, Mel and Medina, they both seemed nice, Mel seemed a little wild though.

We went for a walk around mid-morning on the hunt for food. The girls took us to a little metal shack in a quiet back street selling a selection of grilled meats. It had been raining on and off all morning but had begun to come down quite hard now. We stood under the shelter provided by the stall whilst waiting for several chicken peanut satay skewers to cook. Smoke from the grill filled the air. A passing local approached Kim and struck up a conversation. They were talking in Indonesian, but I did hear "U.K." at the start, so it was a safe bet they were talking about me. I looked at him and smiled, but he blanked me and continued to speak with Kim. She later said he was probably too shy to talk to me, which was kind of strange that a man in his forties wouldn't directly address me. I'm guessing he didn't have much experience of interacting with foreigners. To be fair, there wasn't many of us around to practice on – other than Mo, I hadn't seen any, which for a capital city I found rather unusual. Even in Kuala Lumpur, which is just a country over, there were still a significant number of non-Asians around. The population here appeared to be made up entirely of Indonesians, living amongst a sprawling urban jungle that went on for miles. I realised I would get hopelessly lost in this labyrinth if I ever tried to explore it myself. Worrying I might get lost on my stay, I asked Kim what district I was in, she told me an instantly forgettable foreign word, and said it was a "good quality area". I would have to take her word for it, as the apartment I was staying in did not represent anything to do with quality.

I attempted to sleep a little bit in the afternoon on my single mattress, but once lay down on it, noticed was a bit damp. I needed to sleep off the remainder of my fever in preparation for the night, but it wasn't happening. My bedroom was right next to a mosque which, apparently, a regular feature of Jakarta is having some bloke wailing on a microphone for prayer several times throughout the day (I would later learn as early as 5 AM). This would only be cranked up in time for the Islamic event of Ramadan next week. I laid there annoyed as some man spoke Arabic over a loudspeaker, thinking that if only the European missionaries had worked harder hundreds of years ago and made Indonesia more of a Christian nation, I probably would be asleep now.

That evening I was taken to the south-central business district in Jakarta, (*SCBD* for those in the know) with the new crew, and the differences from the residential area we had come from blew my mind. There appeared to be hundreds of black-glass skyscrapers everywhere, lit up by rows of lights along them, blocking the horizon in every direction. It was nothing like I'd ever seen, it made London look like a town. Our first port of call was a bar which I was told was 56 stories high, and the view of the skyline from there was probably the most impressive modern man-made thing I had ever seen. There were skyscrapers as far as the eye could see. Part of the shock was the divide between rich and poor, which was as extreme here than anywhere else I'd visited. On the street level, you have people barely earning enough to make ends meet, living in absolute squalor – some literally sleeping on the broken pavements. They look up and see these skyscrapers collectively costing billions (billions of proper money – as a billion in the native currency is probably only about a £15!). The people that can afford to enter these skyscrapers are usually loaded, drive fancy cars and can afford to buy a drink at a bar that costs more than what some earn in a single day. There is serious money around in Jakarta, it's just not distributed well amongst the residents at all. We had a few drinks in various bars that evening, again striking me by how trendy and modern they each were inside, at first not expecting to see such a high standard inside the buildings after experiencing the poverty on the streets. Meanwhile, we were chauffeured around with taxis costing us next to nothing. I was experiencing both sides of the wealth divide too, drinking in the fancy bars, only then to return to my horrible little hole which dared call itself an apartment in the evening.

After being a little unsure at first, the city began to rub off on me. If you were poor, no doubt it would be a shitty place to live, among the excessive traffic, supposed high police corruption and pollution. I could imagine backpackers arriving here to break the journey up on their way to Bali or somewhere, seeing all the major tourist spots in half a day, stuck in traffic for the most of it, a dirty, built-up city and going away with a bad impression. I was here for more than just a day like these other backpackers might be, hosted by a local, and because of that I really saw the hidden gems of the city. Much like my time in Koh Phangan, or anywhere else in fact, if you spend long enough there, you'll get that true sense of the place that passing tourists simply don't get. Strong positives were going for it, one of which it was honestly the safest city I had ever visited (I could take an aimless wander at three in the morning, residential areas or otherwise, and if anyone was up they'd wave and say hello – how many other cities can you do this in?), and the party scene was something else. After a night of clubbing, we'd head back to someone's place just chilling out on sofas, watching TV and talking shit together. I'd missed doing this like I would at home, it's something I do with the lads after an evening in the pubs. I decided after only the first weekend I wanted to come back here, I was having fun, so why not? Kim and Mel said if I came back in August, they would have their own place, and I could stay with them as long as I wanted. I did start to make some more concrete plans around this as well. I decided after my upcoming Sri Lanka visit, I would do a few nights in Vietnam. Conscious on some days I was spending like I was on holiday and not backpacking, I knew money would need topping up by September, so after a second visit back to Jakarta, I planned to meet up with Clive from Tioman. He was moving to Australia, renting a house somewhere south of Sydney and had a job working in some dive shop. He said he'd help me find work, so it all started coming together nicely. Mo had decided she wanted in on the plans, so would be joining us in Australia around October. I liked she was joining me again. I was having fun out here with her. With nearly a decades' age difference between us, she became like a little sister to me. I was impressed that someone as young as her was comfortable travelling the world by herself. We'd clash on certain world views though, I'd consider myself mostly on the liberal left, but Mo was an aspiring hippy, and that mixed with a know-it-all teenager attitude, I realised topics like eating meat were best avoided.

The night of the big wedding with celebrities arrived, waiting in the rain by our apartment for the taxi, all dressed up ready. Kim had said it was a big event but had been a bit vague on what else to expect, other than the possibility of a TV crew being there. We hopped in the taxi and after a few moments of silence, the taxi driver turned to me and in perfect English, asked the dreaded question:

"Where are you from?" I dread this because the conversation almost always leads to the same topic. Two things I wish I could have as a traveller is the ability to speak another language and a mild interest in football. Knowledge in the latter would absolutely make travelling easier compared to the former. A typical conversation with a local – not just here in Indonesia, but anywhere– would start like this: "Where are you from?" And for ease I reply with the closest city to my town - "Manchester, in England". This has in the past had the local start to shout a footballer's name, presumably one of the team, something like "Rooney Rooney Rooney!!" but usually it leaves me to answer their follow up question of "*City* or *United*?". In the past, I have had too many awkward conversations started by the fact I'm from England and don't like football. They think I'm teasing, or they just can't process what I've told them. It genuinely gets weird sometimes. The other day at a bar, an American guy said that "We have literally nothing to talk about" when I said I didn't like sport and he walked away. To make my life easier, I have started to lie, so I just say I support whichever team takes my fancy at the time. If the conversation continues around football, I can fumble for the basic football knowledge I have, as I don't want to be caught out a liar, I will then try to steer the conversation into something else, and the crisis is over. On occasion, the local will try and ask more about my opinions on the pressing football topics like the recent performance of *Player X*, or worse, what did I think of the big game last night. By this point, my football knowledge has typically been depleted, so my final shot to drop the topic is to confuse the shit out them. I talk like I would when I'm with my mates in the pub; a lot quicker in speed, words dropped, and slang added, amping up my Englishness. This so far has always worked, and the football topic goes away. The idea behind this technique came to me because I began to realise that unless I put some real effort into how I spoke, some people genuinely had difficulties understanding me. My linguistic skills talking to others, especially to those who have English as a second language have improved considerably in recent months. Those with English as a second language tend to speak it so much clearer because they've learned from textbooks and watched movies (usually leaving them with a slight American twang). I'd never previously considered my accent particularly strong, just a broad Cheshire accent I guess, and it's definitely easy to understand compared the strong regional accents near me like those from Liverpool or Manchester.

Speaking clearer was a little tricky at first, analysing every sentence before I said it, thinking what common words to me will sound like bollocks for the person listening. That is a word there actually, I have to replace "bollocks" with "rubbish", that is until I realised only British people use the word "rubbish" too. Honestly, it's a fucking minefield. At first, I began to feel a bit inferior, only speaking one language compared to the many people I was meeting that speak two or more, and people couldn't even understand me entirely when I spoke it. Kim and Mel both speak Indonesian and two European languages. How bad is it that I live in Europe and only speak one, apparently badly? It's got to be a cultural thing though because no one really speaks other languages fluently where I'm from. It's great knowing English because everyone abroad speaks it, but that causes a lack of incentive to learn another. I hoped to sort this situation out and downloaded software to learn Spanish on my new laptop, but it remains an unopened file. There is more chance of me watching a game of football on the telly than starting it up, if I'm being honest.

There are the things you envisage before coming on your travels. You know that you'll be sat on a white sand beach with a cocktail at some point, or meeting new friends in your hostel, or visiting some impressive Thai temple out in the sticks somewhere. Then there are things you couldn't have even remotely fathomed yourself being a part of. This was one of those moments for me, nervously sat in a taxi on my way to a millionaire's wedding on the other side of the world. Okay, so we have marriages in England all the time, and they're usually big events, with however many people at a church wedding, then more arriving later on for the scran and piss-up. I still don't think I've been to an English wedding that had more than eighty people attending. We arrived at a posh mansion surrounded by highly manicured gardens and multicoloured spotlights, and there must have been close to a thousand people scattered around the foyer and the main area, stood amongst the marbled walls and chandeliers. Who the fuck knows a thousand people? I admittedly have a thousand friends on *Facebook*, but half of them consist of people I barely know like Ayaan back in India, and I certainly wouldn't be inviting a blert like that to my wedding. A small film crew sat stationed in the centre of the room filming the action as it happened, beaming images onto screens across the room. A band were warming up on a side stage. There were probably celebrities buried in the crowd somewhere (Unsurprisingly, my knowledge of Indonesian stars is non-existent, so I wouldn't have recognised any even if I'd bumped into them). I don't know why, but I expected there to be some other white people around. Me and Mo were literally the only two foreigners, me being by far the tallest of the thousand people. We walked sheepishly into the main area and watched the end of the ceremony. I felt a bit out of place, and even Kim, who must have been to enough Indonesian weddings in her time, was surprised at the scale of the whole thing.

The bride and groom slowly walked around in a choreographed fashion, with a walkway which curved round into the centre of the room. Their clothing was particularly striking, dressed in colourful Javanese garments, which entailed golden robes, trinkets, and a serious amount of makeup. The bride's face had so much makeup put on that she resembled a china doll more than a person, meanwhile traditional Javanese music filled the room. After standing around literally like a spare prick at a wedding, it was time for me to queue up and meet the bride and groom to wish them well, who were now stood on the main stage. Mo appeared nervous too, which was actually a bit of a relief as she was normally easy going, meaning my nerves were justified. Kim gave us advice on the traditional Indonesian greeting and how to act once we were up there. Fortunately, as scary as it was, it was instantly relieving when I noticed the bride and groom were down to earth people despite their excessive wealth, and in English told us "Thank you for coming". They were evidently not bothered two total strangers had turned up. Whilst the bride spoke with Kim, the groom turned to me and grinned, then asked where I was from. I gritted my teeth and prepared to pretend to like football again.

As is traditional with Islamic weddings, there was no alcohol available anywhere. Crazy traditions these foreigners sometimes have! The food, an absolute monster sized buffet cooked in front of us by ten chefs to one side of the room was outstanding, and made up for the sobriety I had to endure. It was a highly enjoyable event that I felt privileged to have seen, and you know what? We had a lot of fun, and it turns out you don't need alcohol to have fun at an event after all.

CHAPTER THREE

Yogyakarta, Indonesia – 10th July 2013

Breaking away from my usual form of just staying at a destination for a week or two once I realise there's beer available, Mo had plans to visit the city of Yogyakarta some distance away across Java and asked if I wanted to go for a couple of days. She showed me some pictures of an impressive Hindu temple called Borobudur near the city on my laptop. It looked almost mystical on the photos, so I said I'd definitely be up for that.

It was pushing 4 AM by the time our train got in into Yogyakarta. 4 AM is just a shit time to get in on any form of transport. If you've been on a plane, do you risk inflaming jetlag by going to sleep for a few hours in the morning, or push through the day until night-time, suffering a spaced-out day, groggy as hell? Trains coming at 4 aren't much better, Mo and me weren't sure if we should just look for a hotel or skip a night's sleep. We agreed we couldn't decide on an empty stomach and found a little area doing food by the station. It was surprisingly busy for the time of night, fifty people sat along the whole street. I couldn't work out if it was a really late dinner or an early breakfast that these guys were all sat munching on. You can get some absolutely outstanding street food in Indonesia; soup, chicken satay or fried noodles just for starters. I'm not just saying this, it's honestly great, and usually comes in at less than £1 for a full meal. Some of the vendors are unfortunately stationed near open sewers or busy roads, but the smell of the excellent food usually overrides any of the bag pongs from where they're stationed. More often than not, you do see someone else's street food dinner from last night floating past in the sewer, but what can I say? It's a mere quid to fill your stomach on tasty food, you can't do that at a *Michelin star* restaurant.

We sat on a rug that had just been placed on the side of a road, eating our rice dishes made by a street vendor. It was a curious way to have my dinner/ breakfast, but I completely loved being in a foreign setting to have something to eat, as I honestly can't say I've ever done this at home. I was sat next to an old woman who had an arrangement of edible goods in front of her. She had tried to make some sort of shop on the floor, asleep amidst it all, fashioning packets of dried noodles as a pillow and some were spread out into the street where she had knocked it over with her foot. Some locals were outright staring at the two Westerners who were around at these hours. The guy selling the food gestured with his hand for me to come over and talk to him, so I left Mo and moved over. Kim had mentioned locals really love talking to white guys but sometimes don't know what to say, partially to do with the language barrier, but shyness plays a part as well. It's something I've experienced before when I'd been walking down the street in Jakarta. I will hear something like "Hello Mister", a phrase in Indonesia which everyone seems to know, then I'll turn to look, and there will be two guys sat staring at the floor. Kim had also said locals are usually quite happy when Westerners try their food, especially so at the street vendors, who rarely get foreigners eating there. This particular vendor was positively beaming when I said his street food was the best I'd had out in the country. There's some sort of myth here with a few of the people in Indonesia, especially those from a poorer background, that the white guy is special, maybe even superior. I wish I could take these people to shitholes at home, such as the town of Crewe, and walk them around the overweight and unemployed horrors that lurch around *Poundland* with their faded tattoos and dried remnants of a *Greggs' steak bake* around their mouths that they've pressed into their face for breakfast, who then retreat home to catch up on the day's *Jeremy Kyle,* whilst breathing out of their mouths for the whole duration of the episode. I could then finally shatter this illusion that we're somehow better. Friends, we are all scum, no matter where in the world we are from.

There were apparent differences between Yogyakarta and Jakarta. Jakarta seemed perpetually jammed with traffic, and a little dirty in certain areas, with concrete favoured over any green spaces. Yogyakarta was more much more nature-friendly – multiple trees and plants grew alongside the roads with their vastly superior traffic conditions. There was a distinct lack of skyscrapers and huge shopping malls that are found everywhere in the capital, here were more traditional styled buildings and independent stores instead. Perhaps being a smaller, less populated city explained the better upkeep too, making it easier to keep clean and free of trash. Either way, it was a pleasant city to be in and I particularly liked all the street paintings on the side of the walls – it gave it a somewhat hippy vibe to the place. Mo was in her element.

Lack of sleep, excessive coffee and excitement had me feeling slightly spaced out several hours later, but I was in good spirits for the Borobudur temple regardless. I wasn't sure how busy such a landmark like this usually would be on an island that didn't seem to have many foreign tourists. It was mid-week which may have explained the lack of people, native or otherwise, but we had it almost to ourselves, which was great by me. Mo mentioned that the entire thing was built over a thousand years ago as we climbed up the steps of the monument. It made me wonder what qualifies things to be among the *Seven Wonders of the World*, as this apparently isn't. This place is just as impressive in its own right compared to the likes of the Taj Mahal or the Pyramids of Egypt, and it was almost itself a colossal pyramid but with the top flattened, built with chunky grey bricks, featuring large bell-shaped objects on top. It's a bit hard to describe, for me at least, mostly because I'm shit with trying to explain things in great detail. It's a good job I'm not writing a book. You're better off having a quick search on *Google images*.

There were a fair few steps which we had to navigate via the winding little internal paths and mossy arches of the temple, definitely giving off some tropical temple vibes from *Indiana Jones*. Once at the top, you could see for miles; a slight haze on the horizon; palm trees; jungles; little villages with tiny bits of smoke from them blending into the haze. We took some great photos and just sat back and soaked in the view. Mo couldn't have been happier, she had been keen to come here since she was thirteen (which I had to keep reminding myself that this was only five years ago for her) after reading about it in a magazine, and her enthusiasm for the place was rubbing off on me. The handful of tourists here appeared to be Indonesians who, at times, were more interested in our presence than the temple itself and kept asking for photos with us. I still find it so surreal that people want a photo with some random sweaty people they met on their travels.

I was nearing the end of my stay in Indonesia by the time I had returned to Jakarta. Once Ramadan had kicked in, it killed the party vibe I had previously been enjoying so much. Whilst there's some religious significance to Ramadan, in a nutshell, it is where Muslims exercise their will power by not eating, drinking, or shagging in daylight hours. The strictness of how this is enforced depends on where you are – in Algeria, for example, to do any of these things is breaking the law. Indonesia is around an 87% Muslim majority nation. At the time of writing, whilst the religious fanatics are still trying to push their agenda, it's still a secular society; Therefore, religion doesn't play a part in most of its laws. Whereas it's considered taboo to drink alcohol in Islam, from what I could see, the Indonesian people still have fairly liberal attitudes to alcohol, much like you'd find in somewhere like Turkey. That said, religion is still taken seriously here, so for something as holy as Ramadan, meant that anywhere we could usually buy alcohol, or food during daylight hours were mostly closed. If we'd be able to get our hands on it, at least we wouldn't be breaking the law, it was just finding it in the first place which proved problematic. Myself, Kim, Mel and Mo drove around for hours looking for open bars. Mel is a Catholic and Kim a non-practising Muslim, so all four of us were disappointed nothing was available. I found it weird that Ramadan rules are forced upon others – be you from another religion, have a relaxed approach to Islam, or in mine and Mo's case Atheist, that because we are a minority we have to have our lives disrupted by someone else's beliefs? If someone else can't resist the temptation of eating a packet of crisps in the daytime or *Greggs' stake bake* before sundown, how is that my problem? I could even possibly accept the banning of alcohol for the month, but food in the daytime? I wasn't impressed. Kim knew people who owned an open bar, selling soft drinks, but we convinced them to sell us a beer which they agreed to under the condition we drank it from a china cup and teapot. I kind of beat the system, I just looked a right twat in doing so.

On my final evening, we decided that we weren't going to find any open bar to party at, so created our own. We managed to get a few bottles of vodka from friends, booked out a hotel room and invited a lot of people around. There were at least twenty people there at one point getting blind drunk, rolling around the room. It was great here, I'd made a lot of new friends, and it was such a different way of life to back in England. I loved it and couldn't wait to come back.

Chapter Four

Krung Thep Mahanakhon Amon Rattanakosin Mahinthara Ayuthaya Mahadilok Phop Noppharat Ratchathani Burirom Udomratchaniwet Mahasathan Amon Piman Awatan Sathit Sakkathattiya Witsanukam Prasit.

Bangkok, Thailand - 14th July 2013

For the first time ever on a tropical short-haul flight, there wasn't a hint of turbulence, and it sent me off into a much-needed doze. I awoke to the plane circling over Bangkok at night, and it was great looking at the city from so high above – I've lost count of the number of times I've flown, but it always gets me when I see the epic panoramic view offered by the unnatural heights of flying. At night from above, cities look like little circuit boards, the cars on the street look like electrons moving around on it. I'll admit I wasn't too keen on the lightning forking across the sky whilst being up in the air though, which slightly spoiled the moment for me. Bangkok still looked as enticing as ever underneath. The only real place I could remember visiting from last time I was here, five years ago, was the backpacker hive of Khao San Road. You might as well not be in Thailand – There are lots of American-style shops and places to eat – 7/11s and *Subways* – with the only real give away you're still in Asia are the crazy nests of electrical wiring overhead and street food offerings of edible scorpions.

It's a good starting point for the rest of the country, which is why it's so popular with backpackers who have just flown into the city, with many tour operators working from here to get you to the far-flung places of the country if you desire. Like any tourist hotspot, you can get hassled by local people selling either absolute tat like trinkets or suits (like a backpacker has £200 spare for a suit he has to carry around travelling!). Either way, I remembered it was cheap, which worked out fine for me. I spent the best part of the first few days holed up in a small room having stocked up on the essentials like bottles of water and paprika crisps, living on a pittance, still having not fully recovered from the fever in Borneo. The first couple of days, I didn't leave the room at all. It was just nice to get away from everything for a while and not have to socialise with people. Don't get me wrong, I love meeting people, but it's just nice to have a little time away to recharge your batteries sometimes. I used to suffer from anxiety which comes in a continuous stream of self-doubt and lack of confidence, sometimes manifesting as social awkwardness. Whilst it's nowhere as bad as it used to be, it still does crop up from time to time. Trying to be outgoing and friendly to new people takes it out of me. I find alcohol helps with it, which is sometimes why I drink so much out in social situations. I'd had enough of drinking for a bit.

The break was good for the first few days, but mainly due to poor planning on my behalf, I found I had *too* much time to kill, and the novelty of my self-imposed self-isolation began to wear thin. I became bored with counting down the clock until my friends from England arrived for their holiday. Although my room was marginally better than where I was staying in Jakarta, I could hear loud thumping music from the nightclubs on Khoa San Road from 10 PM until daybreak. There's only so much television you can process in a small stuffy budget room without going delirious from cabin fever, whilst your bed vibrates from the club downstairs. Five days in whilst spending only something like £35 in total, I had depleted all my TV reserves and could hear this big party going on out on the street every night. I thought 'fuck it', let's go out and have a bit of fun before my friends arrive. There was a bar directly opposite my room on the main strip of Khao San, and it was as good as any place to start.

I soon met two French fellas who were friendly enough, and I had some beers with them. I noticed a white guy maybe in his mid-forties playing pool in the corner of the room, who instantly stood out because he was wearing jeans and black waistcoat. People generally don't wear clothes like that out here, okay, maybe jeans, but never a waistcoat, that extra layer of clothing in the tropics is absolutely unneeded. He looked a bit of a twat. He was playing pool with another Westerner who left, so waistcoat guy came over and in his cockney accent, introduced himself as Richard, or as he preferred to be called, Rick. Rick was one of those guys who screamed *geezer* about him. I enjoy people like that sometimes though. If you keep them at arm's length about things like money, then they can usually be a good laugh to go out with – and he was. I hit it off with him right away. After a couple games of the pool, he commented that this bar was shit here, which it was, so I took him up the offer to move to his favourite bar a short ride away. The French lads instantly seemed wary of him and weren't up for it, so I said bye, and we swapped details and made vague plans about meeting up for the full moon next week in Koh Phangan.

Rick's local was about ten minutes away from Khao San by tuk-tuk, I knew I wasn't far away from home, but still, it was an entirely new area of Bangkok for me with a guy I'd only just met. It's worth a mention that tuk-tuks are crazy three-wheeled machines, a sort of motorbike with a little carriage at the back, found not only throughout Thailand but also in a lot of Asia, named after the noise their running engines continually make. The only thing you need to know to drive one is: Always try and overtake whoever is in front, no matter what cost. They're tremendous fun, though. I love it when you see a backpacker clearly on their first time riding one of these, they're usually expressing a face mixed of panic and thrill, wedging themselves into their seat with the use of all limbs, much like they are on a roller coaster. As the journey continued, the surroundings of the city deteriorated, and we were dropped off on a run down and seedy side street. Rick led the way into the bar and judging by his character this place was entirely his sort of thing; a smoky bar filled with cheap neon lights, old decor and the wooden floor slightly sticky, judging by the smell it was dried up old piss. Terrible Thai pop music blasted out of the speakers (that's one thing about Thailand, considering the high amount of tourists they have in the country, they don't usually cater for them musically, locals love to play their own Thai pop music in the bars. It's pretty awful). Half the people there were old ex-pats, and the other half was most likely working girls a third of the age of the men. It was quite likely Rick had brought me to a prostitute bar here. Before we all judge, my local in Koh Phangan was in a red-light bar but, in contrast, it was a small bar conveniently located near our apartment. It was pretty clean, I suppose, and there were huge shutter doors that once opened, allowed fresh air in. Occasionally there was loud music, but generally, the vibe was often quite chilled out. I got to know some of the girls who worked there over time, and each had their own sad story. A lot of them were from Thailand's impoverished north-east region, and I never quite understood the full set up, but it seemed like a lot of them were 'owned' by the boss of the bar, a middle-aged ex-prostitute herself who had bought the girls from their families and sold them into prostitution. That is until they could afford to buy their own freedom. That's what I understood from it all, at least. Maybe it was a sob story from a few of them, but I could definitely believe it happening out here. Thai working girls sometimes have an attitude and a hard way of acting towards strangers, which is understandable given their career paths. Still, the girls there were often genuinely nice people beyond the fake flirty behaviour once they realised I wasn't a potential customer, and I cut through the bravado. Liggy and I would sometimes have lock-ins until the early hours of the morning with them and the occasional *Full Moon* backpackers who had strayed too far looking for a room. They were some good times there, playing cards, dancing about and chatting away until sunrise. Back here in Bangkok, I couldn't imagine having this horrible smelly sweatbox filled with probable nonces as my local.

To the right of the entrance, there was a pool table people were using as a seat. After buying drinks, me and Rick made our way there, and we met what I assume were Rick's friends; a load of equally iffy Westerners and Thais. Although I've been in worse places before, I think after my few days of hibernation and then straight into this seedy place was a bit too much, and I couldn't initially shake the awkward feeling I was carrying. I kept telling myself that half of *Banged Up Abroad* episodes usually start with an innocent backpacker meeting a dodgy character, and even before the second commercial break they're stuffing a kilo of heroin up their arse to smuggle through an airport. I told myself I would flatly say no to anything drug-related if it was brought up. I scanned the room just people watching as the place was full; meanwhile, Rick and his mate were talking about which girls they would like to take home tonight. I perhaps use words like *shithole* too much in my stories, but this truly was. Even the toilets weren't working, and people were just going out of the side door and using an alley as a toilet.

After a few drinks, and once the girls began to back off once they knew I wasn't interested in them, I began to unwind a bit. Rick was a funny guy, cracking jokes all the time. I got talking to his friends as well, a few older ex-pats, a German and a couple of Danish lads. After my initial impressions, they weren't so bad, after all. Okay, they might be lost souls here, and in the case of the German guy have next to no teeth – but who was I to judge? They made me feel welcome, and that's all you can ask for really. One guy I got talking to, another Brit called John, was having a particularly hard time. I've heard similar stories a few times, and it's quite common in Thailand, particularly with the older Westerners; he had overstayed his tourist visa by six months, and Thai immigration charges you 500 baht, around £10, for every day you overstay - so you can imagine what he must owe by now. He decided on a whim to stay out here having nothing to return home to, now he can't afford to leave the country and will get thoroughly hammered by the authorities if he gets caught. If you can't pay, you end up in a Thai immigration jail which in itself is supposed to be fairly rough going, and once deported you're looking at a ten-year ban from the country. John told me he had £200 left to his name and had no idea what his long-term plans were now. Drinking his troubles away, he must have spent at least a tenth of what he had left that night. I thought to myself that if the Thai police raided this bar right now, I bet half of the guys here have overstayed.

Hours passed and only after John left for home, I noticed I hadn't seen Rick in a while. None of the original guys we sat down with was still here. I made an effort to talk to a few of the working girls who were initially part of our group, in the hope Rick would come back, but the conversation wasn't flowing. I said to myself I'd had enough. Rick had probably left to go home with a girl anyway. I decided to use toilet alley and then jump in a tuk-tuk back to Khao San. Mid-piss I heard a moaning sound coming from the shadows. Bangkok is mostly safe, but still, having a wee in a dark alley in a foreign city can still be scary, especially when you start to hear unusual noises. The fear this caused was so intense, it caused me to halt urinating without even trying. I looked to my right, and after giving my eyes a few seconds to adjust, I could see that it was Rick lying on the wet floor.

"Are you okay, mate?!" I shouted. No response. I hesitated walking over, but he was obviously not in a good way. "Rick? Are you okay mate?" I nudged the side of him with my foot which sort of woke him up slightly. I swear he muttered he'd been drugged, which sort of made sense as I didn't really see him drinking much that night. I looked around and checked that I wasn't walking into some kind of trap, suspicious I was getting set up like a mug and bent down to him once I was confident this was legitimate. Fuck. He's pissed himself. I reluctantly lifted him up hoping none of the urine would get on me, when I felt something hard in his pocket, something rather gun shaped. I peered down and could see the top of a small pistol. This guy had a gun in his pocket! Straight away, panicked, I leapt in with "Is that a fucking gun mate?" To which his response was,

"Yep"... I couldn't think of anything to say at first, then asked,

"Has someone drugged you? Who drugged you?"... a moment's silence.

"Arseholes did".

Well, I'm sure that gun will be illegal, but even in the unlikely event he has a licence, what's he doing bringing it on a night out? He was definitely off his tits. I couldn't quite place my finger on it, but I could tell this wasn't the drink making him like this. Was he fighting the effects of something like *Rohypnol?* I'm stood in an alley with a guy I've only known for a few hours. He says he's been drugged; God knows on what, and as far as I'm concerned he's got a loaded gun. I still couldn't leave him like this. I propped him up as best I could and walked him back through the door and into the building, hoping someone in there would be able to take over. He was heavy and took quite a bit of effort not only to prop up but then to walk along. One of the Thai prostitutes spotted us from across the room as we entered the bar again. Seeing his face appeared to anger her. She smashed the end of a bottle on a table, fashioning a rather dangerous weapon with what was left, and came running over towards us, with several other girls following immediately after. Noticing there was a drama unfolding, some fool turned the music off, so within seconds the whole bar was looking in our direction wondering what was going on.

"I told him to fucking go!" she screamed at us right up into our faces, whilst waving the sharp glass in our direction, but mostly near Rick's exposed neck who had his head tilted to one side, being completely out of it. Panicked, I could only shout "Sorry!" on a repetitive loop whilst backing back through the door, easing Rick slowly, and once again returning to the alley. Fortunately, the alley wasn't too far away from the main road, so I struggled with him further, listening intently for the door back to the bar to open, worrying in case the girls followed us outside. The first three taxi guys wouldn't even touch him because he was that out of it, but I managed to get an address out him for a tuk-tuk driver. The address could have been total horse shit, but as far as I was concerned, I'd done my bit, he was gone. We'd never swapped details, and that was the last I saw of him.

The next day I contemplated looking for the bar again to see if he was okay but decided against it. Who knows what another night there would have ended up like if I found it? I decided my best bet was to get a load of *Diazepam* from the pharmacy, which is completely legal here, so I could have a massive sleep over the noise of the clubs in Khao San, ready for my friends to arrive. Still not your average night, but better than dealing with lunatics and weapons – loaded with bullets or otherwise.

Bangkok, but with mates! 21st July 2013

My friends had arrived in the country, and we arranged to meet at where we were staying for the next few nights, a rather nice modern apartment with city views and a balcony. I arrived early anticipating their flight. For me, having hot water showers and access to a fridge was a novelty. It had been weeks since I stayed in a place with a kitchen. I sat around in the apartment with no pants on having beers, enjoying the air-conditioning whilst listening to metal and hip hop waiting for my friends to arrive. That in itself was a pretty good afternoon. When their cheeky faces popped through the door, and it was quite surreal after being away from them for months. My best mate Ding, his girlfriend Jussy, and another mutual friend of ours, Sarah, had all known each other since we were kids. We had a catch up than my role as a tour guide had begun. I'd get my friends sorted with street food using the bit of Thai I'd picked up and informed them about what I have learned about my time in Thailand, about the culture and way of life. It was nice to be able to give something back in that sense. This year alone, people from India, Malaysia and Indonesia had taken me around their countries and acted as guides, so it was nice to be able to be the guide for a change.

The next day would be our only full day in Bangkok, so we got up reasonably early to make the most of it. The plan was to take a speed boat along the Chao Phraya, Bangkok's river, see some temples in the afternoon, then go to a *Ping Pong* show. Bless Jussy's heart, she thought we were going to see an actual ping pong tournament and if you think that's what it means too, then stay innocent and skip to chapter five. For those a little more clued up, you'll know it's where ladies stick things up into their lady-gardens, not just ping pong balls, worryingly, and do creative things once said objects are inserted. It sounded grim, so I really wanted to see it. I had met travellers, genuinely nice people, salt of the earth types, and even they had been to see these shows. So if these good people are going, scum like me certainly isn't going to give it a miss. It's something "you do whilst you're here" everyone kept telling me. I would be avoiding any of the cruel ones that use live animals, though. A friend told me he once saw some woman pulling live turtles from out of her at a show in Pattaya. My morbid curiosity only goes so far and doesn't cover that.

The river ride along the Chao Phraya was tame, for me at least, but that was only in comparison to what I'd seen over the past few months of travelling. My mates loved it. It was their first-ever full day in Asia, and it was nice to see them get excited over the things here that I'd become a little desensitised to. Our longboat, driven by a local, flew down the broadest part of the river, which must be a mile across in parts. In the distance you could see the usual Bangkok gubbins through the hot tropical haze; skyscrapers, billboards, temples and closer to us, tropical plants and narrow marshlands. The river itself didn't look particularly clean, which is to be expected as it's near a busy city, I guess. We turned off down a much smaller side river, taking us through a residential area with rows of shacks along the water's edge. It's unbelievable that people live alongside the river like this – huts on stilts supported by wood that appeared to be rotting away. Some looked like they could literally go at any moment. Anything goes with these shacks too, a mishmash of metal, wood or concrete, all different shapes and sizes painted in all colours, none of which the same as their neighbours. Occasionally there would be breaks in the shacks revealing reed beds, long grass, willows and palm trees, and that too offered a fantastic opportunity to see some wildlife. My knowledge of tropical river bird species lacks so I can't name them here, but there was a great variety of them around. And this is where the wholesome part of our day ends.

It was now night-time, and we were in a tuk-tuk heading to a *Ping Pong* show. I had pre-organised the excursion with a little Thai chap I had become friendly with during my week of near isolation on Khoa San road. Although I had no idea where Rick's bar was in the city, this area we were being taken to had a similar feel to it. We could well be only a street over for all I knew. Our tuk-tuk dropped us off outside a small building which looked like it could have been a factory in a previous life, the whole of the surrounding area just looking as seedy as you can get in these type of places. We were in a proper red-light area, flashing neon lights and prostitutes on every corner. Inside the building for the *Ping Pong* show, the standards continued to drop further. My friends asked if we were safe here. I told them I think so, but really, I didn't have a clue.

There were only two types of people working there, fat old Thai blokes taking the money, and fat old Thai women in thongs. This is definitely not my scene anywhere in the world, never mind in Asia, and I wondered if it was a bit of a mistake to have come. I am usually quite okay with weird situations, and generally keep my cool, but something about being there didn't feel right, and fuck knows what my friends must have thought heading here with it only being their second night in Asia. Entering in through the cigarette smoke, there was a dimly lit main stage surrounded by chairs with a depressed-looking overweight Thai woman in a thong dancing on the stage. I had the same pitying feeling for her as I have for animals in small enclosures at zoos. Thankfully, I spotted some other Western people already sat down, albeit looking a little uncomfortable too, which always makes me feel better that there are at least a few other definite tourists here. I don't know why I find seeing fellow palefaces such a big comfort in weird places abroad. Perhaps I feel like they'll know what to do if it gets fucked up, or there's less chance the locals will target me if this is a scam of some sort. They were sat there in contrast to the front row of seedy looking, grinning Chinese men on the other side who looked like they were really enjoying themselves.

The first 'dancer' who was on stage was one sorry person to look at. She must have been pushing fifty for a start, so her drooping bits just looked wrong stuffed into skimpy clothing but doing this job every night for years must slowly eat away at your soul. I think she had managed to completely switch off her feelings and whilst her body shuffled slightly in time with the music, hence 'dancer' in quotation marks, nobody was there running the controls and autopilot mode was truly on. She could well have been on drugs. The smoke and heat increased as the room filled with punters, and to my surprise, there were many types of people there. All the Westerners were around my age, but the variety of Asians there shocked me: Middle-aged women, businessmen, teenagers, old grannies, young men. Even an entire family arrived at one point, which was really strange to see a mother, father and two adolescents. When I was fourteen, my family used to go to Blackpool for a day out on the beach. Have a stick of rock and maybe get to ride a donkey. This family here are watching an overweight Thai woman grind her minge up and down a pole in a red-light district. Once the room had filled, the first 'dancer' left and then the show really started to fire up. Two slightly younger girls got up on stage and began to stuff ping pongs up into their fannies and fired them out and into cups placed around the stage. It was odd but somewhat impressive how many they got in there with such accuracy. Whilst this was going on, Jussy turned to me whilst laughing, partly with shock, I think, and asked,

"Where the hell have you taken us?!" It was a fair point. A bit weird this, innit? But we were here now, might as well make the most of it.

More women arrived, and shit just got weirder, and they began firing darts from there (everything was front-bum based activities). The darts came out with such force they were able to pop balloons mounted on the ceiling. Obviously, with that sort of pressure, blowing candles out was a piece of piss, which they did on a birthday cake. Whose birthday was it? I don't know. They began cutting the cake into slices and offered it out, the only thing I could think was how you could eat anything that's been in this sweaty room and had fanny air blown on it? The weirdness continued with writing messages with a pen held impressively by the lips. One girl managed to store six metres of thin rope which was pulled out and later danced with. I never knew fannies could make a little melody on a penny whistle until today. Then a girl tried to get one of the seedy Chinese blokes sat at the front to put the whistle in his mouth to have a blow, at first he wasn't sure, but she was insistent on it. The Chinese guys ended up passing it around and licking it, whilst the family of four sat behind were clapping and laughing, the dad encouraging the two kids to go up for a closer look, clearly a highlight of the visit for them. The highlight of my family outings was getting to see the illuminations in Blackpool. And then full-on intercourse! Out of nowhere, some guy leaps out on stage wearing nothing but a condom and starts nailing one of the girls. They were clearly fans of the *Karma Sutra* by the looks of things, some positions I didn't even know existed. I think for me the most notable point of that part was her upside down doing a handstand whilst he was upright nailing her. I honestly wasn't really expecting it to end up in full sex, but it was the last little bit of craziness that put the icing on the (ping pong show birthday) cake. To be honest, I could have just watched my group of friends trying to process what they were seeing, their faces were funny enough.

To summarise my experience there: I would definitely never go to it again, but I'm kind of glad I did see it. I don't know if people are supposed to find a woman using her clout for storage as some kind of a turn on. If anything, it's the opposite for me, but still, it was interesting to see in its own fucked up way. I just hope the women there aren't all messed up on drugs, and my money hasn't gone into feeding their habits and keeping them stuck in that life. I like to think they're just good at switching their minds off when they're at work, it helps my conscience if I think about it that way.

The next ten days we had a blast in Koh Phangan, it was great to go back and catch up with my friends I'd met on my first stint, and do the highlights of the island with my friends from home. It's not all just about the *Full Moon Party*, there's quiet expanses of beach, The *Loi Lay* bar that floats on water, a full replica of an English pub with roast dinners, and a place called *Amsterdam bar* where you can view epic sunsets and smoke a joint in the process if that's your bag. I was hoping to catch up with Liggy but having his bar idea not work out, a few weeks before our arrival he'd decided to leave the island and do some travelling. He was currently in the Philippines and rapidly running out of money.

And that was that, before I knew it, another fantastic *Full Moon Party* was under my belt, my friends were waving me off at Bangkok international as I boarded my next flight to Sri Lanka.

Chapter Five

A wanka in Sri Lanka

Negombo, Sri Lanka – 3rd August 2013

Sri Lanka wasn't even on my radar when I first set off from the UK all those months ago. Meeting those young Sri Lankans in Borneo had planted the seed, and it had grown into real plans of being here. I had done little bits of research on the interwebs over the past week – I knew I wanted to go to Hill Country in the centre of the island, with apparently epic scenery. Other than that, though I would just go with the flow. If there's one thing I'd learned about this solo backpacking malarkey is that I would almost certainly meet a travel buddy who would then have a strong influence on where I'd end up visiting. During the flight, I was sat next to a lad from Sheffield who was returning home after two years away, on a connecting flight in Sri Lanka. As we chatted, it became clear that he really wasn't keen about heading home, whilst out of the plane window as the sea ended and Sri Lanka started, it begun to look positively enticing with lush green landscape. Whilst both of us gawped out of the window looking at the new foreign land he muttered,

"Wish I was goin' Sri Lanka with you now mate, not Sheffield." I couldn't blame him. Going home after travelling is a mixed bag of emotions but returning to Sheffield of all places is pretty grim. I thought to myself that I wished he was coming, too, if only for the fact I'd have a new friend to tackle this place with. The worry of being by myself crept up slightly, taking on a brand-new country, stepping off the plane into unknown lands, ready to fall victim to some scam or get lost in the middle of nowhere. To put some more unease into me, I'd heard the country is culturally similar to India – which as you know holds the record as the wildest place I had ever been to. I wished my new friend a safe onward journey and sailed through the airport.

Stepping out from the airport to flag a taxi, the outside temperature here seemed even hotter than Thailand. My destination now was Negombo, a coastal town north of both the airport and the capital, Colombo. I had either read somewhere or heard from someone, that it had a great backpacker vibe, so there was a good chance I would meet a travel buddy. The town itself was nothing special but was obviously one of those places that was a cheaper option for backpackers as opposed to staying in the capital. The sea was close by which explained why the roads were so sandy, whilst colourful bungalows and palm trees were either side of the streets. I took the best part of half an hour exploring whilst looking for a room, happy to take my time as it was so pleasant. I was delighted that locals were just being friendly, saying "Hello" and then didn't seem to expect money after it, which is usually the case in parts of Asia. As a cyclist went past, a pedestrian jumped out in front to give him a scare, I think they were mates or something. It was funny to see, but the scarer turned to me and said he was "Sorry for the inconvenience" as a joke, making it even funnier. There was just such a buzz going along the street. I wasn't sure if people were being so friendly because I was a foreigner, because surely nowhere in the world is this naturally happy? If they were, then great! I walked with a smile on my face too, waving back at the friendly locals. I spotted a small alleyway to the beach, and on to the right there was a sign that simply said "Rooms". My backpack was getting a little heavy, so this would be as good a start as anywhere I thought.

Use of the word "Rooms" was a little ambiguous - they were cheap and a little on the shabby side, a simple bed in a small breeze-block walled room, with ripped curtains and itchy bed-sheets. Mosquitoes could fly in freely, but the bloke who ran the place couldn't have been any friendlier. He oddly referred to himself in the third person as 'Nightman'. I would have paid the £3 I did for the night's stay just to have a chat to him. I towered above him as he was only short, and in his fifties. He spoke English brilliantly, and with it filled me in on the recent politics of the country. Apparently, the government had been shooting peaceful protesters only four days ago but it wasn't making big waves in the news. The incident was over a large company leaking ammonia into the national water supply, and people were protesting this being allowed to happen.

"Why do they bring the military in for a peaceful protest? Nightman doesn't approve of this at all!" he scorned. It was fascinating to hear his stories of life here, and after politics, he then gave me a detailed orientation of the country. He said it is mostly safe for tourists, and more than anything I needed to get into Hill Country whilst I was here (which was the only major plan I had anyway). I should avoid the extreme north as it wasn't very safe with the current political situation – infighting between the government and a militant group fighting for independence. After telling him I had only two weeks here, he said that should be enough to scratch the surface.

Now the room had been sorted, first things first – Food. I had become a right bloody foodie since getting out here. I think the turning point was that night in Tioman I touched on briefly earlier, where locals caught that fresh fish in the evening and it was on a barbecue within an hour later, stuffed with garlic and tomatoes. I miss a good Sunday roast now and then, but thinking about it, I'd become a bit bored with food at home, eating the same things every day. Largely pre-prepared frozen food. Since that fish in Tioman, I realised there was no excuse for letting myself get bored with what I ate. I had started to eat a little more adventurous too. When the locals told me the eyeballs of the same Tioman fish were just as tasty, I thought why not try it? And you know what, it had an alright taste if I didn't overthink it being an eyeball. Clive had also got me into calamari which previously I had dismissed as weird meaty onion rings. I love them now. Out here, I couldn't contain my excitement thinking of the entirely new gastronomic delights that awaited. I found a restaurant a short walk away from Nightman's and outside on a board it boasted "Sri Lanka Curry". It seemed a little bit generic, but I thought 'fuck it' and sat down for it. It was awesome. Instead of one flavour of curry and then the rice like what you may get with a 'normal' curry, there were loads of little pots of curried chicken & green beans. It was terrific, and the flavour not a million miles away from an Indian style curry I guess, and it all went down well with a local bottle of beer. I ate like a king for £3. The man who ran the restaurant was so nice too, making sure I was constantly happy with the food. It's times like this I want to leave a tip. I still think tipping should be optional. None of this 20% service charge or whatever. What if your meal was shit? I still have to pay extra? Aside from it being a great way to indicate to the staff if you've been happy with the service and the food, doesn't tipping show genuine appreciation? How can you show that if your tip is enforced? As the meal was so cheap and plentiful, I paid double, and the waiter couldn't have been more thankful.

Negombo was a lot quieter than I expected on the tourist front. I walked around the streets, having a nose around little trinket shops and seeing if there were any bars with people in. I didn't see many other backpackers, and those that I did seemed like they were hurrying on their way between places. Disappointed I hadn't met a travel buddy yet, I went to my room and watched *Django Unchained* with Nightman in his living room on a small black & white cathode-tube television for something to do. I had been speaking regularly with Kim and Mel in Jakarta about plans for my return to the city, and we had a chat for half an hour or so on *Skype* after Nightman left for bed. I checked my email and noticed my Sri Lanka mates from Borneo had gotten me in touch with one of their friends, Tashiya, a local from the capital. We agreed to meet in the city at 3pm the next day and whilst having a beer or two she could give me some travel plan ideas in regard to the country. Great!

Early the next morning, I had a chat with Nightman over some toast about my options for getting to the capital – I wanted to get a tuk-tuk to Galle Road in Colombo, this was where my hostel was. The cost of this was 1500 Rupees – nearly £8 – but Nightman suggested a better alternative would be to get a tuk-tuk to the bus station in Negombo, then a bus to Colombo, then finally a tuk-tuk to the hotel. Although there was a bit of faffing about compared to going there directly, it would work out the cheapest option by far, at around 400 Rupees. I thought doing the Nightman route could possibly give me something interesting to write about for my travel blog. I have a huge aversion to public transport abroad, with all the potential to get lost or taking the last bus to the arse end of nowhere, but this route in Sri Lanka seemed pretty straight forward, so what could go wrong?

The five-minute drive to Negombo's station surprised me a little as the town extended quite a bit on from the coastal area I'd spent the night at. There were busy expanses of markets, street-side sellers with lots of fruit and vegetables, and large residential areas. Arriving at the bus station, I was instantly greeted by a local as I stepped out of the tuk-tuk.

"Colombo?" It was too sudden, so I was wary about who this guy was. "It's okay", he said, picking up my hesitation, "This is bus to Colombo." He was asking for 100 rupees, which seemed incredibly cheap for the distance. Great. He led me to a small bus which I had to crouch through the door to get inside, which was already packed with locals. There was nowhere to really put myself other than try to squish up between people and having nowhere to put my backpack, I had to sit with it on my legs. The engine rumbled into life, thankfully bringing on the air conditioning with it. We chugged along out of the dusty car park and off to our destination. Strangely, considering the dilapidated state of the bus, it still offered TV mounted at the front, and even better, it had *Mr Bean* on it, which I could just about see from over the top of my backpack. Everyone on the bus was lapping it up, including me. *Mr. Bean* has to be one of the biggest exports out of the UK, repeats from the classic 90's show I'd seen all over Asia. I believe the international appeal lies in the lack of words spoken – it's just a silly man bumbling about from disaster to disaster, simple enough for anyone of any age to understand. Engrossed in Mr Bean's caper at the hairdresser, circulation cut off to my legs from the weight of my backpack, I hadn't really paid much attention to where I was. After about twenty minutes of driving, the bus driver turned around and shouted down the bus corridor to me,

"Okay. You, Mister white man. Your stop". Seemed too early to be here, but whatever, I must be here if the man said it, so I got off. The complete dickhead that I am didn't even think where I was, I just trusted the guy that I was where I needed to be. As the bus pulled off and left a trail of dust, my first impressions were that the surroundings here looked a little quiet for a capital city, and there wasn't a single building in sight. I quickly realised this was a motorway with nothing but a load of dust either side. Weirdly there were a few tuk-tuks, and their drivers sat near an intersection. I walked over to them.

"Colombo?" I said, sweat beginning to form on my head in the heat. One of them laughed.

"Colombo many miles away!" I looked around he was probably right, this obviously wasn't anywhere near the capital, or human civilisation, by the looks of things.

"How much to Colombo then?"

"Three thousand, five hundred". £15.

"You what, mate?" This was some sort of scam, wasn't it? Drop the foreigner off miles away from anywhere and then charge them a fortune to get back. I could afford 3500 but wasn't going to pay out of principle, so stormed off the same direction the bus was going. 3500! What an arse! I still hadn't got a phone sorted so awkwardly had to load my laptop up on the dusty footpath next to the busy road to check the time. It was pushing 12pm, I still had three hours to get to Galle Road to meet Tashiya.

The midday heat was intense, not to mention carrying my backpack. Trying to negotiate large junctions in the road with speeding drivers at the wheel was a challenge in itself. I was stuck with my thoughts wondering what had happened back there and did notice the airport was a left-turning near to where I was dropped off. It would have made sense that this wasn't actually a scam and that the bus driver assumed I was going to the airport. The tuk-tuk drivers were probably waiting at the intersection so people could get to the airport without walking. It would also explain why they were charging so much for the journey to Colombo, as the airport is a fair old drive from the capital. The guy on the bus said Colombo though, not bloody Colombo airport! A couple of tuk-tuk drivers pulled up from the highway and tried to take advantage of my situation and offered five thousand to take me to the capital. Yeah okay, you can have my firstborn child too if you want. After looking like a lost tourist twat for a further twenty minutes, buildings slowly started to appear along the road, and finally, I came across a bus stop, and the people waiting there told me the next bus was for Colombo. A local man in his mid-sixties, with short grey hair and glasses who made me think he looked like he could have been a doctor, was keen to fire up a conversation with me. His English was superb, he told me that if I wanted to go to Colombo, I needed to get on the same bus as he does but to hurry because it's a fast bus and doesn't wait at the stop long. I soon knew what he meant, it never really stopped but slowed down enough for a few seconds for people to get onto it, he leapt onto it like a 100m hurdle athlete. I barely had my footing on it before it pulled off again with furious acceleration, swerving into another lane in the process. The bus driver drove like he was being pursued by the police, either only having his foot fully on either the brake pedal or the accelerator. There was no middle ground, no staying at a nice speed. This was made even more intense by the weaving in and out of the traffic on both sides of the lanes. On these travels, I'd climbed the taxing peak of Tioman, jungle trekked in the humidity, walked for miles in the blistering heat and swam like my life depended on it (which it did). And yet negotiating the gangway to a seat on the number one bus to Colombo with my backpack was the most demanding physical task I've done so far. I had toyed with the idea of renting a motorbike to see the country with but after this little experience, no chance. As good a driver I consider myself, it's the mentals like this guy that are the risk.

An hour flew by as quick as the bus rallied towards the capital. I turned to look at the old Doctor guy, and he was asleep. I couldn't remember if he said he was getting off at Colombo too, I was pretty sure he did, but I didn't want to wake him up to ask. The ticket inspector was a young guy running up and down the bus collecting money from the passengers. As he passed, I took the opportunity to ask "Colombo?" and gestured with my hand the direction of the way the bus was travelling. He looked confused. I tried again but got nothing. I began to worry that after well after an hour now we still weren't there when I was told it was only a forty-five-minute journey from Nightman. I was so confused, feeling like I was living a story straight out of an episode of *Mr Bean*. After some time, the bus reached the end of the line at a built-up area, and The Doctor told me to get off here. I had an hour and a half to meet Tashiya by this point, and with no way to contact her that it was looking like I was going to be really late. I pride myself on my punctuality, plus if I was too late and she'd left without seeing me, what else was I going to do today? What was I going to do for my insider Sri Lanka travel advice? I still had to get to my hostel, wash all this sweat and despair off me, and then get to the bar she was at. Time was running out. As I left the bus, the heat hit me again. No wonder people are always laid back in the tropics, being anxious or in a rush in this heat just doesn't work. Twenty tuk-tuk drivers swarmed me the second I stepped off the bus and started hassling me to go with them, some pulled on my clothes trying to get my attention. I was getting a little bit overwhelmed and annoyed with not having time to think. The Doctor hadn't left, I think he pondered leaving but waited around anticipating I wouldn't have a clue where to go next. He fought through the crowd to get to me and said he'd take me where I need to go. If anything at first, I only went with him to get away from the mob. I showed him my address, and he said we had to take another bus. I didn't know if I should be trusting him, I mean, I couldn't imagine older people as scammers, but I'd only met him an hour ago, which most of that time he had spent asleep. Another bus? Did I have time for this, even if it did save me a bit of money? That said, there was just something trustworthy about this man, I mean, he looked like a doctor after all.

The Doctor led me through small claustrophobic markets selling fabrics and food, rammed with people. I had to duck several times as everything here was not built for tall foreigners, and further along the streets until we reached another bus stop. We talked about England on the way, and he said he had a brother that lives in Surrey who works, I shit you not, as a doctor. As the pair of us jumped onto yet another moving bus, I caught The Doctor paying for my ticket. It was only forty rupees – twenty pence – but still... He wouldn't let me pay him back. Why was he helping a stranger like this? Fifty minutes to go. The bus reached Galle Road, and The Doctor pointed out some points of mild interest as we passed. This looked like a nice part of Colombo, it had all been relatively nice, but here especially so, as traversing these open and clean streets with the beach on one side. I realised this was probably the most affluent part of the city, and arguably the country. There were restaurants, banks, western fast-food outlets and a couple of expatriates on the streets. The bus finally stopped, and the walk was another ten minutes to the hostel. I expected The Doctor to ask for money once we got to the destination, especially seeing as he paid for my bus fare and spent nearly an hour out of his day doing this. But no. We got to the hostel, and he said,

"I hope you enjoy your stay in Sri Lanka", and "do not trust everyone here". He even pointed to where the bar that I was meeting Tashiya was – literally across the road. I thanked him profusely, offered to buy him a beer, which he rejected, and then he waved and walked off. I hate that I was so suspicious of him. I think travelling the world has made me a little wary of people just being overly friendly like that, they're usually after something in exchange for their time. I have no doubt Sri Lanka has a few people ready to rip tourists off, but I have never experienced such generosity like that before. I would have taken that whole trip in a lot more relaxed state if I knew the Doctor was such a good person doing his good deed for the day. I'd let him examine my prostate any day, doctor or not!

I got to my room, rushing to sort some fresh clothes from my backpack. A young guy was already in the dorm, sat on the bed watching me come in like a whirlwind. He was in a mood for a conversation, telling me he was from Saudi Arabia and he'd been here for a week trying to get a job, and wondered what I was doing in the country. I apologised I didn't really have time for a chat right now. He said I should relax more, and a bit snappy I said he shouldn't assume I've had a difficult day! I reached the bar with ten minutes to spare – Tashiya was actually the one who ended up late! The bar, called *Barefoot*, wasn't just a bar, but also sold clothes, books and ornaments upstairs, all with a slight hippy vibe to them. The bar area was great, a large open area in which some effort had gone into the decor, with a band playing lounge music outside. I was embraced by a chilled atmosphere upon entry, a perfect place for locals and expats alike to unwind on a Sunday afternoon. Tashiya arrived with her friend Raj, we greeted and shook hands and sat down for a couple of beers, whilst they suggested a travel route to get started with. Again, nice of the locals to spend time with a foreign visitor and help him get to grips with the country. I'm really grateful for all this help you know! After our discussion, the first stop I decided would be to a town called Kandy, south-central of the country, in the hills. From there I would continue through "Hill Country", in the centre of the island by taking the trains, seeing Sri Lanka's "Eighth wonder of the world" and the highest point of the country with "the best views in the country". There was a lot of things in quotation marks there, and each one sounded fantastic.

After a couple of hours of chat and beer, they dropped me off along the beach, north of Galle Road and wished me a good time here. The weather wasn't outstanding, a little windy and overcast if anything, but that didn't stop the Sri Lankans. There were hundreds of them, having a dip, playing cricket, flying kites. It was really nice to see everyone having fun late on a Sunday afternoon. I was the only foreigner around. People smiled, said hello, inviting me to get involved with their games of cricket. I found a good place to sit along the wall of the promenade and got stuck into a *Cornetto*, watching the world fly by. It wasn't particularly late by the time I returned back to the room, and I had full intentions of catching up on a bit of TV. However, perpetually tired as I was, I fell asleep on the top of my bed-sheet in my boxers. My lad managed to slip a little bit out of said boxers and lay there exposed, just as some new residents were checking into our room. I've never been woken by the screams of a startled Swiss girl before.

The next day I woke up early to get on the first train to Kandi, anticipating it taking most of the day. Tayisha had mentioned yesterday that the rail system here is antiquated; it *will* get you from A to B, it just takes time on the old and slow train network that's not improved much since the Victorian colonial era. As I was checking out of the hotel's reception and asking for directions to the train station, my conversation was overheard by another backpacker checking out at the same time. She was an attractive girl from Germany and introduced herself as Kate, she was travelling by herself and looking to go to Kandy. She asked if we wanted to travel together. Brilliant! A travel buddy! We spoke on our walk to the station, and within half an hour had already formed plans together as a new team. It is literally that easy meeting people when you're a backpacker, it's great.

Two hours into the train ride, the track rose with the altitude and continued alongside a mountain. The initial cityscape and had turned into sky-high panoramic views of incredibly green tropical mountains with small villages with plumes of smoke coming out of them from below, heading towards the centre of the island. Inside the carriage was just as interesting as out the window; there's enough seating, but people choose to dangerously hang slightly out of the doors of the carriage whilst the train was moving for fun. Strangely, some locals scream as we passed through tunnels, not in the carriage thankfully, but out of the windows. It creates a weird echoing wail. Also, in the neighbouring carriage, there was a full band playing some music. The train rattled down the tracks into the deep green unknown. The real journey of Sri Lanka had finally begun.

Central Sri Lanka – 7th August 2013

To really kick off our journey with a great start – we missed our planned stop for the town of Kandy. The return route left us for some hours waiting for a train in the town of Gampola, and by the feel of things, it seemed like we were the first-ever tourists to visit the place. The main street was narrow and claustrophobic; dirty buildings leaning inwards with tuk-tuks and pedestrians pushing past, offering nothing much for tourists. The only noticeable thing around here wasn't even in the town itself; there was a panoramic mountainous backdrop in the distance, although you couldn't quite see it all with it being an overcast day. I got to know Kate a bit more with the free time as we walked around. She was really friendly and easy to get along with, had excellent proficiency in English (like all the Germans I met on the road!) and had already done a significant amount of travelling in South America and Hawaii before coming here. She had come to Sri Lanka enticed by the famous beaches and surfing on the east coast. The lack of efficiency on Sri Lanka's trains was often commented on by her, though, as our train back appeared to be late, adding more time around the town. I guess that Germans are just too used to punctual public transport because it runs like clockwork in their home country. Late trains are nothing out of the ordinary for me, the fact the train here eventually bothered showing up made it one better than British trains. Our trip from the capital which should have taken three hours took nine. But it was okay, it was mostly our fault, and we weren't exactly pushed for time. Finally checking in at our hostel in the hills surrounding Kandy late evening, a trio of Scots arrived at reception the same time as us, so we got to know them over dinner.

Kate and I woke pretty early to tackle a day of sightseeing in and around Kandy. Unfortunately, overnight one of the Scots had been taken to hospital with a mystery illness. The sick one was part of a couple, leaving their mate Dave at the hostel unsure what to do with his day. He was seated at the breakfast table by himself, looking a wee bit glum, so we asked if he wanted to join us for our excursion, which he took us up on. He was an amiable guy, but interestingly he had a real punk look about him, most notable of which was a mohawk radiating nearly a foot from his scalp– which he had fully styled today. As the three of us walked on through the town, every single local person was drawn to the unusual hair. The reactions would range from having a good gawp, groups of people alerting others and pointing, stopping him in the street to take photos, and just outright try to touch it. It literally stopped traffic. Some bloke pulled up in his car, wound his window down and drove alongside us as we walked, wanting to know all the details of how it was styled. This would have all been all well and good had there not been a queue of cars behind all going crazy with their horns, trying to get through winding roads of the town. They were all just pushing for their go of a photo. It was all harmless, I suppose, and the locals admitted they had never seen a hairstyle like it before. It quickly became annoying. I think the breaking point was in a narrow market, and a mass of locals came for photos, followed by more, blocking the exits as they pushed closer to have a look. We were overwhelmed. It felt quite rude of us to barge our way out of the rabble, but it was either that or be lost to the market crowd forever. It was then I understood how annoying it must become for a celebrity. This was the first day, and already the novelty of having this extreme attention from the Sri Lankans was wearing thin. Dave can wear a hat, and it's over. You're a celebrity and have been for years? Even nipping to the shop for a packet of fags would be a hassle. As lovely as all the wealth that comes with being a celebrity must be, getting constantly harassed by the plebs in the street must spoil it.

Kandy was a pleasant city to be in. It was very green and pretty, with a large lake and river running through the centre of it, although perhaps a little hectic with the traffic and pedestrians the down-town parts. There were a handful of things to see on the tourist check-list, mostly based around the spiritual and nature. Our first major stop was the *Temple of the Tooth* – a temple said to be featuring some of the actual Buddha's tooth. How the hell they obtained it, I don't know. It was £10 to go in to see it, so I didn't bother. Kate did though, after a massive queue, and even she said it wasn't worth the money. Boom, tenner saved! The Kandy botanical garden on our next stop was again a little on the pricey side to enter. A Victorian English mansion in good repair sat in the middle of trimmed lawns whilst local kids played cricket. Beyond this lay many separate gardens with a considerable variety of plants and animals. This had obviously been a British colonial building with extensive grounds back in the day. It was good that the Sri Lankans had converted it into a decent tourist attraction, I found wandering around an agreeable way to spend a few hours with Kate and Dave (with his hat on).

That night at the hostel, we managed to get ice cream delivered by tuk-tuk. We stayed up eating it and were joined by a travelling family from the Faroe Islands. I can honestly say I've never met anyone from that part of the world before, and least of all expected to meet some in Sri Lanka. They were fascinating people to talk to as they explained how remote and sparsely populated their country is. You're never more than three miles away from the sea, they told us, and the prime minister's home number is in the phone book! Sometime after dinner, everyone went to bed other than Kate and me. She wasn't much of a drinker, but I convinced her to have a few cocktails with, feet up on the railings of the hotel balcony, watching the world go by whilst slowly getting pissed, as two new mates in a new part of the world. The sights you see and things you put yourself through whilst on the road are amazing, but for me, sat here with effectively a group of strangers from around the world in the hills of a foreign country, eating ice cream, drinking cocktails and swapping stories, well, it's nights like that which make travelling so worthwhile.

Our plan the next day was to get to the town of Dambulla, the furthest north we were to go to on this trip, and onwards to what the Sri Lankans proudly describes as the eighth wonder of the world – Sigiriya – an ancient fortress carved into a massive rock, at nearly two hundred metres high. Laying there since the 5th century, again like the Indonesian temple I saw with Mo last month, it made me question what criteria makes a world wonder become one. I'm told Christ the Redeemer is one of the actual *Seven Wonders of the World*, I haven't seen it, maybe it's awe-inspiring. But, it was still built in modern times, and correct me if I'm wrong, it's nothing much more of a giant statue of a man. Only if it's still there in another fifteen centuries, then it can qualify, surely? Why can't the Sri Lankans have Sigiriya? We swapped details with Dave as his friend was still in the hospital, and took the bus to Dambulla which took a whole two hours and cost us the equivalent of thirty-five pence. Bargain.

Upon arriving at our destination, some differences between mine and Kate's styles of travelling had begun to show. Any room would have done me really, just a cheap, shitty place to dump my backpack in. Whereas Kate had her heart set on checking out certain higher-rated hostels further out of town, at a higher cost of course. Whilst she was happy to spend more on the rooms, she would have no issue haggling with the tuk-tuk drivers for as little as twenty-five pence sometimes – although admittedly, twenty-five pence does go a long way out here. I did wonder if the likes of myself being happy to pay extra was setting a precedent for future travellers, and maybe it was worth demanding we pay local prices. That said, I was tired and stood at the bus terminal in the sun with a heavy backpack on, breathing in the fumes from the traffic. Personally, I wouldn't think twice about giving them what they asked for at these prices, maybe more if I didn't have the right change. There wasn't much in Dambulla to look at either, as I waited for Kate to haggle the equivalent value of a *Freddo bar* down from our tuk-tuk, just a dusty long street with rows of shabby-looking shops and restaurants.

We settled on the place and price on the outskirts of the city. I forget the name, but it looked a little quirky in Kate's travel guide book. The tuk-tuk pulled up at the hotel, and instantly we were greeted by what I assumed was the manager. Problem was – and I know I shouldn't mock here – but his eyes were both facing outwards. Like extremely outwards, one looking to the far left and the other to the right. Like some sort of human chameleon. It was so noticeable that I had to stop myself from saying "whoa!" out loud when I first looked at him. I dubbed him Bozz Eye in my mind, and he was actually alright to be fair, and gave us a reasonable price in his strange little hotel in the sticks. He had the knack of being able to look at both me and Kate directly even though we were stood far away from each other. In Kate's guide book, the hotel boasted a swimming pool, but sadly when we got there, we noticed they had chosen to fill it with fish, rendering it into a pond. Advertised on a board outside the hotel was a "Gym" which, tucked into the corner of the restaurant, comically consisted of a lone bicycle machine and a single dumbbell. As Kate and me were inspecting it, Bozz Eye walked over and said,

"Good, no?" as if it was some sort of test of our politeness.

"Yeah, very good", I said, "I might have a go later", lying through my teeth, and having no intention whatsoever to even look at it again, never mind go on it.

The afternoon was a bit of a let-down. We headed to the main attraction in Dambulla, a temple, but Kate couldn't get in because her legs were exposed, like most holy places in Asia covering up body parts was a requirement. There was a £10 entry fee anyway, so that was another tenner saved as far as I was concerned.

That night, I suffered from the worse mosquito attack of my life. Bozz Eye had assured me no mosquitoes would be able to get into the room during a tour of the hotel earlier in the day. I asked about a suspicious-looking vent in a corner of the room, and where it led to, I was told not to worry and assured no mosquitoes could get in. I awoke after about an hour of sleep to a furious itch on my hand and arm, two bloody bites within five minutes. Exhausted, I peeled myself out of my bed and fumbled in the dark not to wake Kate up looking for the mosquito repellent. I sprayed a little around the vent and on myself, and I tried to sleep, only to hear the unmistakable buzz around my ear a short while later. I smacked hard where the noise was coming from, trying to kill the mosquito but only hitting myself on the head quite hard, again feeling like I was in a skit from *Mr Bean*. More buzzing around my ear. I could feel my anger rising, finding it even more annoying that I knew Kate was sleeping soundly. Remembering my video camera was in my bag beside my bed which could act as a back-up light for night filming, I reached just to see if I could spot the tormenting little bastards. As I moved the camera across the wall, I was horrified to see maybe five or six mosquitoes all sat there just on one wall alone, looking positively terrifying with the long shadows they cast from the light. They weren't just small mosquitoes either, they looked closer to crane flies that we get back home! The *only* good thing about the bigger mozzies is their size;

it's harder for them to manoeuvrer out of a swatting hand. These ones also seemed stupider than their smaller counterparts, so they just sat on the wall and I only needed to put my finger on them to kill them. There's something satisfying about squashing a mosquito, especially if it's just fed, which two of these had, and just seeing them pop like a zit. With the vent looking blocked, there were no noticeable gaps around the doors or windows. Buggered if I know how they were getting in.

All squashed and dead. I tried to get back to sleep but just lay there, still a bit wired from my killing spree. After about an hour, I began to hear buzzing near my ears again. Knowing they were all getting in somehow, and there was no way to stop them, I wrapped myself up into a little ball of clothes and blankets. It was almost unbearably hot, but with only a little bit of my face popping out, I had minimal skin exposure. I don't know why, perhaps it was my state of mind from lack of sleep, but I assumed my face would be okay and the mosquitoes wouldn't want to extract blood from it. One of the little fuckers bit my eyelid. I mean, my eyelid man, come on. In case you've never had a parasite feed off your eyelid before, it's a particularly sensitive piece of skin that likes to swell up like a water balloon when anything irritating has gone near it – and that's precisely what happened here. By morning, I had managed only a couple of hours sleep, with my massive swollen eyelid, Bozz eye was the looker between the two of us. What I lacked in numbers of hours sleep I made up for in mosquito bites – twenty-two. Although Kate hadn't been bitten once, she woke up with a sore throat and a cold, so I wasn't the only one feeling like shit for our excursion to the rock fortress of Sigirya.

Upon arrival to the site some hours later, and after having successfully avoiding unnecessary payments to see temples and bits of old tooth over the past few days, I was horrified to see the entrance fee was well overpriced. I mean it's fair enough to charge a bit, but this was £30, expensive by even western standards just to walk up an old rock. This might seem like peanuts to you reading this, but when you're backpacking, you have a daily budget that you try to adhere to, something this expensive can shorten your entire trip by up to two days. Now I think about it, the botanical gardens we did in Kandy were probably four or five times the price they should have really been. After the civil war ended in Sri Lanka in 2009, only four years ago at the time of writing, tourism was hit, and you genuinely get the impression that they're still finding their feet with the whole industry. I'm sure a few big chain resorts are operating by the coast no doubt, but I'm talking about elsewhere in the country, more so the independent tourist attractions and hotels. Some of the guys who run the hotels like Bozz Eye, although genuinely nice people with good intentions, they still seem like they are learning as they go along, which to me are signs that tourism here hasn't been running all that long. That gym of his was a joke. There's a running theme for ridiculous prices for tourist attractions in the country, and honestly, they're usually a rip off for what they are. A tenner to see a bit of broken old tooth, whereas places in Thailand just accept donations to enter. It just puts me off wanting to go. We had made the trip to Sigiriya now so kind of had to pay the money to enter but still, come on, make it reasonable. And where is all this money going, too? Thirty quid is a lot in Sri Lankan rupees, and there were a lot of tourists at Sigiriya toady. They must have made thousands on that day alone. Who's sat at the top raking in all this money, because the man on the street certainly isn't seeing any?

All that said, once we had climbed to the top of this ancient fort, some of it winding steps clinging to a face of the cliff, the view was striking. The surrounding land is pretty flat, with the rock of Sigirya sitting in the middle of it all, which I guess makes it a sensible place as any to stick a fort on. We could see for miles once we had made it to the top. Kate and I enjoyed climbing around the fort's old brick remnants at the top of the rock, after soaking up the views. The whole thing was impressive. Not thirty quid impressive, but you can't win them all.

Impressed with the natural beauty I had seen so far, I was sure the views in Sri Lanka wouldn't get any better - I was wrong (this has been know to happen once every now and then). Done with Damballa, we were now heading south, deeper and higher into the island's mountain region. Considering we were in the tropics didn't matter, I almost felt the need for a coat as our train chugged along higher and higher on the tracks. In fact, for a moment I felt like I could have been in the Alps in late spring rather than by the equator. The standard tropical plants like palms were nowhere to be seen, giving way to coniferous trees and buses. Although having months in the tropics, all of it had been spent around sea level, so experiencing a notable drop in temperature was a little strange. I'd sometimes get a glimpse out of the train window of an old Victorian-style mansion like what we get at home, further removing the feeling of being in Asia. The only major giveaway I hadn't left the continent was the endless rows of the tea plantations on the side of the hills. We were pressing on next to Nuwara Eliya, a town founded as "Little England" back in the Victorian era. I knew for a fact the locals had moved in since the English moved out, but I wondered if it had retained any of its Englishness, and if it would leave it a weird mash-up of Victorian England and Asia.

Our train stopped around halfway through this journey for no apparent reason. There was countryside all around, so this obviously wasn't an intended stop. I'd heard other passengers say it was likely that the train might have broken down, so we had no idea how long we'd be waiting around for. After around half an hour sat on the floor of the carriage, Kate said she was hungry and had noticed a man had walked past on the tracks earlier selling food. Ever the gentleman, I offered to go and look for him to get her something to eat. I stuck my head out of the carriage door, which is forever open on these things, and checked to make sure there wasn't another train coming on the neighbouring tracks. Once confident all was clear, I slowly climbed down via a small ladder and onto the tracks below. Of course, sod's law, a train started to come from around the corner mere seconds after planting my feet down on the ground. On the other side of the tracks was a steep drop down, leaving me only the ladder I'd already used to climb back onto the train to get out of the way. The problem with this route was an older tourist had begun to climb down too. She became confused as people from the whole carriage began shouting at her to get back on board, some shouting through the carriage window at both of us that a train was oncoming. She didn't know which way to go, hanging midway on the ladder like a moron whilst the oncoming train continued its pace. Suddenly a rather stocky backpacker appeared above the ladder and plucked the woman off with such force she fell on the floor of the carriage, clearing the way up for there with only a few seconds to spare. I scrambled up, and the same guy rather unnecessarily pulled me up with the same force, bringing me crashing down on top of the woman. I rolled over and lay on my back next to the cries of the woman on the floor, who I had almost certainly elbowed on the tit during my landing, just taking a breather to process the mad minute we had all had. As the noise of the passing train died down, Kate said she could probably wait a bit longer for food.

CHAPTER FIVE

Sri Lankan Hill Country – 8th August 2013

Sri Lanka's Hill Country had been a welcome change from the rest of Asia. At two whole kilometres above sea level, the cooler, sometimes overcast weather, coupled with the big green hills almost looked like were travelling somewhere in mainland Europe. There are significantly fewer insects there too, repelled by the altitude – no annoying little shites like flies pestering me or trying to land on my food, and the lack of mosquitoes had been the best part about it. Whoever designed the train route is a genius too, planning it not to be down below, but alongside hills or mountain ridges, so the beautiful scenes can always be enjoyed whilst in transport. I love taking the train in Sri Lanka, it's actually a fun experience in itself. Britain could learn something about how to run trains like these. Okay, they might be packed with people beyond safety sometimes, stink slightly of shit, and they're definitely always late. But don't let that put you off. The highlight of any train journey here is you can hang out of the doorway whilst the train is moving along the tracks, having most of your body swinging outside, occasionally with a long drop down right below you. It's fucking quality. Also, the prices are unbelievable for the distance. A two-hour train journey costs only forty pence. Think of that! Our trains in England are still late and stink of shit but cost you a hundred times more. In England, we have electric doors that open and close automatically. Big deal! Here, sometimes they don't even bother with boring stuff like doors at all!

With train prices so low, anyone can afford to use them, and you often find yourself rubbing shoulders with some of the country's poorer residents whilst in transit. I noticed an old man sat on the floor looking like he could well be homeless. He was obviously keen to make conversation with his limited English, bless him, firing off a wide variety of questions like did I like being tall, and if I had any pets. He then asked where I was from, and when I replied "England", he began to shake his head weirdly as if he was disapproving of it. Listen, mate, I know England has a history of being a shit abroad over the centuries, but it's not my fault! It was only later on when someone else asked where I was from and they did a head jiggle too, it dawned on me that it wasn't a head shake saying "no", but it was the same head wobble that they were doing in India. I had seen it when Riya was talking to people. It's hard to describe exactly over mere words but imagine a classic head shake that means "no" but with a slight jiggle to it too. It's widespread out here; it means approval or acknowledgement, and some people literally do it all the time during a conversation. It's weird for me from my western perspective, because it looks like everyone is always saying "no" whilst you're talking to them. There were many little quirks like this I noticed Sri Lanka shared with neighbouring India. The countries are culturally aligned in many aspects, I'd even heard of Sri Lanka being described as "India Lite" from other backpackers as it's so similar, but not quite as dangerous or busy, and I would therefore argue the more enjoyable of the two to visit.

Nuwara Eliya meant we were into deep Hill Country territory, arriving late evening after a full day's travelling from Kandy. Nearly getting squashed by the oncoming train earlier had been an icebreaker with a young English couple, Thea and Tom, who had also left the train at the same stop as us. They had been travelling for some time now, made evident by the classic scruffy backpacker look about them that some people seem to embrace, hair long and wild. They were genuinely friendly, and we formed into a small group walking through the town looking for somewhere to stay together to save on cost. There was problem after disembarking the train late in the evening; there had been a local event on or something, meaning many of the rooms were already booked out by the Sri Lankans. The group of us must have walked a good mile or so, knocking on several hotel doors in the process of inquiring for rooms, slowly taking us further out of town as each one rejected us. Whilst it was slightly annoying not just being able to dump our bags off somewhere, it was at least a pleasant walk. Well, for me anyway – with the cool temperature and surrounding mist, in addition to the trees that could look like they'd be at home in England, it had a very slight autumnal feel about it. I stuck my hoodie on and was loving it, which is more than can be said for Kate. Being a native Bavarian, the region of which contains the German Alps – It was a bit cold and wasn't a fan of it. She'd come to Sri Lanka for the beaches, sun and surfing, whereas for me, this part of the country offered me a welcome break from my four months in perpetual heat.

It was getting well past 8 PM by the time we had checked in and sorted a room, coming across a large rustic hotel that accommodated all four of us in the town's hilly outskirts, and decided because of the time it was better to eat at the hotel. The four of us sat around a table and ordered our dinner and a bottle of arrack to wash it down with. Arrack is the local grog that is brewed from, I'm told, fermented coconut flowers in Sri Lanka. You may well have heard of the word *arrack* if you've been around South East Asia before. Several countries from here all the way to the Philippines have adopted it, and whilst the principle is the same, each country has its own methods of brewing and flavouring it. Any variant of it is cheap and gets you very drunk.

The hotel appeared to double up as a more upmarket restaurant for the wealthier Sri Lankans, which I thought it sat at a juxtaposition as it also sold cheap, unlabelled, home-brewed arrack on the side. It was great drinking with Thea and Tom, I love bumping into fellow Brits on the road. You can just chat to them like you can't do with anyone else. Making irrelevant jokes about things like, say, *Ian Beale* or those massive *Sport's Direct* mugs, that only a British person would get. Plus, you know you're in for a late-night on the piss with them, which appeared to be on the cards tonight. Several bottles of arrack later and the girls in bed, me and Tom continued our session in the hotel's kitchen with the waiter and chef, both Sri Lankan males in their twenties, who had lured us from the dining area with yet another bottle of home-brew. Their English wasn't brilliant, but through the language barrier, we still could have a bit of fun with them. They provided a crash course on the different types of fruit and vegetables you can get in the country, pulling out draws and knocking things off shelves in the kitchen looking for things. "Niviti!" One of them shouted, holding a handful of spinach up to our faces trying to tell us the name, clearing having way too much of the ol' arrack for the night.

In hindsight, it was pointless booking a room. I woke up in an uncomfortable heap just after dawn, on the floor of the hotel's dimly lit reception next to the waiter and an empty bottle of arrack. God knows where Tom had ended up. I staggered back to our room to see Kate packing her bags, she was making a break for the beach of Arugam Bay on the east coast. It would take the best part of two days' travel to get there from Nuwara. I'd enjoyed travelling with her, but I really didn't want to go and leave this new and interesting place after only just arriving. Thea and Tom were up for staying around Hill Country to my delight, so I hugged Kate goodbye and said we'd meet up at Arugam in a few days.

Now only the three of us, the first stop was Nuwara Elyia town centre late morning, seeing it for the first time in daylight. It's was a quirky, if slightly strange town visually, remnant buildings from the old English colonial era interspersed between the compact together newer wooden buildings made by the Sri Lankans. It was easy on the eye though, and some care had gone into its upkeep, more so than other towns I'd see on the ride over. It was curious to see all the Sri Lankans wearing coats, some even had hats and gloves as opposed to the usual shirts and sarongs worn by the coast. Sure, it was a little cold here, but not hats and gloves cold! The town's post office was arguably one of the main attractions, it was one of the first to be erected in the country during colonial times – built in striking bright red brick in a quaint Tudor style, boasting a clock tower on top of the two stories, leaving the building almost disproportionately large for a town of its size. It was a historic structure from the outside – I was happy to see it was a little more contemporary once we had entered, and it offered comedy postcards featuring photos of elephants with massive erections. I bought a few and sent them to my mates at home.

Surrounding the town lay the ever-scenic, deep green tea plantation covered hills. Somewhere amongst it was Pedro tea plantation, the next stop on the list, five miles away from the town by tuk-tuk. Once there, we trekked for hours into the fields, up into the hills, and got the highest point we could physically get to. The view was breath taking – actually, I think my breath was taken from walking uphill for hours on end! There was nothing but tea plants, acres and acres of them growing across rolling hills and around streams and waterfalls. I knew it grew out here but never really gave much thought to the extreme quantities they must have to grow to match worldwide demand. Then on top of growing it all, there's the time and effort to pick and ship thousands of tons of leaves, all of which then only makes enough tea to fill a single *Sport's Direct* mug (see, you'll get that joke if you're British). Occasionally, we would bump into a villager who looked puzzled to see us three slightly hungover tourists well off the beaten path. It struck me these financially poor villagers could still speak English, I mean it wasn't fluent, but there was still a decent level of education going on around here somewhere. Some would be carrying stacks of wood on their heads back home – one guy in his early sixties stood talking to us for ten minutes, just friendly in curiosity, but did so with the weight of a huge log on his head. I think I would have struggled to carry it around from A to B at less than half his age, never mind stood around having a chat, taking the weight of it throughout. All this green tea, fresh air and walking in the hills must keep you fit!

The log guy escorted us along the dirt path to his village. This village appeared to be where those who worked at the tea plantations stayed with their families. Their housing looked simple, single-room structures made from either concrete or breezeblocks, yet it was nice to see that they'd made the most of what they had. They'd used paint on the walls to cover up the dull colours of the building materials. Their gardens looked fantastic, growing whole rows of carrots, potatoes, and what I could proudly recall in the native tongue after last night in the kitchen – *niviti*. Everyone stopped to say "Hi", giving off a real sense of welcomeness to the three foreign travellers. It touched me a little that the local kids would ask us for a pen, and not money as they would elsewhere in Asia. I wished I had brought my stash of pens I robbed before I quit my job, luckily Thea and Tom brought a few to hand out.

On the outskirts of the village late afternoon, an old man came over to us and introduced himself as Joseph. I found this quite usual for the ever-polite locals, but Joseph went a step further and invited us into his home. I was admittedly quite curious to have a nosey inside one of these buildings, so we agreed to follow him. Joseph told us he was a retired lower manager at the tea plantation so had a little more money than your average villager. It certainly showed too when walking around his house which was bigger than all in the area; there was a bedroom, a living room, and a little office – small rooms, sure, but still well furnished with carpets and ornaments. The tiny kitchen had seen better days, and they relied on a small wood burning stove, but still, I was impressed. We were greeted by his elderly mother sat in the living room upon our entry. She was eighty-two and certainly looked her age but was positively gurning with excitement at the arrival of us. She didn't speak English, which I think was actually fortunate because she was borderline deaf, and I reckon trying to have a conversation would have been a challenging exercise. Joseph would shout questions at her in the native tongue, I'm guessing along the lines of "WOULD YOU LIKE A CUP OF TEA MOTHER?", and she would just look at him gurning away, completely puzzled.

With his proficiency in English, Joseph was able to explain that the government pushes the language hard on children from an early age in schools, even in these rural areas. The cultural remnants of being an ex-British colony, I guessed. This was a great experience because I could ask all sorts of questions of him and get into the detail of life here. I've stayed in rural villages in developing countries before, the Berber villages in the Atlas mountains of Morocco springs to mind, but there I couldn't communicate to the locals much as the people rarely spoke English, and you get the feeling you're missing out on some of the experience. Joseph happily shared all details of life in the Sri Lankan hills, as we all sat around in his living room. He openly told us a day's wage at the plantation is a mere £2, spent bent over picking tea leaves in all sorts of weather. There was a moment's awkward silence when he started asking *us* the questions and wanted to know what religion we were – and all three of us said Atheist. I hear in some countries they are not even aware of the concept of atheism, or they can even find it offensive. I couldn't quite gauge his feelings on it, but it was certainly an unusual concept for him. Yes mate - we all die and become worm food. The end.

His mother brewed us some tea grown from the local area, made with water collected from a nearby stream. I was a little hesitant about drinking water that hadn't been treated, but he assured me that everything was unpolluted here because of the high standards it has to be to grow the tea. It was a quality cup of tea, and if anything, it settled my belly a little from all the alcohol last night. Satisfied we'd had a great day in the fields and having our fill of some culture, we thanked Joseph for his hospitality and headed back to Nuwara Elyia to get twatted on the arrack again.

It was late in the evening, and darkness had begun to creep in by the time the three of us had returned to town. There's a distinct lack of street lighting in Nuwara, so once the sun departs for the day, it requires some focus to negotiate the streets in the dark. We were disappointed by the handful of pubs and bars we found that sold alcohol. Usually, the bars were empty rooms with only a few tables and chairs dotted around, lacking any vibe, or people. One was more in line with a doctor's waiting room than somewhere you'd want to get drunk at. A local man in the street we quizzed pointed us to a bar off the main road which edged slightly into a residential area, and we were told its where most of the locals head to in an evening. It was even worse than the other bars once we got there– Grimy black walls and floors, dirty chairs and tables cut out of misshapen wood, with an atmosphere thick with smoke. A near-pointless single 40-watt light bulb flickered away in the middle of the room, it was nearly as dark as outside. You could kick the floor and chunks of thick black dirt would come up with your shoe, Tom wiped his finger along the wall, and it was black. There was no initial signal to me that we had made any sort of mistake coming here at least, although three Westerners, one being a girl, did turn some heads at this place where clearly only local fellas went.

In the corner of the bar, a scruffy middle-aged bloke in a little hat sat there fucked up, like he'd had way too much arrack, not necessarily tonight, but across his whole lifespan. His eyes never left Thea. Sitting there quietly supping our drinks, we noticed people stopping their conversations, and we eventually became the focus of every single person in the room. We'd only been here for a couple of minutes but we agreed we had best neck up and leave. I could feel the eyes on us as we got up and awkwardly shuffled back through the room in front of the twenty drunk men.

There was a slight feeling of defeat by not being able to find a decent pub after what had otherwise been a great day. The roads were quiet as we decided to call it a day and head home, trekking back up the dark foggy hill to our hotel. It was therefore striking to hear several tuk-tuks abruptly coming all at once from behind, disturbing the peace of the lane. They didn't pass once they'd reached us, and rather notably began trying to box us in alongside the road. One tuk-tuk got in front then began to slow down, whilst another came up to our side and another up from our rear. Twelve men had appeared, and I recognised one of them as the scruffy twat in a hat back at the bar. Fuck.

"Hey, you! You want lift?" One shouted with clearly no room for us to fit in any of the tuk-tuks. Some of the men left the vehicles and edged out towards us as if they were intending to grab Thea, but didn't quite seem coordinated enough amongst themselves and retreated back inside the tuk-tuks. I clenched my fists ready for some sort of arrack fuelled attack and had my eye for anyone who might try to grab her. Tom looked equally prepared for what might be coming next. We carried on walking, didn't say a word, and weaved past the front tuk-tuk in single file, with Thea between both me and Tom. They hovered behind us for a minute, edged into the middle of the road, then for some reason turned around and went back to town. I honestly don't know what that had been about, if our confidence by just continuing to walk scared them off, or perhaps they were unsure what to do once faced with the situation. Either way, we thought ourselves lucky and it was a little reminder that although we were having a fun time here, we shouldn't allow it to take our guard down, wandering around anywhere for a drink, like the pissheads we were.

It was a relief to get back to the hotel. I saw the waiter and chef from last night's session talking in the lobby. They were still on shift, but the restaurant was dead. I was beaming to see them again and went over for a handshake and a chat, but they seemed a little off with me. I later learned the poor fellas had a bit of a bollocking from their manager for staying up drinking with customers whilst ruining the kitchen. I was a bit upset seeing them playing it cool with us after our fun night last night. It was time to move on out of this town, I think. I wasn't quite ready to leave Hill Country though, nor were Tom and Thea for that matter.

After studying a map over breakfast, the following day, the map showed us the town of Haputhale along the train tracks, which was the closest town to *Lipton's seat*, which I will explain more about later. Haputale was my favourite bit of Hill Country, the journey there alone you could have sold to me as an activity for the day. Our two-hour train ride carved through the most impressive mountain scenery I had ever seen in my life. Rural villages, valleys with waterfalls, rows of deep green tea plantations and forest – all stunning scenery in every direction for the full journey. The three of us took it in turns to sit in the doorway of the carriage, legs dangling out, swinging into the air (and pulling them in quickly whenever entering a tunnel). If there's one thing that you ever end up doing after reading about my travels, make sure to take a train in Hill Country.

Admiring our fun on the train during the ride, we were greeted by a local bloke who introduced himself as Ramal. He was a rather tall, skinny man, perhaps somewhere in his mid-fifties, with wavy grey hair and huge lines around his face. He spoke English well, and was likeable enough. He said he had a guest house with "the best views in town" at our next stop, at a reasonable price, just a short walk away from the station. With no plans arranged once we got into town, we decided going with him was as a good choice as any. To get to the hotel, we had to partially walk along train tracks to get there, which is a perfectly normal way to get from A to B in Sri Lanka – you'd get a fine and possibly jail back home in England for trying this. You don't have any other option sometimes in Sri Lanka, you just have to be ready to bail onto the embankment as the occasional train passes by.

Ramal wasn't lying about the views. They were even better than the tea plantations yesterday. I honestly reckon we could see as far as thirty miles away, entire villages on the lowland plains below appearing just small specks, the land beyond faded into blue to the sky in the distance. I had never seen anything like it in my life. It was almost like the view you'd get from being in an airplane, but still having your feet on the ground. We were even higher than the clouds. In my head, I had already planned my nights here, sat on this balcony with an arrack and coke in my hand, waiting for an epic sunset. My plan was to get so drunk tonight I'd get double vision, so I could see these beautiful views twice.

Originally from Scotland, Thomas Lipton was one of the original pioneers of the whole tea movement in Sri Lanka way back in 1890. The tea plantation estate here was only a mere part of Lipton's worldwide empire, but he understandably had a real fondness for Hill Country and decided here was the best place for his 'throne', named the ego-inflating *Lipton's Seat*. Sat here, he could relax and enjoy the more scenic views of his property. As it sits at two kilometres above sea level, you can imagine the views were unreal; Despite the fact we were miles away from the sea – two hours by car south, on a clear day it was rumoured you were still able to see it. Still a touch hungover from a street festival in town we'd been lucky to come across yesterday afternoon, we had managed to get up at 5am to from Haputale to catch the sunrise on the seat. Even the hike up to the seat was excellent after the tuk-tuk took us as far as he could go, and here were great views of rolling hills poking through a foggy soup once we made it to the top. I could just image Lipton on the arrack up here getting off his barnet on his days off. Maybe there had been too much arrack going around between the three of us over the past few days, but on the walk back down the mountain Thea began to feel sick, and by the time we got back to Haputale she was crippled in pain. It came out of nowhere, which was all the more alarming. I got the tuk-tuk to drop me off in town so I could go to the pharmacy look for something to help her whilst Tom took her back to the guest house, but by the time I'd got back with the meds she was so sick that Ramal had taken her to hospital.

The day's events continued to spiral downwards from there, and I didn't like just watching the afternoon's events unfold out of my control. Unbeknown to us at the time, Ramal was, in fact, an alcoholic and whilst Thea was in the hospital getting checked over, to pass the time he took Tom to a nearby pub and got wasted on proper piss-head drinks – several pints of 8% beer with a double of gin in it. Bear in mind this was at ten in the morning, surpassing even me at my worst over the past few months. Usually, I would think 'what a top lad', but this brought a new side out to Ramal which wasn't pleasant. It appeared Thea needed to spend the full day at the hospital, so after getting tanked, Ramal and Tom returned to the hotel to pass the time. Ramal started freaking out when he got back – he began crying and kept referring to Thea as his daughter.

"Why has God put her in the hospital?" He screamed, falling out onto the balcony shared by all of the rooms, taking out all the plastic tables and chairs with him. With nothing to do whilst Thea and Tom were away, I'd anxiously been waiting around in our bedroom and heard a commotion outside. I came out wondering what was going on, and I could see Ramal wrapped around tables and chairs, shouting gibberish, blood coming out of his face whilst Tom was stood further beyond looking exhausted. Ramal became aggressive once he got back up on his feet, at first threatening to kill Tom and then turned to me.

"Why didn't you come with us to the hospital, you?!" and swung to punch me, in doing so fell into the heap of plastic furniture again. I slowly backed off into my bedroom with Tom, both of us not really knowing how to deal with this situation other than to barricade ourselves in our room. Through a crack in the curtains, we could see Ramal's daughter help him up, and then he vanished for several hours. We hoped that was that, but he was back out causing a fuss once it was time to pick Thea up. We politely asked which hospital had she been taken to so we could retrieve her ourselves, but he wouldn't tell us unless he went. In fact, one of the conditions for telling us the hospital name was it had to be him and Tom only, or no one. I even offered to at least drive as he was in no fit state, but it was a definite no. Tom and he both set off again, and as Ramal's little white car slowly bumped off down the dirt road with him behind the wheel, I just thought it was a terrible idea and was left to wait around the guest house once again. I realised I had started to get a bit protective over Thea and Tom, they were considerably younger than me, and I felt like Ramal was putting them in a dangerous situation. Later Tom told me they'd both had a fight on the drive, Ramal having an outburst which nearly ended up in both of them throwing punches at each other whilst the car was moving.

Thea came back feeling miles better, and once the three of us were together, we barricaded ourselves in with one of the beds moved up to the front of the door. We sat on the floor of our room hearing Ramal screaming at other guests over something, whilst sat there in silence in a dimly lit room with the curtains drawn, looking at each other. We pondered the safety of staying another night here but agreed it was getting a bit too late to be looking for another room. If he tried to get in, then we'd have to leave. We didn't really sleep well, hearing him outside trashing around, falling out, and over, with the plastic furniture again.

We made a break for the train station at the crack of dawn, being as quiet as possible not wake Ramal and have to deal with him again. Tom mentioned on our walk along the train tracks that Ramal had settled the hospital bill yesterday, which made him even more of a riddle to me. Perhaps he was just a good guy all along, who lost it when he had a drink.

I'd only known Tom and Thea for three days and it had been pretty wild time with them both for the whole duration of it. They had plans to stay in Hill Country, whilst time was slipping away for me, so I made the call to meet up with Kate in Arugam Bay on the east coast for a few days. I didn't want to leave Hill Country, especially to go to a beach town, but I thought I might as well make an effort and see as much of the country as I could. Plus, even if it was just a beach, Kate was fun to spend time with. Hill Country had been one of the best places I'd visited, not only in Sri Lanka, but possibly during my whole travels. The people were mostly friendly, or if not then at least interesting, and the views alone topped anything I'd seen in my life. I will be back one day. I will just be giving Ramal a wide berth, well, unless I need any hospital bills paying.

Arugam Bay, Sri Lanka – 14th August 2013

It says a lot about how long I've been travelling when I say going to the beach is not a priority any more. When I first started my trip all those months ago, the only thing I wanted to do was go to a beach and sit in the sun all day getting drunk with Liggy. Now, I find myself openly admitting that the beach isn't really my scene, and many things bug me about it. Sand gets everywhere, there's nothing worse than trying to enjoy a *Cornetto* that been sprinkled in sand whipped up from the wind, and if it's not on your food then it's chafing your arse cheeks by making its way up there somehow. Sun cream? Forget it, it's an absolute sand magnet. If the wind isn't blowing sand about, then it's flapping the pages of your book or newspaper rendering the pages unreadable. I can't get comfy lying there either, as much as I try to make a pillow out of sand it spreads out as soon as I put my head on it. When you've hit a breaking point with the sand and make your way into the sea for a change, things don't improve. I'm continually watching people walking by who looks like they might try and take my stuff, or if not on the lookout for people, sharp hidden rocks, or animals trying to bite off a toe or inject some mad poison without an antidote. And don't go too far out otherwise a current will sweep you out without a trace.

I arrived on the east coast of Sri Lanka, Arugam Bay, in fact, and whilst this large bay with a clean tropical beach and palm trees certainly seemed visually pleasing, I felt disappointed. I thought to myself "I've left Hill Country for a bloody beach". I've heard that you "find yourself" whilst travelling and I always dismissed that as hippy pap but being out here made me realise that I'm a country boy through and through. I love my fields, lakes and forests. I certainly wasn't in the best of moods either. I'd re-entered a hot, sweaty climate after having endured a long day's travelling. Arugam Bay annoyed me because it was an okay beach, but people I'd met on the road were absolutely raving about it like it was the holy grail of sand and saltwater. I can't surf either, and there were loads of these tanned, cool muscular surfer dudes with their shirts off which made me look like a flabby weed in comparison. It was so expensive to be there. August and September are considered high season on the east coast so the cheeky Sri Lankans are just cashing in. Walking down the main street checking out prices and vacancies, a bog-standard room, with no air con, would cost at least £30 a night. It was an absolute rip off. £30 in most other Asian countries, even in the capital cities, I'd be able to get a half-decent room for £30. I was so annoyed, no one would budge on the price too, despite most of the rooms being empty. Kate was staying here for a few weeks and had been priced out of finding somewhere – she found it cheaper to have bought a tent to sleep on the beach with. It was like an oven inside during the daytime.

Arugam Bay was your standard beach town. The beach ran parallel alongside the main road with shops selling wristbands, sunglasses and fridge magnets. There were hotels, restaurants, shops and bars between these too, but ultimately, there was nothing notable worth travelling hours for. After walking up and down the main road like a complete prick for half an hour in the heat looking for a room and getting rejected by a few surly Sri Lankans, I accidentally stumbled into someone's house by the beach thinking it was a hotel. I spoke to a young woman who lived in the house with her mother, and after a brief conversation and the realisation that this wasn't a hotel, the daughter said I could still stay in her bed, and she could sleep with her mother in her room. It was perhaps a bit unusual, but as we agreed on £20 a night, which was still a lot for the standards of the place, it was a tenner saved on the going rate elsewhere. My bedroom was modest once she carried several armfuls of her clothes out; a room crafted out of chipped breeze blocks and a straw roof, daylight could be seen where the wall and ceiling crudely met. Within the room: A bed, a fan, and a mosquito net with holes, making the use of it absolutely pointless. The kitchen was a bare concrete room with a slab of raised concrete on the floor for storing utensils on and a fire stove for cooking food on. The bathroom again was all concrete and breeze block, and although the largest room of the house, there was nothing but a squat toilet sculpted out of the concrete and a showerhead above it, which of course had no temperature settings – just set at permanently hot from the sun baking it in the underground pipes. I'm just slagging off someone's house here; There was a roof over my head, I probably should be grateful.

Another thing that pissed me off about Arugam bay was the people there. The rest of Sri Lanka had genuinely lovely locals, almost knocking the Indonesians off the top spot. Here, they were often rude. I stopped and asked a local for directions, he told me and then asked me to pay for it. I think he needed to meet my mate The Doctor about how to give directions to guests in your country! Even the woman whose house I was staying with tried it on during my second day of staying there. After I got back from the beach having spent a full afternoon feeling inferior to the cool surfers, she told me to follow her, sat me down in the living room and presented me with a plate of rice cakes. The way she was acting, very friendly, rubbing my arm as I passed, I first thought she was coming onto me or something. She went on along the lines of I could see she was quite poor – her life is difficult etcetera – so, could I pay her 20,000 rupees, around £100, to paint the walls. I just flatly said no, I was slightly offended that she'd done this set up asking for money and then had to cheek to ask for such an extreme amount. Trust me mate, if I had £100 spare I would most likely be staying at that proper resort down the road! I think I may have spared enough for a few tins of paint if she'd asked for a sensible amount, but she'd already had sixty quid off me to sleep here. She even charged me for the rice cakes she'd offered during our sit down. Maybe this party-beach lifestyle for Westerners attracts some of the wrong sorts of Sri Lankans. I really hope it wasn't just our influx of money corrupting once lovely people. I was so close to just getting on the bus back to Hill Country, giving a middle finger out of the back of the bus window to everyone in town. It was only because I had plans with Kate, and the Scottish trio I'd met in Kandi that I decided to stay a little bit longer. Once I met up with them all for dinner one evening, I moaned as I did with you guys for the last three paragraphs. Kate disagreed, she loved it here, saying this not long after introducing me to some muscly South African surfer fella she had befriended on the beach.

It wasn't all shit, but the only real highlight was going on a safari ride with mohawk Dave. We hired a tuk-tuk, and the driver took us into the sticks behind the bay and into a national park. With it being the dry season, the park was really nothing more than a dusty expanse with yellow dried grass, with the occasional body of water, attracting all sorts of animals; birds, elephants and a creature called an Axis deer which had a little mohawk down its back to brilliantly match Dave's. We spotted two wild elephants on the side of a dried riverbed, a mother and a baby. We ditched the tuk-tuk and sneaked up to them through the bush, being careful not to disturb, because as you can imagine, mother elephants can get protective over their calves. We managed to get close, but I had a moment of realisation that this had the potential to become very dangerous. Either way, it was incredible watching a wild animal of such magnitude go about its business. It was quite the adventure, but endangering your life slightly always is. The risk of danger increased as we entered the bushes looking for crocs hiding from the intense midday sun. I was a little worried about how qualified your average tuk-tuk driver is in taking tourists around wild human-eating animals. I mean, come on, going through dimly lit bushes containing numerous meat-eaters and saying nothing but "be careful" hardly warrants as a genuine safety tip, does it? The bush area became noticeably dark once we were inside, making it harder to spot them lurking about. Any time one got too close, the driver threw a rock or a bit of a stick at it to scare it away. Any crocs that moved would often bail into a murky river that ran through the bush and would vanish completely. It was a bit mad being here, and I loved it.

Time in Sri Lanka was nearly up. I was on the east coast and needed to get back to the west. In England, I'd be able to complete this distance within half a day on the network of rail and roads. It must have only been 250 miles, tops. Here, with the uneven, winding streets and antiquated railway network from the Victorian era, it was going to take two full days or more. It's worth mentioning actually how old most of the technology is in Sri Lanka. It's like stepping back in time. The bus I had to take back into Hill Country clearly was brand new – in 1982. It was struggling with the constant up-hill drive back into Hill Country and began overheating with the sun on it. No problem – this was easily remedied by the wily driver. There was a large hatch at the front near the engine which opened up, and every now and then the driver would pull up alongside a stream or waterfall, fill up a large bucket, bring it back to the bus and tip it down the hatch. You could hear the "HISSS" of the water hitting the engine even from within the bus. A colossal amount of steam poured out, but it worked! It's not just transport that is as old as the hills, mobile phones used by the locals, generally speaking, are at least ten years behind in technology. I'd see someone texting away on a *Nokia 5210* occasionally, anything else could be even older models than that. I sat there jealous looking on because I just wanted to play the original *Nokia Snake* game to pass the time of this painfully slow journey.

Back in Hill Country, I now had a ten-hour train ride back to the capital. Some of my Australian or American friends laugh about how British people find ten hours to be such a long journey – ten hours barely makes a dent in the massive continents they call a country. A ten-hour drive in England doesn't exist, even going from Newcastle to Penzance! It's mad that within ten hours of driving across those large countries, accents won't change either. Within a *single hour's* drive in England, you will find two or three strong accent changes, and the name for bread rolls will have changed eight times with it.

The whole journey back through Sri Lanka was kind of a nostalgic one, passing through all the towns I had stopped at on the train ride, half wondering if I'd see Ramal again at Haputale station waiting for his next group of unsuspecting tourists. I went back to the same hostel I stayed in at during my first night in Colombo, by pure chance they had set me up in the same bed in the same dorm. I was surprised to see the Saudi guy was still there after two weeks waiting to hear from a job interview. I didn't do this intentionally, but it was a Sunday afternoon, two weeks precisely after I arrived in the capital and wandered along the beach again seeing all the families playing cricket and swimming in the sea, although the weather was considerably better today.

On my last full day, I made my way back to Negombo for close proximity to the airport ready for tomorrow's early flight to Vietnam. It was a no brainer staying at Nightman's place again, who was made up I'd chosen to stay at his home. To finish off the complete retrace of my steps, I even had the same bedroom, and it appeared I had the same bedsheets! My last night in Sri Lanka was spent on a quiet beach behind Nightman's, watching a small group of local lads playing cricket, enjoying one of the great things about the west coast of anywhere – a great sunset. I was by myself, but it didn't matter, I'd made friends here to tackle the past fortnight with, plus I was happy knowing they were still out there somewhere enjoying this great country. It was a chilled-out last night, and I wouldn't have wanted it any other way.

Sri Lanka might not be your classic destination for a two week holiday, but it really offers true gems to see for those that make the journey.

Chapter Six

Billy some mates

Ho Chi Minh City, Vietnam – 21ˢᵗ August 2013

As much as I loved Sri Lanka, I was ready for something new by the time I moved on; I just wasn't expecting the culture shock of Ho Chi Minh City. There had a complete shift into top gear from the relative calm of Sri Lanka. It was quite disorientating. Entering downtown on foot, people, cars, rickshaws and bikes were whizzing around like ants on amphetamines. Often, I would see hundreds of mopeds attempting to pass a single crossroad at the same time from all directions, with no traffic lights either to help ease the problem. Street food vendors were utilising every inch of pavement, often pushing me out onto the busy road to get past, which made negotiating my way around the city on foot tricky. The Vietnamese in the street wore those light yellow conical straw hats that are associated with this part of the world, which I found rather endearing. The owners of said hats were often pulling wooden carts behind them filled with vegetables, and their mere presence further contributing to the havoc on the busy roads. The electrical sky-spaghetti also known as outdoor wiring, found across Asia was particularly bad here, thick layers of wires around single wooden poles. Whilst hot like Sri Lanka, the air felt stuffier, likely made worse by all the exhaust fumes, and I'd quickly get a sweat on being outside.

Although not the capital city of Vietnam, it's still the country's central financial hub, and whilst nowhere near the scale compared to Jakarta, there were still several skyscrapers around. It did have a more appealing 'greener' feeling to it as there were large areas of land just left as nature, and several parks, something which Jakarta didn't offer. Vietnam is currently undergoing a substantial economic boom, and whilst out in the countryside it is still developing, some would say twenty years behind regional neighbour Thailand, the cities themselves are booming with scaffolding, building many new skyscrapers and industrial parks. I was once again dealing with unnecessary zeros of the local currency, one British pound bought me even more numbers than it would in Indonesia, around 30,000 Dong (yeah yeah, we all laugh the first time we hear its name).

After walking around aimlessly for some time just absorbing the vibe, I decided to find out what the food was like. I knew nothing about Vietnamese cuisine, and that's because growing up in a small English town manages to shelter you from most of the world's food. You want Indian and Chinese variations of food rendered for a British palate? Sure, we have lots of those. After any authentic Vietnamese, Korean or Brazilian? You best get on that train to Manchester. I guessed the food here would be like Chinese or Thai, maybe a mix of both, either way, I wasn't expecting anything particularly new or different. I found a little restaurant, and once sat down a waitress came over to take my order. I asked what her personal favourite was, and whatever it was, I'd have it. She brought out a crispy, savoury pancake folded over, the contents within from what you'd find in a spring roll, along with some decent sized prawns were thrown in for good measure. Alongside the main dish was a bowl of a clear liquidy sauce with a kick to it, followed by a massive plate of leafy greens, none of which I recognised except for mint. It wasn't just a case of eating it all individually but filling a large green leaf with some of the pancake and some of the smaller leaves, rolling it up tight and then dipping it into the sauce. It was admittedly a slight struggle, and I'm sure there was a technique to it all I had yet to master – leaves would never be my first choice to hold what is effectively a wrap together – but when I actually got it all together in one and into my mouth it knocked my socks off! Fuck me, it was tasty! I was amazed I had got to 28 without trying this style of food before. A curious thing also is that the old French colonial era still has an influence on food and drink in Vietnam today. You can get baguettes on the street food stalls, which is pretty strange to see.

Getting a street butty in Asia was a new one for me, with some recognisable fillings like ham or spreadable cheese, but then complimented with oddities like chilli sauce and beansprouts. Also, they love coffee strong enough to run a small motor on.

Satisfied I'd had a great meal, I really didn't fancy much more walking around today, plus I was fairly tired from my flights. Staying in the backpacker area of the city, I found a local bar for a beer. Well actually, I say "found", that's a lie. A Vietnamese girl, clearly there trying to pull people in, grabbed my arm as I passed and stuck me into a seat on the street right outside the bar, managing to catch me before the other girls at other bars did. I had nowhere else to go, so why not? She was petite and in her mid-twenties, with short-cropped hair, most noticeably rocking a rather large scar along the side of her face.

"What you want", she asked.

"A beer? How much are they?"

"Nine thousand Dong, you pay".

"Okay, go for it". Whilst she was off getting a beer, I had a discreet fumble through the change in my pocket from my meal earlier ready to pay, trying to act like I wasn't new to all these notes in case one of the other bar girls was watching me be all new and foreign, and therefore a potential rip off opportunity. When the bill came with the beer, it took me a few seconds to realise it must have only cost thirty pence in British money for a whole pint. That can't be right, can it? Whilst Asia, in general, had always been cheap compared to back home, I had yet to find beer prices that were this low at a bar. Thirty pence for a pint of beer! I mean, come on! You could get properly off your tits for a fiver! Fortunately for my liver I was only going to have a couple today, as at this price things could get messy.

The girl got herself a drink and sat down next to me. "Here we go!" I thought. She was rather friendly after I got over the weirdness of her deciding to sit at my table, and as time went on, we started talking a bit. It wasn't lost on me she was likely a prostitute eyeing me up as a customer, plus she was a little rough, and I couldn't stop staring at her facial scar. It beat sitting by myself, so I was okay with it. We started playing cards for most of the afternoon whilst continuing to enjoy the wonderful beer prices. Before I knew it, the time had taken me to early evening, and I'd lost count of the beers I'd had, but I'd spent a massive £3.

Sometime in the evening, a stocky Caucasian guy came swaying down the street, mopeds swerving out of his way, blood gushing out him. Even in the frenzied streets of the city, he stood out above everything as blood leaked down from his face and onto his shirt. He attempted to get into some of the bars before ours, but the locals were pushing him away and telling him to move on. He got to our bar, the bar girls here didn't seem too bothered about him dripping blood everywhere, and let him in. They brought him a beer and some tissues for his head. Well, this guy was absolutely obnoxious once he sat down and started talking – and worse still, he was the certain type of Australian that we all avoid out here.

From my understanding, Australians tend to have a bad reputation around South East Asia, and it's because these types of arseholes give the rest a bad name. I'm no saint and definitely get up to bouts of mischief when I'm away, but there is a time and a place for it, and these guys are on another level. Thankfully our equivalent, the trouble-making, pissed up *Brits abroad* stick to various locations in Spain, descending on short hauls flights to Benidorm and Magaluf for their yearly reign of terror in the sun, fuelled by fried English breakfasts and pints of cheap lager. Having to embark on a long flight to even leave the boundaries of their country, their Aussie counterparts like to upset a broader area, case in point, this absolute blood-drenched dickhead sat in front of me. He started mocking everyone, shouting out pretty derogatory words for the Vietnamese, despite the fact they were trying to fix the cut on his head. I couldn't settle with him nearby. He kept saying to me what a "funny cunt" he was. "I'm the funniest cunt you'll ever meet.... aren't I such a funny cunt?!". Hilarious mate. What are you doing out here by yourself in this state? Then he necked his bottle and threw it on the floor, shattering it. Either from alcohol or blood loss, several minutes later he then proceeded to fall off his seat backwards knocking his head pretty hard rendering him unconscious, luckily for him the glass he had smashed earlier had been swept up. I think everyone had enough of him by this point, so no one was really in a rush to help, so we all just watched him for several moments splayed out by the edge of the street. I was looking around as if to say "What do we do now?" before one of the bar girls walked over and put her hand into his pocket, pulled his wallet out, helped herself to all of the notes within and threw the wallet back down onto his chest. I sat there and watched with my eyes fixed on her. I had just watched someone getting robbed. I may have said something had I been a little more comfortable with my surroundings but having been in the country a mere ten hours or so, I decided it was best to stay out of it. He was a 'cunt' anyway, so if anyone deserved to be robbed, it was surely him. Just at that moment, a moped crashed into a little street vendor's coffee shop across the road. This place is proper nuts.

It got to 10 PM, so much for an early night. The bar girl, who I had not bothered to learn the name of so simply dubbed her "Bar Girl", had stuck around and the pair of us had been bar hopping most of the evening. I knew she was a bit of strange friend to have with me, a prostitute with a scarred face, but if anything my time in Koh Phangan taught me about working girls is not to judge a book by its cover. She took me to a street food vendor between the bars for a feed. As we were sitting, enjoying our fresh spring rolls as people passed us going about their business, out of the crowd, a scruffy elderly man approached and asked if I wanted a cheap massage. I wasn't so sure, but Bar Girl insisted I went for it. I reluctantly agreed. It was a bit surreal getting my neck and back rubbed by what may have well been a homeless man whilst trying to eat food. Still, the real shocker was when he suddenly turned my head to the side to crack my neck – I wasn't expecting it at all – which I guess was his intention, the crack in my spine was even loud enough for Bar Girl to hear it. She turned with a look of horror on her face. I never really get why people crack bones for pleasure, knuckles, spine and the like. It's worse than a fart to me, keep it to yourself because I don't want to hear it, you utter creature.

Intoxicated and new to the area, unbeknown to me, we had looped around via various side streets and road, and a couple of hours later found ourselves walking up to the original bar we started at. I was fully swaying around by this point, maybe the beer, maybe blood building upon the base of my brain from my earlier spine massage. There was a new set of girls on at the bar, I didn't recognise any of them. Some of them started arguing with Bar Girl the moment we arrived, and then after a few heated words and pushing her around, she fell to the floor, and six of them began to kick the shit out of her. They had her curled up on the floor and were kicking her head and body. It would have been a fun fight to watch if this person hadn't become my friend slightly over the day. I'm not usually the type to stand idly by and let something like this happen. Still, at the same time like with the drunk Australian getting robbed earlier, I've been here a few hours, I don't know what I'm getting myself into here if I get involved. As she lay there covering her head, getting kicked and punched by a gang of prostitutes, I wondered to myself, does this sort of madness just attract me whilst I'm away? Is it my fault, do I go to places that most other backpackers avoid? Wasn't only a few weeks back I was dealing with Rick drugged up in an alleyway and his gun? And Ramal swinging for me in Sri Lanka a few days after that? A fellow Englishman was sat at the bar watching the fight, and he turned to me and said,

"I can see what you're thinking mate, leave it, she's a tit and owes all these other prozzers money". She got up on the first chance she could and ran off, and that was the last I ever saw of her. I was able to find my way back home across the area and through the foreign alleyways and roads. I'm like a homing pigeon when I've had a few though, always finding a way back, usually doing it in England picking up a kebab in the process despite everywhere being closed. Thankfully all my new dorm mates were still awake and as I hadn't quite introduced myself properly to them yet earlier in the day, coming in comically drunk was a bit of an icebreaker. I spent the following days with them out in the city, seeing the sights in the afternoon among the bleary-eyed hangovers then start partying away once the sun set. Three English lads from Blackburn in my dorm were a great laugh, and we all encouraged each other into days of heavy drinking. Perhaps I'm more of a *Brit abroad* than I would care to admit.

A guy from my dorm worth a mention rocked up one afternoon halfway through my stay. He clearly was of Asian origin, but I could tell he had been living on the North American continent somewhere because of his dress sense. He introduced himself as Don and after a brief chat revealed he was actually Vietnamese, but he and his family left the country when he was only 5, and moved to Canada. Now aged 29, this was his first time back to his city of origin. He commented it was strange being here as an adult, effectively to a brand new and alien place, but knew so much about the culture and even spoke the language. Having just arrived, he didn't really know what to do with himself now he was here. I had plans to meet a local, she was called Vy and was a friend of Kim from Jakarta who had kindly organised for us both to meet up for dinner to show me around. Despite befriending countless people on this trip, it had been done on random encounters, but arranging to meet a complete stranger at an agreed time left me a little nervous. I asked Don if he wanted to join me to ease the worries, sure, he's a stranger too, but we can all be strangers together. Ten minutes into meeting him and he's agreed to go to the other side of town with me – great news, a new mate and a translator rolled into one! The problem for me now was that this was the night after a party at the hostel and having only three hours of sleep last night. I was far too hungover. Vy had emailed me that afternoon and said for dinner tonight, we were to have a genuine Vietnamese experience: A place where snails were on the menu. I'd never seen a cooked snail before but had now seen them on various street food vendors here, some of them the size of my fist. They looked absolutely grotesque. All curled up and glistening, looking like a piece of thick black leather stuffed in a shell. The hangover was rendering the thought of eating something familiar like beef was turning my stomach, never mind a garden pest. We don't eat snails in England, it's not normal, and if anyone from England does, it's because they've escaped from their specialist care home and into the forests where they're just putting anything they find on the floor into their mouths.

After getting to the address, Don and I arrived at not only a snail restaurant but a whole road dedicated to it aptly called *Snail Street*. There was no escaping it. The road had so many restaurants along it, in fact, specialising in this type of food that it took me and Don a while to actually find our meetups. Vy had come with two of her friends, also Vietnamese, all in their mid-twenties. I was the only Caucasian, not just at our restaurant but on the whole street – all the other backpackers were probably away having something normal like a *KFC* whilst I'm here in weird food land. Like elsewhere in Asia, I was getting a few glances from the locals. Although thinking about it, this time was probably more do to with how funny I looked sitting in the small furniture I had been provided – think of a child's plastic chair and table set you would stick in the garden at home. It was fine for the 5ft Vietnamese and their small builds, but for me being the big over-sized lurch I am, I wasn't able to sit in the chair properly with my knees up to my chin, nor fit my legs under the table, leaning over the table like a crane. It's hard to make a good first impression when you look like this much of a wanker.

The table filled up with all sorts of boneless blobs... mussels, clams, snails, crabs. This was supposed to be an authentic Vietnam culinary experience and to be fair if they were anything like the rest of the food I'd had in Vietnam then this place was probably the best place to have them. I looked at them though, curled up and yellow in their shells. They're not going into my mouth today, sorry. I managed some crab and a mussel which were okay, but mostly I just filled up on bread. The street was loud and bustling with people, and although the girls spoke English well, I don't think they could understand my accent entirely over the noise. I'm glad Don was there as it might have been a little awkward without him. After the meal, the girls asked Don and me if we wanted to watch an orchestra in the posh part of the city. We said sure. I'm not joking how posh it was too. Although small, the area Opera House district was like being in a fancy part of a European city. It was like we had stepped out of Asia and into Paris. Clearly built in the style of the flamboyant French colonial era; beyond the Opera House lay elegant white brick buildings, hosting expensive Western branded outlets. I was impressed with it all, if only for the contrast to the rest of the city.

There was probably just shy of a hundred people on stage for the orchestra – a mix of European and Asian – and they didn't just launch into a full tune but spent some time explaining the different components of a symphony. A German guy did most of the talking and in English, explaining in detail about Beethoven's 5th before playing it to us. I was interested in the first hour, but the thought of this going on for another two quickly made me realise it was not my scene. I think me and Don would have been happy there if we could just get drunk, but strangely enough, cans of lager didn't appear to be sold at such a classy event. Don whispered in my ear "Should we head out for some beer?" I thought he'd never ask. We thanked the girls for the night, which if I'm being honest the evening had been a touch on the awkward side with them, and headed to a grotty part of Ho Chi Minh with the lively bars, feeling thoroughly charged to be back at something more our scene. You know what I said earlier about do I bring on all this madness myself? Thinking about it, I probably do. The fact I could have had a cultured evening at an opera house with three lovely and well educated Vietnamese women, and instead decided to get drunk with my mate among the cheap neon lights of a run-down part of the city probably says it all. Shortly after me and Don entered the district, two girls pulled up on a moped and drove alongside us for some moments. They were weighing up if they could steal anything from us, but we were already clued up to their game. The crime rate is high across the city compared to most of South East Asia, and several people in our dorm had been victims of snatch and grabs over the past few days alone, usually done by people on passing mopeds. I quite assertively told them to "fuck off", and they did. Ah, that's more like the people I'm used to dealing with!

The evening continued, and we found ourselves sat on the street outside a bar, with plastic child's furniture again joined by eight other Vietnam lads. Their ages ranged from around our age up to sixty, and we'd met them by chance just choosing bar at random. These were really top guys – their English was pretty limited, but Don's translation skills came in handy. They wanted to know what I thought of Vietnam, "it's brilliant" I told them, and they began buying beers and food for us. I wanted to buy *them* drinks for letting us sit with them and giving us a great night, but they wouldn't let me put my hand in my pocket. One of the older blokes was the most notable of the crowd. He stole the show by singing Vietnamese love songs for the group. He wore denim clothes with a flat cap and interestingly I noticed a little American flag badge on his sleeve. I wondered how the feelings of the Vietnamese were today in regards to America after the war. This guy must have been around for it all and yet seemed to hold no grudges, clearly if he was wearing an American flag badge. I admit I didn't know much about it though or what it was really all about, that is, until I went to the city's Vietnam war museum, and discovered what an actual shit show it was.

To have spent days of partying with people, it was a rather sobering end to visit the war museum on my last day. The museum was understandably anti-American biased, but even so, you couldn't deny the photo evidence or facts of what the Americans got up to. I've always been pretty wary of US international politics anyway, but after going through the museum, I was horrified. The Americans visiting the museum must have pretended they were Canadian or something out of embarrassment. It's a bit hard to fly through a seventeen-year war in a light-hearted travel book, but some parts really stuck with me. By the early '60s, America was getting beat by the Vietcong, who had amongst their advantages over America, were using the dense jungle cover to hide. America's "great idea" was to destroy the jungle and thus the hiding spots of the enemy. They had recently developed a new range of chemical weapons and decided now was the time to test it out in the real world, spraying it across the Vietnamese countryside to eradicate the jungle hiding spots. If the museum is to be believed, the substance they used, *Agent Orange*, is by toxicity the deadliest chemical known to man. Eighty-five grams could wipe out a city of eight million people. It wiped out plants and wildlife where it was sprayed, destroying crops and other agricultural lands, forcing the mass displacement of the natives. It eventually seeped into the water supply and caused horrific genetic deformities of Vietnamese newborns, a couple of million of these people are still living with the shocking effects caused by the chemical. I won't describe what I saw on the walls of the museum, I'll spare you the horrific details here, but if you want to look for yourself, an internet search of *Agent orange* will leave your jaw on the floor. It didn't stop with *Agent Orange* either, Napalm was also developed and tested for the first time on the Vietnamese. Napalm, of course, being the highly flammable sticky gel.

I like to think that most of the Americans fighting in the war, like the rest of the world, were against what they were doing there. I was therefore sad to see the museum portrait stories of troops entering villages and murdering and raping large groups of women and children, performing torture on the men, and then burn their villages down afterwards. It was a hard day reading all this and certainly opened my eyes to a lot the atrocities. Whether you agree with America's ultimate intentions of the war, the way it carried itself out over it should not have been allowed. The whole thing had me pissed off with America for a brief time with their fucked up international politics that are still affecting the world today.

As a remedy to my anti-American mindset I had been plunged into, I received a call from Mo after getting back to my hostel, an American herself, who wanted a catch-up and it sort of brought me back around that your average American isn't so bad. Some of them a little dumb though, no doubt, but it's their leaders and their terrible calls who give the country a bad name. Mo, of course, is beyond your average American, and she had some news she would be moving in with Clive and me once we got to Australia, so I'd be seeing her again soon. The Tioman three would be reuniting!

Jakarta again – 31st August 2013

I arrived back in Jakarta just in time for Kim's birthday party. It was great to see a big group of familiar faces. Likewise, people genuinely seemed happy to see me again, welcoming me back into the city, which was kinda nice. Drinking shots of *Grey Goose* vodka in a trendy nightclub, I still couldn't quite wrap my head around that this city is in a Muslim majority nation and yet it was hands down the best place I had ever been for nightlife. The nightclubs were bigger than anywhere I had been before, and there was genuinely a great selection of bars to party across the city. My friends were a large group of mostly Indonesians, male and female, plus a handful of French and American expats, but always without a doubt, I'd be out partying somewhere with Kim and Mel. Two of my mates from back at home, Rob and Marsh, said they were overdue a visit out to see me and were considering my next stop at Australia. I said no lads, get yourselves out to Jakarta next year when I'm back in Asia. You will love it here, and they said fair enough. My plan, for now, was to head to Australia after Jakarta, meet up with Clive and Mo, get a job over the Australian summer and then get back to Asia with a ruck of savings. I now had dates to stick to as these mates were coming to Jakarta in the new year. Money had begun to get a little tight, which was my own fault as I was spending pretty recklessly, so I didn't have much in the way of options left. I had to go to Australia to work soon or face the prospect of going home.

Kim and Mel had a small rented apartment in central Jakarta, which is called a kosan here. A kosan is basically a single room with a bed, TV, air-con and fridge, a separate small bathroom and a shared kitchen area for use by everyone in the other apartments. Not that anyone would usually cook in the kitchen, it was so cheap here you could afford to eat out every night. Okay, not eating out in the traditional sense – it was only sat at street food vendors, which I've already mentioned before, some of them have questionable hygiene, but all are delicious. Whilst the girls were at work during the day time, I would have a mooch around one of the city's whopping 170 malls (finally buying myself a cheap phone after three months without one!) or explore the shanty areas of the city. I ended up in districts where I assumed tourists never go, and in these places, people would often stop me in the street just try and talk and be friendly. It was rare the language barrier wasn't there, but a smile and wave are international and goes a long way with people. My love for the city only grew and grew. I had heard people moan it was corrupt, dirty and polluted. It didn't bother me in the slightest; the people, safety, food, nightlife – the positives, just overwhelmed anything bad. On occasion, I would cook dinner for the girls for when they'd return home, giving them a taste of English food (it was definitely a task getting all the ingredients to do a cottage pie!). I'd clean their apartment up, and on occasion unblocked drains, fixed their cars or changed the flat tyres. I became somewhat a live-in housekeeper that partied with them at night.

One evening on a weeknight as it was reaching 11 PM, Kim had crashed out with the TV on, and I was nearly asleep myself when I noticed my new phone buzzing. It was a text message from Mel, she was finishing work and asked if I was up for some beers with her after she finished. It wasn't like I was up to anything important to do the next day, so I said sure. She arrived at midnight with a large crate of the local *Bintang* lager. There wasn't anywhere to go in the room without disturbing Kim, so we sat outside of the kosan, on the floor of the balcony with the many skyscrapers of Jakarta's impressive skyline glowing around us. I don't think either of us intended to stay up so late, but we were having such an in-depth chat about our lives, and at times having to tell ourselves not to laugh so loud as we'd wake Kim up, that before we knew it, dawn had rolled around. We only really noticed the time when we heard the early morning call to prayer, the Imams from the various mosques in the area blasting Arabic over the speakers. I realised that I was actually talking to a really cool girl here and pondered for a minute what she would say if I asked her out in the near future. She had mentioned during our talk though that she was having trouble with her boyfriend, she was still in a relationship, so I guessed it wouldn't be sensible to ask.

Leaving my group of friends in Jakarta was as bad as leaving my English friends when I set off in April. It's quite a profound feeling to meet people whilst on the road by absolute chance, and they end up being as good friends like the ones you have at home. I appreciated that they came to see me off at the airport, and those that didn't at least made an effort to text me goodbye. It was 6 AM back in the UK, and no one back at home was available to talk, so I sat in the departure lounge by myself feeling glum. I don't know what came over me, but I didn't really want to go to Australia at this point in time, and just wanted to stay in Jakarta. If there had been a way to swing an extended visa, I might have stayed. The fun, free-roaming travel was coming to a temporary end, and there was considerable anxiety about looking for a job once I landed. Still, at least the past few months had gone better than I ever could have imagined. Travelling by myself had been fantastic, definitely a little wild at times and certainly character building. I'd made it through the other side though, and I don't know what I had been worried about.

Chapter Seven

The Pisswizard of Aus

Jervis Bay, Australia – 29th September 2013

I have to admit that it was such an exhilarating feeling as my plane flew over some of the gorgeous beaches of North Sydney and the realisation that this country was going to be my home for some time. The Australian summer hadn't even started, yet out of the plane window it already looked like it was a beautifully sunny day. I could feel my Jakarta blues soon slipping away.

Clive had finalised the paperwork for our rented home. We weren't staying in Sydney but rather a two-hour drive south of there, in an area called Jervis bay. He had considerable knowledge on the area, annually returning for a few months during the town's busy summer season, which packs out with Sydneysiders looking for a break. He worked in the local dive shop but told me there should be a lot of work opportunities elsewhere there for the high season. Meeting him to get set up here in Australia, rather than an attempt by myself, was a no-brainer. I had met some unlucky travellers who had spent time in the country on a working holiday visa, working long hours in shit call centre jobs and sleeping in ten-bed hostel rooms in downtown Sydney, trying their best not to spend money. Others had taken low wages on fruit picking jobs in remote areas, all day spent bent over in the blaring sun. It sounded awful, and you might as well stay at home if life's going to be that shit. Thanks to Clive, I'd be hitting the ground running here in an affordable house with my own bedroom with multiple job opportunities on my doorstep. On top of it all, he was a good laugh, we got along, and we both loved a good piss up.

It had been a good few years since I was last in Australia. I recalled it being a weird mash-up of feeling a bit culturally like England, but visually more aligned to the USA. On my journey down to Jervis Bay (or J-Bay as the cool kids call it - I'm not cool so won't be referring to this term ever again), there were Americanised shops like *general store* or *liquor store*. The building architecture resembles North America, and there's probably some reason behind it too that I'm not going to delve into here. Wide roads and intersections, residential areas with spaced out bungalows and tall palm trees, which didn't look hugely different from parts of Los Angeles. British similarities underlie all these though; they drive on the same side of the road as us, have proper pubs and bacon butties, have the Queen on their notes, and most importantly, say *arse* instead of *ass*.

I met Clive at the train station, and he took me around for a tour of the town. I couldn't believe I was going to be living here. A small, but picturesque town in Jervis bay itself, running alongside a beautiful coastline. Miles of pristine beaches, lots of warm sun, and people seemingly happy to be alive in such a nice town. The bastards – it certainly beats the cold and pissed-stained streets of northern England where I am from.

That evening, a few of Clive's local friends held a dinner party a few miles out of town. I had been awake for a day and a half already, including the flight from Indonesia, and was feeling a little bit spaced out. I still managed to get stuck into the booze on offer, introducing myself to Clive's local crew. A conversation between British and Australian cultures started up. One of the biggest myths I encounter with the less travelled Aussies is that we drink warm beer in England like it has been purposely heated before being consumed (I think they are referring to room temperature ales you can get in the old man's pubs, which is unheard of in these hot climates!) I'd heard people confuse Wales being part of England before now as well.

"I know what a *billabong* is" I proudly proclaimed (a small area of water), but it didn't really impress anyone, and no one says it here apparently, despite it being an Australian word. I mentioned to Clive that I had missed strong cheese and hadn't seen it since being away from home, and low and behold, our hosts whipped out a smorgasbord of strong cheeses, olives and crackers! Fuck me, I'd missed cheese, getting only plastic cheddar knock-offs throughout Asia, if at all. I celebrated by eating almost all the blue cheese provided.

Clive and I drank a bottle of vodka each, plus some wine in boxes, affectionately called *Goon Sacks* in Aussie lingo. As the early hours came around, drunk and tired, we thanked our guests and pondered our route home. As we couldn't get a taxi by this point, (ah, the memories of small-town problems came flooding back!), it was suggested that we take a bike each and ride the three miles back to our place. Not the best idea as we could hardly walk, never mind operate a light vehicle, but we didn't really have another option. A short distance into our drunk bike ride, Clive excitedly shouted "Kangaroo!!". I was thrilled because it was the first one I had seen since getting here. Instead of focusing on moving as fast as the residential speed limit, I watched the 'roo bounce across the road and began to lose control of the bike, getting dangerously close to falling into a small body of water at the side of the road. I slammed my breaks on, collapsing into a big heap on the floor, inches before crashing into the water.

"I nearly fell in the fuckin' billabong lad!" I shouted over, happy the word I knew had actually come into use. I was in a lot of pain from hitting the floor though, I'd have been better off landing into the billabong to break the sudden speed of the bike.

When we got home, I thought it would be fun to ring Mel in Jakarta, blasting all of my new Australian phone credit on an international call. Instead of throwing up in a toilet like a normal person, did it in the sink, blocking the drains in a feeble attempt to get the partially digested olives and cheese out of the plug. Finally, I passed out on the bathroom floor as my knees gently bled from my fall earlier—a great first night in the country.

The bungalow Clive had sorted offered three bedrooms, a large living room and an even bigger back garden. The real highlight of the place was the minutes' walk from expanses of quiet white sand beaches next to deep blue waters, and lengthy nature trails in the hills behind the estate. I loved having my own bedroom again, well, for the first few weeks at least. My friend Jen from home was stuck in a rut and fancied something different. I said she should come out here for something different, and to my surprise, she actually did. She quit her job and came out to Australia. Fair play to her for that, it was a fair trade sharing my bedroom for the effort she'd made on that one.

Over the following few weeks, we slowly got our house kitted out, starting off sitting on the floor for mealtimes, and gradually acquired appliances, bedding and furniture. Whilst doing this, I was applying for as many jobs as possible. I could feel routine creeping in with it all. Whilst still going out for drinks occasionally, I was settling down – and even started going to bed at regular times! I clocked myself in the mirror whilst leaving the shower one morning and saw the fat mess looking back at me, body abused from a half-year bender. With literally nothing holding me back, lots on the time and money, but empty on willpower, I'd been a total pisshead. I'd flirted with the idea of trying to be healthy back in Borneo, vaguely recalling something about some apples or something, but had instantly dismissed it all as soon as the glistening dew from a beer tap caught my eye on the next hot day. "Right", I thought to myself "Now is the time to get into shape you twat, because if you don't do it now, you'll never do it". I was somewhere around 115kg standing near two metres, and after many unsuccessful attempts to get in shape in the UK, I thought that this was probably my last opportunity to do it. It's sunny every day here, there's no excuse to not go for a run at some point of the day.

I went for my first run in years around the neighbourhood. I was out of breath within seconds and got a rash between my fat legs, but I told myself I was determined to stick to it as I arrived back at the bungalow wheezing for breath.

The months rolled by. My first ever Christmas day abroad, hours of which was spent talking to Mel over Skype in the evening, then partying on the beach with the gang for New Year's Eve. Then it was getting well into 2014. I had carved a new life out for myself down under over. I was initially hoping to get into something like engineering work, but after realising the jobs around the area were all tourism-based, I'd probably have to settle for something in hospitality. After a brief stint as an ice-cream man, I later became a waiter at the local stone grill restaurant for some months, bringing out cuts of meat on a hot slab of stone. It's a slight novelty, but the food was pretty good. I enjoyed my hours working there, but the highlight of the job was socialising with the customers who were either locals or the occasional foreign traveller. My British accent was always an instant conversation starter. As standard for Australia, the wages were much higher than back in the UK, even as an ice-cream man I was earning a whopping $18 AUD per hour, around £11, which had me replenishing my bank account in no time.

My shifts at the stone grill would sometimes have me working past midnight. I'd have some beers and pizza with my work colleagues in the car park, or if we were lucky to finish early, have a couple in the town's pub. Australians like to think they drink like the British – they don't. Jervis bay's town of Huskisson had two proper pubs, whereas my town of roughly the same size back in England has *fourteen*. We aren't even a tourist town like Huskisson either which should offer places like these for people to visit; we're just a small English town filled with pissheads. Maybe it was only the area I was in, but everywhere would close down and most people would go home after close around 11 PM, which for me is when the fun nights begin. As Jen was the only other English person with me, more than once we had stayed up drinking past daybreak just as the locals were getting up to surf.

Don't get me wrong, the Aussies did party, it was just on a lower level. I put it all down to the weather. In Australia you can get up at the crack of dawn, it's already warm outside, and you can go and enjoy an outdoor activity to a nice sunrise before work. I don't care how much people say a bit of rain doesn't bother them; There's nothing pleasant about being up early to endure a cold, wet English morning, standing in a field, kidding yourself this is a fun hike, when you could still be in bed, or rather, still up drinking from the previous night. It rains a lot in England, even during our summers, so it's nice to go somewhere to socialise, sitting inside a pub with mates whilst the rain is coming down in the middle of July. The summer I had that year in Australia, it rained maybe six or seven times in total. It got so hot there that we were nearly evacuated because of the raging bush-fires nearby, putting us on alert for several days. I couldn't believe people were planning barbecues weeks in advance, knowing it was most likely going to be nice weather. Usually in England, we get maybe three days of notice before we are due to have a decent spell of weather (which is that much of a big deal it often makes the news), and have to plan our barbeques accordingly.

The weather was undoubtedly a benefit, and I couldn't often justify sitting inside watching TV when I wasn't in work. I'd be off in the sea or running, cycling, hiking. My local friends all had active lifestyles, and that rubbed off on me, some days I'd go hiking and snorkelling on the same day. Some weeks passed without me drinking alcohol. I even signed up at the local gym, something which had been an alien idea to me back in England. The weight completely dropped off me, 25kg in fact. I felt great, I was finally getting into shape, so much so that when Liggy finally caught up for a visit, he was gobsmacked how different I looked. He was in Australia for good now, staying with us for a few weeks whilst he got himself set up in the country. Here with me now was a group of friends, old and new. Various people me and Clive had met in Asia would come and visit for a few days, enticed by friendly people with somewhere free to stay. Jen was enjoying herself, whilst Mo and Clive were working various jobs as well, whilst we all lived in this great house by the beach for barbecues and beers. Life was pretty good.

The vast differences between Australia and England continue beyond the weather, and Australia certainly offers a greater diversity of wildlife. We get knobhead swans and squashed roadside badgers. They get great white sharks and kangaroos hopping around on the front lawn in the evenings (which never got old for me). I saw a couple of spiders, including a huntsman, which are so large they forgo webs and hunt small mammals and birds directly! Large cockatoos, multicoloured lorikeets, and numerous other parrot species would fly into our garden every day. Whilst their colours are extraordinarily vibrant and pretty to look at, it's like they know they're good looking so don't have to bother making any efforts with their bird song; usually relying on a loud squawking noise to let everyone know they're in town. Early morning is the best time to hear all the beautifully layered birdsongs of England. The humble blackbird, literally just a bird named over its distinct lack of colour, has one of the nicest birdsong of them all. I heard nothing like that in Australia, just always horrible screeching noises of parrots going apeshit on my patio. I had a regular run-in with a native bird called a Wattle Bird, known as *Nature's Alarm Clock* locally, sounding more like my *Spectrum 128k* from the Eighties loading up more than a bird. There was a tree outside my bedroom window which the same sodding wattlebird every day decided to park its arse on at dawn every morning, waking me up with its awful call. One morning after a couple of weeks of these rude awakenings, I finally snapped, I stormed outside and shook the tree with all the might I had. The neighbour was off out to work and just looked puzzled to see me in my boxer shorts shaking a tree violently so early in the morning. He asked if I was okay, and I said no, not at all. The bird flew off but was back the next day.

Jervis bay's towns shared something with the little seaside villages we have running along the coast of Cornwall in southern England: They get by every year with the summer tourism boom. Mostly dead and quiet during the winter months, then for the school holidays over the summer it just blows up crazy with crowds of people, flocking down for the beaches, ruining the town for the locals who have had to put up with the town for the rest of the year when the weather's been shit. Up to half of the houses here are reserved for the rich Sydney folk – empty in the winter months, yet house prices are insanely high as it's a desirable place to live. Because of this setup, it leaves the town population to fall to 40% in the winter months. Staying in this town for so long, as you would anywhere, it began to feel like home for me. I'd been living there for a few months, arriving before the season started, now one of this year's 40%, and it felt like *my* town. Who were all these strange out-of-town arseholes, causing huge queues in the local supermarket, clearing all the fresh produce out like a plague of locusts, leaving only one gammy potato left for me? Why should I have to walk at the pace of zombie on the high street with the crowds of people, or make a reservation to eat at my favourite restaurant a week in advance? Or share my beach with a load of teenage pricks playing shit music loudly on tinny portable speakers, and kids that run around screaming and kicking sand everywhere?

There were issues here beyond the economy's reliance on summer tourism, notably a huge drug problem. Use of *Ice*, or crystal meth as it's also known, is pretty rampant and many of my local friends had been affected by losing family or friends to it. Fortunately, that particular drug isn't so much a problem at home in England, we're still happy with the classics like coke and smack. Nothing is apparently quite as addictive as *Ice*, so I'm told, and it evidently was a huge problem here as a lot of people were affected by it.

A lot of *Ice* users were *Bogans,* Australia's answer to a *chav* – residents with a lower social status, to put it politely. They are particularly disliked by the general population for being unsophisticated and often troublesome, but I quite enjoyed their visits to the restaurant. There was never a dull moment when they were in; If they weren't throwing food around, they'd be letting their kids up on the table to run around, and similarly to myself, swearing and drinking a lot. Also, there is a noticeable *Hell's Angels* presence in the region, which I thought was a joke when I was first told about it (like *drop bears)*. This is small town Australia, not California! But sure enough, they'd roll up to the restaurant on their Harleys every now and then, the owner practically falling over himself to hand out free food. I wasn't aware if they were causing trouble or breaking the law, yet the majority of the people here didn't seem to like them.

Another group with the lower social status tag (and sadly so), are the native Aborigines. There's a reserve on the outside of town where they mostly kept to themselves; generally, outsiders were not allowed in. Some did leave the reserve occasionally and made their way to the high-street, only then to wind up drunk fighting in the street. Hey, other races of people do it too, but seeing as there's only usually a handful of the indigenous people ever spotted in the centre of town, and when they were, they were often drunk. It just fed into the stereotype that they all have drinking problems. I was saddened that a couple of the customers who I otherwise got on with well found it funny when a group of Aborigines came in for dinner one night. A while after I'd taken their order, I was asked if they had ordered grubs and worms. I was surprised those attitudes still existed, although it doesn't help that the Aborigines weren't considered full citizens of Australia until 1967 and were unbelievably still classed under "plants and fauna" before then. England is in no way perfect, yet even in my little white-wash town in the north, people are generally tolerant of different races. I still feel Australia has a bit of a way to go on this front yet.

I dwell a bit on the negatives. Overall, it is a fantastic part of the world. Australians have a good standard of living there, and they know it. I was lucky to have experienced a piece of it and let it change me for the better.

Hitting the road again – 27th February 2014

When I was last in Australia, I did a road trip around part of the country, driving the equivalent distance London to New York in just twenty-one days. This current visit had been the complete opposite, having spent over five months in the same ten square mile area. I was ready to get back out on the road when the leaving date had finally come. It had been well worth coming here; I had replenished my bank account and was in great shape to boot. To avoid falling into any traps of staying in the same place for weeks at a time, Jen and I made a proper route with flights already booked and paid for, taking us through an epic route of Indonesia, Malaysia, Thailand, Cambodia, Nepal, Jordan, Cyprus and Italy over the rest of the year. I was ready for the next chapter of the adventure. In the meantime, Jen was going to have her final two weeks in Australia, visiting her nephew in Brisbane, whilst I was going to fly back to Indonesia, and have a two week holiday there with my friends Rob and Marsh who were coming over from England especially for it. I was going to take the opportunity to ask Mel on a date or something as well. We had spoken most days since I last saw her in person, hours at a time sometimes. The thought of asking her made me a little nervous, but I'd kick myself forever if I left Indonesia never doing it.

We had a final weekend of partying in Sydney, I said bye to Liggy for the second time on this trip who took a break to see Jen and me from his new job as a chef somewhere north of Sydney. I was also saying bye to Clive, Mo and the rest of the gang I'd spent a memorable summer with and departed from Australia. I was back to being a nomad once again.

Chapter Eight

Trouble in the Tropics

Jakarta, yet again – 5th March 2014

If I could peg a single smell to Indonesia, it has to be that of Kretek, the sickly-sweet clove and tobacco cigarette that's smoked everywhere in the country. I personally find it too intense to smoke, leaving a thick yellow, syrupy paste on my lips on the occasions I'd ran out of cigarettes and asked an Indonesian for something to smoke. The locals here love it, young and old, often opting for it over regular cigarettes. The smell of it in the air isn't too bad though, and I caught the all too familiar aroma mixed with the warm tropical air as I entered the airport terminal. Look at the airport staff smoking it indoors! Australia had recently started to clamp down on smoking, covering cigarette boxes with pictures of grotesque tumours and relegating smokers to designated spots far away from public spaces. Watching the Aussies stood puffing away from the crowds was a sad sight. Seeing people smoking indoors back in Indonesia, staff and disembarking passengers alike, filling the terminal with carcinogenic plumes was the first moment I noted I was back in a country where rules and "health and safety" always take a back seat. Rules are boring anyway, they just make life difficult.

I made my way down-town, thrilled to again see the mass of shanty towns and weaving mopeds against the ever-impressive skyline of Jakarta's hundreds of skyscrapers and shopping malls. I checked into the three-bedroom apartment with a roof-top pool which was to be our home for the weekend. Jakarta, it was good to be back! Mel was on her way to the apartment, joining the lads and me for this weekend in the city, and then onward for a week in Bali. There was a few moments of anxiety as I waited to see Mel in particular, seeing a person I was attracted to after nearly half a year apart. I'd started to learn some Indonesian in Australia to try and impress her and was keen to try it out. I met her in reception, she ran over and hugged me. I tried to say "welcome" in Indonesian and messed it up. Rob and Marsh arrived a couple of hours later, brilliant to see mates from home after nearly a year. My travel buddy Jeroen who I had not seen since Borneo was coincidentally in town with a new job, so he joined up with us too. There was a good group of party animals here ready to hit the city for the weekend. Me and Mel made sure we took the group to some of the best clubs and bars I had enjoyed during my time last year.

Undoing all my hard work of exercise and eating right in Australia, I awoke a bit of a mess but ready for day three of a fun-filled alcohol-fuelled bender in the city. We sat around the apartment's pool, forming plans for the evening. We'd ticked off most of the decent clubs and bars, and there was nightclub which Mel had been pushing for us to see. I wasn't so sure about it from her description last year when she wanted to go then, it sounded like the sort of place that young, wealthy Indonesians go to spend *Daddy's money*. Mel convinced us to include it on our list of stops tonight. There'd been one or two of these posh clubs in Jakarta that I had visited previously. The Indonesian clientele there were all business, rather pushy individuals who I rarely saw smiling, sipping from bottles of spirits costing well over a week's wages for the average man on the street. I can't afford to drink in the bars and clubs that host the obscenely rich in my own country, and even if I could, I still wouldn't go. My type of nightclubs are those where the music's good, the beers are cheap, and the people are fun. That said, with the comparatively lower prices here in Indonesia we could afford to have a one or two in this snobby club – who knows, this new one might be alright. The five of us all looked the part at least, as the first stop was at the wedding of a friend of Mel, so me and the lads were all in shirts and ties and Mel in a figure-hugging black dress.

We entered the club around midnight, and straight away I noticed it wasn't even a night club in the traditional sense I'd seen elsewhere in Jakarta. Instead of a huge dance floor that even the other posh places had, there were only seats around tables here, where the privilege of just sitting at a table was something extortionate like $50USD, plus the drinks on top. Young, attractive and absolutely loaded Indonesians sat around tables drinking champagne whilst our group of ruffians stood around the outskirts like outcasts, drinking the slightly more affordable beer – which was still $10 a bottle. People were dancing around the tables a bit, but the whole thing just didn't have the same vibe to it as other clubs I had been in, and it sucked. Rob and Jeroen wandered off to have a look around.

Contemplating whether we should buy our second drink, I noticed it had only been me, Marsh and Mel for some time now. I tried to call Jeroen to see where he and Rob had got to. He picked up after several attempts to call and to my surprise, sounding agitated down the phone, said Rob had been in a fight with some of the locals, and it was pretty serious. I asked for details but couldn't really hear much over the shit music of the club. The call ended abruptly.

"Rob's been in a fight" I shouted to Marsh and Mel.

"What?" Marsh shouted back.

"Rob's been in a fight" I tried again.

"Rob's not alright?" he replied. Christ that music is loud! I gestured for them to follow me outside the club so we could talk properly, so the two duly obliged. Once outside I got another call from Jeroen sounding more frantic than earlier.

"Rob's been in a fight mate, what the fuck it was crazy, some guys had him in a circle, and they were going to punch him. He's already been hit once. He's got up and run away!"

"What the fuck? Where is he now then?"

"I hope on his way home". Lost for where Rob was, we arranged to meet Jeroen back at the apartment. The remaining three of us waited anxiously around in reception which had sobered us up - without hearing from either of the two, their phones were ringing out, but no one was picking up. Jeroen arrived by himself shortly after and filled us out more with the story. It was quite an eventful half-hour they'd had since they left us in the club.

Rob had gotten into an argument with a gang of lads after accidentally entering their private area looking for the toilet, which had led to a fight. A few punches were thrown, Rob and twenty others then spilled outside into the car park, and Rob found himself quickly surrounded by them. He was forced on his knees, and the aggressors demanded to see some identification so, dazed and weary, he pulled his driver's license out. Someone yanked it off him and took a photo of it whilst Rob remained on his knees. With the foresight this could potentially escalate further, Jeroen made the decision to pull him up from out of the crowd, which he was able to do without too much of a fightback. By chance, a motorcycle taxi was close by, so once on their feet, Jeroen ushered Rob onto it and got him to leave. There was some vocal protests from the gang of lads that Rob has just got up and left but they didn't seem to do much about it.

Just as Jeroen had finished explaining the story, Rob turned up at the apartment on foot, with a black eye and comically, the bike helmet still on his head. I was astounded he had managed to navigate his way home in his drunken state, somehow coherent enough to explain to a motorcycle taxi the exact area the hotel was, with his meagre knowledge of the streets of Jakarta and still leave without giving the helmet back. Well, that was an exciting end to the night! Crisis over, we retreated to the room for some sleep before our early flight onwards to Bali in the morning.

Mel and I were sharing one of the bedrooms at the apartment, as two close friends might. With the lights off, both lying in bed ready to sleep, I tried to tell her about my feelings and ask her on a date, but it started to come out wrong with my nerves taking control. She told me I was drunk, and I should just go to sleep. Well, that was a total disaster – six months waiting for that.

Bali, Indonesia – 9th March 2014

In the morning we bid farewell to Jeroen who had plans to meet other people elsewhere in the city with the ultimate intention of going out for beers again today. I couldn't have thought of anything worse as I was dealing with a hell of a hangover. It was now Sunday, and our only real plans were to get to Bali and sleep the weekend off. We stopped at Kim and Mel's old apartment on the way to the airport, having pre-arranged to leave some of our clothes and other bits off there that we didn't need for the week. Kim being the sole tenant there now, she took our bags and joked that we all looked like shit.

During the flight and sobering up, we spoke about how mad the end of last night had been, now finding some amusement in Rob's black eye and took some photos of it for social media. Joking aside though, I thought it had been a lucky escape, and he'd been lucky there. I'd witnessed some fights in the posh clubs even over the few weeks I'd been in the city, seeing some getting an absolute pasting by groups of ruthless individuals. From what Jeroen said, there had been a few fists swapped at the bar, it had all escalated so quickly. Rob had still managed to get away from twenty angry lads with only the black eye. We picked up a car rental once arrived in Bali, drove to a hotel near the airport, and all four of us slept for the best part of ten hours.

When most tourists think of Indonesia, they think of Bali, and much to the annoyance of the Indonesians, some tourists don't even realise Bali is *in* Indonesia. The country's only Hindu island means its one of only a few places in the predominately Muslim nation which shares, or at least tolerates, Western attitudes towards alcohol and partying. If you're a little more into the culture, there are centuries of history and ancient landmarks, and like any topical island, fairly decent beaches and a jungle interior. In the south lies the island's main airport, and in the nearby the town of Seminyak you can find street after street with many European and American style bars and clubs along them. I get the impression many of the tourists don't venture too far from the south of Bali, especially those from Australia who come just for a cheap getaway due to its relative proximity. There's enough to do there if you're just after hot weather, beaches and cheap alcohol, which we were looking forward to at the end of the road trip. For now, we'd settle on the cultural central/northern regions having a vital few days of sobriety and activities.

We made our way through the island's iconic areas such as the artistic town of Ubud, and the impressive Lake Baratan with gorgeous mountainous backdrops, swimming below waterfalls, trying new foods and avoiding the sodding macaque monkeys. Each morning we'd wake up and have a look at a map over breakfast and decide on the next stop for the day. If you've ever made a road trip like that, you'll know it's the ultimate feeling of freedom. A particular highlight had us at a beach called *White Beach* on the south-east coast. It was a lengthy drive to get to, and once there, we had a hard drive getting the car downhill through a jungle. The effort once there paid off, during the daytime we had a fantastic swim snorkelling in the water, seeing all sorts of creatures lurking around in our snorkelling gear. The litter in the water spoiled it a bit. I'm told with the way the currents work, all the shite that ends up in the waters of Jakarta is swept out to sea and collects around the neighbouring island of Bali. The locals here aren't much better either, often dumping litter themselves. I mentioned earlier about the lack of rules in the country, it's not all rosy and stricter laws for littering here would do the island wonders.

Along the entirety of White Beach were a few shacks acting as little barbeque restaurants, and the smell of grilled meats and fish enticed us in for dinner. After a fantastic day of sunbathing and swimming, we finished the last of the daylight off with beers and barbecued fish under palm trees, it was cooked to perfection and reminiscent of the top tier eating I had once done on Tioman. Sat with my three friends, I was so happy to be travelling again, kicking it off with what had been a phenomenal start. We spent the last couple of days around the party scene in the south, and I couldn't help find myself liking Mel even more despite that weird, really drunk conversation the other night.

On the last night sat in the hotel getting ready to go out, we received a strange text message from Kim. She said that an owner of one the well-known bars in Jakarta had tracked her down and asked if she knew Rob – and wanted to know he'd come in for a job interview. They apparently liked his style whilst he was drinking in there last week, and he'd be perfect for a new role. Rob had no intention of coming out here to work, let alone attend the interview, and whilst the whole thing seemed really odd, I couldn't help feel a little jealous. I wanted a job in Jakarta, and here's Rob getting people tracking him down for an interview!

The last night in Bali entailed beers and shots, partying with people from around the world, alongside night clubs and live bands. It was great, and unbeknown to me at the time, the last decent night out I would be having for a while.

CHAPTER EIGHT

Jakarta for the hundredth time – Sunday 16th March 2014

Due to work obligations, Mel had to take an earlier flight home, leaving the lads and me waiting for our afternoon plane back to Jakarta. As we had wrongly heard it might be *St Patrick's day* today, and the lads weren't due to leave for England until midnight, our plan was once we landed was to pick up our gear from Kim's and then make our way to one of the city's few Irish pubs for a few hours. It'd be a nice evening to finish off what had been a fun holiday.

Waiting around for the flight in the departures lounge, Rob took the opportunity for some sleep. Through a mix of boredom and wanting to make Marsh laugh, I wrote *I am a drugs mule, arrest me* on Rob's lower leg in permanent marker. We woke him up and the three of us laughed about the huge letters in marker pen, got on the plane and were off to Jakarta. The flight was smooth. Stood at baggage claim, we noticed a real rock'n'roll looking Indonesian guy, who stood out with his skull and crossbones shirt and dyed long blonde hair. The majority of Indonesians don't dress like this, usually opting for clothing that doesn't make them stand out from the crowd, so we couldn't help but notice this guy lurking around near us. We carried on to the cash machines within the terminal, taking it in turns to get cash out, laughing at the rock'n'roll dick loitering around near us. Maybe he's after a photo with the foreigners, one of us joked. Jog on mate.

From previous experiences with leaving through the airports doors in Asia being Caucasian, I am often hounded by taxi drivers desperate for business, it's pretty standard, and it was no surprise that I could see a group of men running over to us now as we stepped outside. "Here we go," I thought to myself. This was a bit different this time though, they began to grab me pretty forcefully, and I could see some of them began twisting Marsh's arm up behind his back just in front of me. One grabbed for my wrists, I shouted "Don't touch me!" and swerved in a way to make his hand release me, only to be grabbed again, but harder. These lads seemed desperate to give us a ride! One of the men shouted "We are police!" and it took a moment to process what they said before an overwhelming feeling of panic set in. Just then I noticed the men were carrying guns in holsters around their waists. Even the rock'n'roll Indonesian guy was holstering a weapon, evident now he had been an undercover copper who had been tagging us since we got off the plane. Actually, wasn't he on the plane with us as well? For a few seconds, your mind starts going into overdrive, what is this about? This must be mistaken identity, surely? Maybe drugs have been planted on us?! If they have, then we could be looking at the death penalty here!

"You there" one of the police pointed at Rob "You were in fight last week. The man you punch now in a coma. This very big problem" I could not believe it. This is over that fight last week? I was expecting drugs being planted on us more than this. Really, all this over that relatively minor fight? He was in a coma now?! Selfishly, I admit I felt a little relieved this didn't directly involve me, as this appeared to be developing into a pretty serious situation.

Several minutes had passed as the police restrained Rob, and by this point, there was a large crowd watching us, one, maybe two hundred Indonesians waiting idly outside the arrivals terminal. Foreigners in Indonesia are stared at anyway but being foreign and having the police arresting one of our group was overload for them. Once the police had Rob, they weren't as physical with Marsh and me but still had no issue talking to us in a bossy tone.

"One of you", said the guy who seemed like he was in charge here, pointing at Marsh and me "One of you come to station with your friend here. He in big trouble" and begun to lead Rob off. Knowing Jakarta best out of the two, I said it was probably best I went with Rob. As I crouched down on the floor flapping in a panic, writing Kim's address down with the spare key I had for Marsh, just for as somewhere for him to head to, I looked up and could see Rob getting handcuffed and thrown into a van, whilst hundreds of people were snapping the incident on their phones. What the fuck was going on here, seriously? This is mental. It crossed my mind for a moment that perhaps these weren't even police; what if this was some sort of an elaborate set up by the guy Rob hit, just a trick to get him into a van, drive him to an abandoned warehouse and proceed to kick the shit out of him? I asked one of the police for ID, which to my surprise he presented. If I'm being honest though, the ID didn't look very genuine, a laminated card which was mostly handwritten with a few details on. I couldn't contest the legitimacy of the ID though, I mean, I had nothing to reference it to. I wouldn't even recognise real police ID if I saw it in my home country. Least of all, I'm not going to argue with men carrying guns whilst on the other side of the world. I couldn't leave Rob either with whoever these people were, so I reluctantly got into the van with him. They stuck us in the back of a people carrier and closed the seats in front, effectively locking us in.

CHAPTER EIGHT

If I was frightened, I couldn't imagine how bad it must have been for Rob.

Having our mobile phones confiscated from us, me and Rob were sat in the back of the van with four police in front of us, two each in two rows. We were told to keep quiet unless we were spoken to, and not to move. The van left the airport and joined the highway. Some conversation started after about ten minutes of silence. They asked if we knew any of the Indonesian language, called *Bahasa*, what our professions were and how long we were in intending to spend in the country. They elaborated a little more on the incident, and we were told there was only one guy Rob hit during the scuffle, but the guy had lost his vision from the punch, and then took a turn for the worse the following day in hospital, which had developed into a coma. I guess it explains why they met us at the airport due to the severity of it? Still, it took eight armed coppers to arrest him? Were they expecting some sort of violent criminal? My biggest question was how did they know when our flight was coming in? Rob had a flight out of the country in just under eight hours. The police said that if he co-operated in an interview, there was a chance he'd still make it, which gave me a little hope there still might be a way out of this. I hadn't mentioned to Rob that I had my doubts that these were genuine police as he had enough on his plate, but I was having my own panic where this van was taking us if they weren't. He whispered to me, "Mate I am so scared", to which I had nothing to say other than "It'll be okay, man", which I felt was a total lie. The police started speaking in Bahasa, laughing, going on *Facebook* on their phones, which seemed very unprofessional, again having me think this was a setup.

I happened to look down and noticed the *I am a drugs mule, arrest me* written on Rob's leg from earlier. Shit! This needs to come off right now! Sat in silence with police in the van, I had to discreetly lick my thumb and wipe the permanent marker off his leg, which was difficult to do, focusing on smearing the trouble inducing words of *drugs* and *arrest* first, trying my best not to get noticed by the police over the process of several minutes. I would say it was one of the strangest times of my life, and at the time it was. Unfortunately, things were about to get a whole lot weirder.

To my relief we were taken to a genuine police station and not the beat-down warehouse. It was, in fact, a vast complex, several acres of various buildings dedicated to all things police, and as far as I could tell, a hub of enforcing the city's law and order. As the van's sliding door was opened and we stepped out, the afternoon tropical heat mixed with Jakarta's thick pollution hit me like a thud. Rob, still handcuffed, was ushered straight off into a building and into an interview room, leaving me a bit lost for a few moments waiting for the police to deal with me. They scribbled down the British embassy's number in barely legible writing and told me to ring it. I asked if they could do it, or at least use their phone, they laughed and said "no". One of the policemen appeared to get increasingly annoyed with my presence, so I took it as my hint to leave. I had no phone credit. Not recognising the area of Jakarta I was in, finding somewhere I could top my phone up took the best part of half an hour looking for a 7/11. When I could finally make calls, sweat dripping from me from the excursion, I called the embassy which had already closed for the day, so I contacted the emergency line. It put me through all the way to London, a man on the phone said he'd be able to get a representative over from the embassy tomorrow. The next day wasn't really good enough, but Rob won't even be here by then, hopefully. At least now the embassy was involved it would be easy to get him out of this situation, wouldn't it? Surely they'll make the police see we're just tourists caught up in a drunken scuffle.

I made my way back to the police complex to see if there were any updates. Getting around in this heat on foot was something else, it's no problem when you're bar hopping through air-conditioned buildings or lazing by the pool, but being physical and moving about in it was tiring. Hungover and covered in sweat, I tried to ring Marsh and Mel to let them know what was going on. I found it hard to hear my calls as I was near a sectioned off part of the car-park where the police were unbelievably pulling handbrake turns for fun, whilst scores of people looked on and cheered. Marsh was having his own lousy time. The spare key I had given him didn't work at the address.

"I can't get in the room, mate, have you given me the right key?" He asked.

"Definitely. Room fifty-six, right? You remember going there before the airport? Did you go up a small embankment through a gate?"'

"Yes, people have started to come out of their apartments wondering what I'm doing. I can see our stuff through one of our windows! This is the right place!".

"Is Kim not there?"'

"Doesn't look like it." I wasn't sure what was going on. Not that we needed this going on right now, so I rang Kim who had told me she had been kicked out of the apartment for not paying rent a few days ago, in doing so the landlord had changed the locks, shutting our stuff inside. Fantastic Kim, nice one for telling us! I told Marsh to hang fire, go and find somewhere to have a drink and I will figure out what we're doing next.

I waited around at the police station chain-smoking fags until I was finally allowed to come in to see Rob. I came into the smoky interview room to see him looking exhausted and frustrated with a translator. They were currently giving a statement about that night. I would later learn that the translator was awful at her job title – translating – and that it did the job of giving his statement difficult. He tried to mention the part where the local lads surrounded him whilst he was on his knees, but the translator didn't know what the English word for "knees" was, so Rob had to re-enact the moment. I think that if your job title is actually a translator for the police, then you should know essential body parts like the word for a "knee". I compare this to my local friends who speak English perfectly, and there are many of them in Jakarta – people who speak English well do exist in the city, so why was someone so bad at it used? The police had slowly warmed to him over the interview process, and they started posing for photos with him in the shot, even the rock'n'roll Indonesian guy was in on it, saying they were both brothers because they both had long hair.

The police lead throughout that if he issued a statement, he'd be allowed to leave. It was all a ruse. After all the photos with the police were done, they said "No flight. Now you go to jail". That was it. An industrial sized can of worms had just opened; he was missing his flight home and spending at least a night in a foreign country's jail. There was nothing else I could do for him today, and after waiting around the station kicking my heels for another hour, I finally realised it. I just hoped he was going to somewhere with his own cell maybe, or at least one with placid inmates. I had some friends who lived near the huge *Grand Indonesia* mall in central Jakarta, which wasn't too far away, so I sent the address to Marsh, and we met up there. We sat around my friend's place and had a few beers, talking about the crazy afternoon we'd had, getting tiny bits of information throughout the evening from the emergency line in London and the translator who didn't know the word for "knees". I was told from them that Rob was looking at two years in jail. Two years! Marsh's day had been shit, yet he took some persuading to go home once the time rolled around to go to the airport. I told him that there was nothing he could do that I already couldn't, he had a job to go back to whereas I didn't. There'd be at least one guy here for Rob, and it would hopefully only take a day or so before he was out.

That night I went out for dinner with my friends at the street food stalls. Surrounded by modern skyscrapers, yet here we were at street level eating tasty chicken noodles in a shanty town, the contrast is one of the things I love about Jakarta. I'd seen a new side of it today though, and it scared the shit out of me.

Monday 17th March 2014

I'm not sure if it's a cultural thing, but some of the Indonesians I know loved sharing a bed together, no matter how uncomfortable it gets. After last night's noodles, I assumed everyone would be going home with them all having work the following day, but they all decided to have a sleepover. The sleeping arrangements were for all five of us to unbelievably share a single bed. I didn't sleep much, partly because I was crammed on a bed with an elbow in my face, but mainly because of Rob. I kept thinking about my mate going through a night in a foreign jail and focusing on getting to him after sunrise. I'd been trying to find out information from a whole assortment of numbers, some unknown, who had calling or texting, drip-feeding me information over last night. I was relieved to find out where he had been transferred to yesterday, thankfully not too far, it was in the same complex he was at yesterday but had just been moved to an internal jail there.

I took a taxi as soon as I could there. I looked out of the window as it slowly steamed up from a building electrical storm building outside and thought to myself how crazy all this was. Could he really be in there for two years? Was the guy who he hit really in a coma?

Finding the jail was a big hassle, as I said earlier, this complex was huge, with multiple different buildings scattered around the complex, any signs or text displayed in the local language. I wasn't entirely sure if I was allowed to wander around freely by myself as some of the police stared at me as I walked past, but again it could be down to just being a foreigner. From what I could gather, there were two main jails on the complex, one for where Rob was held (with fraudsters, murderers and rapists) whilst there was a second, more intimidating jail dedicated solely to drugs dealers and users. I found my way with the help of a policeman who spoke a little English. Once I arrived to the entrance, I was met with sharp looks from three guards through the thick steel bars doors leading inside, all of which already giving me an unneeded dose of intimidation before I'd even entered the building.

"Why you here?" one of the guards at the gate asked.

"Robert" I replied. The guy looked confused and pondered for a minute. I thought to myself there can't be many other white guys in jail here. I'm here to see the only other white guy this side of Bali, mate. He waved his hand to allow me to pass. I was relieved of my phone and driver's license by another guard, told to put them into a tray, and proceeded to walk through another large steel door. Through the door, there was long room – a corridor of sorts, with some scruffy looking inmates, sat on the floor, and a single guard sat behind an old wooden desk. It was a dimly lit room with metal bars across the tiny windows, the walls slightly yellow from years of build-up from the kretek smoke, the yellow tar seemed to absorb what little light there was. The humidity and low light gave a real grim feel to it, and I couldn't have felt more like a foreigner like I did right now, eyes from all of the inmates and guards fixed on the white boy who had rocketed out of his comfort zone. From this corridor, one of the doors led outside, a small roofless yard area for the prisoners, then beyond that, a roofed seating area where inmates could sit with their visitors on the floor. Further on still, there was another section for the female inmates, C-wing, which it seemed I could have walked in and interacted with if I wanted to. There were a couple of other small wings adjacent to the courtyard too, A and B wings. With no real direction, I wandered out onto the yard and amongst the inmates, assuming that was where I needed to go, completely overwhelmed by being in a foreign jail.

A young inmate bounced up to me and said something in Bahasa. I assumed it was along the lines of "Why are you here" so I said "Bule Robert". Bule (pronounced Bu-lay) is the Indonesian slang word for foreigner, and in this instance, it was pretty handy to know, as again it turns out it wasn't so apparently obvious that the new white guy wanted to see the only other white guy. He nodded and ran off into the cells, another room from off the yard, and some moments later out came Rob, looking worse for wear. I hugged him, then we found a little clearing on the floor by a corner of the visiting area amongst the people and sat down and talked. It was a tense time. We filled each other in over our past eighteen hours, and what our next steps from here were. Rob had spent the night locked in a small bed-less, squalid room with several other inmates, and was let out by the morning in time to take a visit from a representative from the British embassy. The embassy didn't bring good news: The help they could provide would be limited, the bottom line being they can't get involved with another country's legal system. They brought some books to pass the time, provided a list of lawyers and said they could relay messages on to his family. They told him to prepare for the worst. Hearing this shocked me a little, as in my naivety I assumed once the embassy was involved, they'd be able to pluck him out of jail. Now it seemed that wasn't going to be the case and it threw my hopes out of the window.

We sat looking around at the assortment of characters in the jail, working out if there was any threat to us here. There was occasionally a guard stood around observing the visiting area, but he would often vanish, wandering off for minutes at a time leaving us with the inmates. The inmates were somewhat diverse, mostly male, a few females, all ranging from their late-teens to sixties, the overwhelming majority looked younger though. The males had to shave their hair as standard for entry, yet curiously Rob had somehow avoided this. Fortunately, most of them didn't look threatening, almost all under-fed and rather scruffy, some sat with their families, others sat alone. The female inmates sat in small groups keeping to themselves. The group I didn't like the look of were the large, stocky men with tattoos and scars who stood around the entrance to A-wing, containing the cells for the rapists and murderers. There was no barrier between them and us, so they were free to come over to talk to us if they wanted to.

There was one inmate in particular who must have had so much influence outside that he was able to walk around with a taser gun in his pocket which I saw him set it off towards a passing guard for fun, who had to move out of the way to not be touched by it. Not retaliating to the aggressive action of an inmate with a weapon, the guard put his head down and walked on. I was dumbfounded on what I'd just witnesses. Taser guy was well built, wearing new and trendy clothes and bright white trainers, which stood out compared to the other inmate's scruffy clothes, or bright orange prison-issue shirts. His hair was not shaved either. I would have guessed his ethnicity was from Papua as he didn't look like the Javanese Indonesians from around these parts – also not looking Javanese were the two European boys sat in the corner, which had piqued his interest. I could see him watching us, and I knew it was only a matter of time before he came over. Sure enough, after about an hour of us sat there, he came swaggering over. I didn't like the way he spoke, surprisingly with some English, but he was too cocky and arrogant. Still, he was relatively friendly to us (I considered the taser gun holstered instead of being in his hand whilst talking to us a good sign). He scared the shit out of both me and Rob, so we just kept being polite and pretended to be interested in his photos he was showing us on his smuggled in phone. Later on, I would see him walking around the yard randomly setting off the taser again, scaring inmates and visitors alike, metaphorically slapping his colossal dick around in everyone's faces. A passing inmate sweeping up told Rob and me that even the police were scared of him, which explained why the guard didn't do anything after nearly being tasered earlier. The man was best avoided (Rob had heard the Taser Guy's real name passed around the yard which he relayed to me. I searched online once home and could see his name in the news, he was, in fact, a Mafia-esque hitman that had been busted for shooting dead a Korean businessman who owed money to the Mafia. He was on the run for two years, getting caught and then thrown into the jail).

It was a rough few hours there on my first visit. Credit to Rob, he had kept his shit together and appeared mostly calm and composed, which is far better than I'd be in his situation. I felt terrible having to go at 3 PM when visiting was over, leaving him by himself again. We decided he needed a lawyer, so that was my first task when I left the jail. I could try the list of lawyers that the embassy had given us, plus one of my local friends said they knew a lawyer and suggested we use him. The lawyer, named Aadit, said he would do "mate's rates" as a friend of a friend. Aadit was prepared to meet that night, so it sounded like a good move, and to get the ball rolling straight away. I met him that evening at a restaurant, and although he preferred to talk through my friend as his English wasn't so good, he said he'd be there at the jail tomorrow and to talk to the police.

Tuesday 18th March 2014

After hardly any sleep again, early morning I sat in my boxers on the balcony of my friend's place, twenty storeys high overlooking central Jakarta, smoking a cigarette for breakfast and going through the e-mails from the previous night. These were mostly from friends and family in the UK, plus one from the embassy, all after updates. By this point, I was beginning to get irritable from lack of sleep and sharing a small bed with other people who decided on a sleepover again. I needed to sort out my own space. Suddenly I heard a click of a camera, I looked up and saw a startled woman on the adjacent balcony, I think she wanted a photo of me but didn't expect the camera to make such a loud sound. Usually, taking pictures of or with me is kind of cute, but today I just wasn't in the mood for it, and it actually annoyed me quite a bit. I'm here stressing out, and some idiot wants a photo of me in my boxers on their phone for some weird reason. So, dealing with it rationally, I gave her the middle finger accompanied by a clearly aggravated face. She went inside and closed the door.

The corruption from the some of the guards' desire for money leads to a strange set up in jail. Whilst you need to buy your own food and water in there, as well as a cell if you want a decent one, you must pay with your *own* money. The problem with this is you are not allowed to be seen receiving money from visitors, keeping up this stupid charade that everything is run legitimately. The head honcho who ran the jail told Rob on his first day that "Everything in the jail is free" which simply was not true. *Everything* had to be paid for there. Food fit for human consumption (true they did offer food, but everyone advised against eating it), water, somewhere decent to sleep and unfortunately, basic human rights all had prices. Like money, the same went for notes or messages too. We were told passing anything between visitors and inmates was forbidden, and there would be punishments if we were caught doing so. I had a note on me that I smuggled in today, without access to a printer I had to handwrite a letter I copied word for word from his girlfriend over e-mail. I was loosely searched at the main entrance but assuming the search would be the same as yesterday, it was nothing more than tipping out my pockets. I could have easily brought in weapons or drugs if I wanted, obvious to me now how that Taser Guy had obtained his. I put money and the note in my socks and realised they were a great place for sneaking in contraband. Once I arrived at the yard area, we sat directly underneath the security camera which had limited scope, both of us would have to scout for any guards and in that moment when all was clear discreetly passed it to each other. Rob asked me to bring out a copy of his documents issued by the police and get it to the British embassy. Whether this was supposed to be done by the police but wasn't because of a lack of organisation, I don't know, but for some reason, they wouldn't do it themselves. This was a pink slip of paper which effectively contained what he was charged with. *Assault with permanent damage.* It made my socks bulge quite noticeably, but I was still able to get it out without issue.

I mentioned to Rob how surprised I was that the jail conditions weren't as bad as I thought they'd be here, clearly adjusting to them on my second visit. I said this, trying to cheer him up, but I was honestly expecting much worse for a developing country's jail. The Western world's depictions on TV of foreign prisons had painted an image in my head, and it wasn't entirely matching up with what I could see. It was kept continuously clean of litter or leaves, and a small guy was walking around with iced mango drinks that we could buy. The A-wingers mostly kept to themselves, whilst others seemed a bit shy but friendly. As it was visiting time, there were families there too, seeing kids and mothers in there took the edge off from the scary people outside A-wing. Rob said the visiting area was a bit deceptive, the outdoor visiting area wasn't so bad, but the cells were dirty, small, and not at all comfy.

We waited all day, and Aadit said he'd be there for 1 PM. Then 2 PM. I had to keep going to the main gate to check my phone looking for updates, which was annoying the guards. Then by the end of visiting hours at 3 PM, he told us he would be there by 4 PM. I'd see missed calls but sadly they weren't from Aadit, Rob's anxious family who was constantly ringing and texting me on what his progress was. After visiting, I sat outside the cells waiting for Aadit for around an hour in the heat, just for him not to show. Mel had finally made it to down-town Jakarta for a catch up, I had not seen her since Bali, so it was good to see a friendly face. By the time we got to each other, from stress, lack of food, water and sleep, exhaustion had fully kicked in, I was swaying and slurring my words like I was drunk. We waited in her car for another hour for Aadit, but Mel decided enough was enough and called him directly herself. I couldn't tell what they were saying, but I could tell by the tone of the conversation it wasn't positive. Aadit initially told her he had been too busy to meet today. Still, when pressed for more information on his whereabouts, he just kept repeating "I'll let you know", "I'll let you know" which really fired up Mel's attitude (one thing I learned since being here, don't get on the wrong side of Sumatran girls, some of which are renowned for their fiery temper!). Aadit finally agreed to meet, but I had to go alone, and I had to get to the other side of town soon. Desperate just to meet a lawyer today, I agreed, and hurried off.

There's only one way to travel if you need to get around Jakarta quickly: Ojeks – motorcycle taxis that get you from A to B fast, with a little bit of fun and danger thrown in. They weave in and out of the heavy Jakarta traffic whilst the cars are travelling at a crawl. I would advise the use of a breathing mask though, as travelling on them during the rush hour smog means a twenty-minute ride feels like you've smoked a full pack of cigarettes. It would take too long for Mel to drive me across the city, so taking one of these bad boys was the only option for me. The ride there was the only enjoyable thing of the day, there were some dramatic views of the skyscrapers in the distance with another electrical storm rolling in at the backdrop. Hanging off the back of the ojek, I got a text saying he now couldn't make it at all and had cancelled today. I was furious that an entire day had been wasted, so got the ojek to take me to a nearby 7/11, I'd be able to get a beer there. I sat outside the shop, drank a few cans and tried to call my mum but couldn't get through. I was sad that I had left Mel after only seeing her a brief time. I just started crying a bit, sat there alone, feeling completely lost. It had been a shitty and tiring day, I thought my choice of lawyer had let everyone down, and Rob had wasted another day in jail.

Wednesday 19th March 2014

Angry with Aadit's attitude yesterday, I tried several of the lawyers provided by the embassy. I'd got through to Indonesian speakers on the phone who I couldn't communicate with, and the couple I got through to who spoke English who didn't want to touch the case. We were desperate to just get anyone to get the ball rolling on the legal side, so – through a friend of a work colleague of Mel, we were put in contact with another lawyer, named Rimbo. I spoke to him and instantly thought he sounded keen, so keen in fact that he wanted me to miss the jail visit and to meet him on the far north of Jakarta right away. In the hope Aadit would come to the jail today I wanted to be around, so told Rimbo I'd send him the details of the case via e-mail when I got home, and we could make plans to meet tonight.

Around an hour left of visiting, it looked like it would be another no-show day from Aadit, and as if we didn't have enough to deal with, Taser Guy had been watching us again for most of the day, and eventually came over and addressed Rob.

"I want to see you tonight after visiting hours are over. Come to my cell. Come alone" This was of course in terrifying A-wing, where Rob was told to avoid from other inmates on B wing. After Taser Guy swaggered off, Rob turned to me clearly frightened,

"What will he want?!"

I was scared for him, that guy could have wanted anything, a dry bumming was on the cards for all I knew. I literally had nothing positive to say about it, I fumbled some words that "I'm sure he only wants a chat".

It was immensely frustrating that Aadit was late, it had been a repeat of the day before. "I'll be there by 10 AM". Then we were told 11 AM, and it carried on until he got there just forty-five minutes before the end of visiting hours. Little did we know at the time, but Indonesians have a thing called *Jam Karet* or in English translated, *Rubber Time*, meaning that time isn't really fixed when setting meetings here. Meet at three? Maybe. If I'm not there, then *Jam Karet*, see you at five! It doesn't help that it's usually quicker to walk than use the highly congested roads of Jakarta too, so even if someone had all the intentions of meeting on time, Jakarta's traffic would see to it otherwise. This guy was taking the piss with *Jam Karet* though, we had waited two days by this point to see any lawyer so were both anxious to find out what was going on, and if it was at all possible to get Rob out. Our thinking was at a minimum we'd be able to bribe the police to get him out on home release today if possible, the pressure to get him out now intensified because Taser Guy wanted this night time "chat". Aadit rolled up, a man in his mid-thirties, teeth stained yellow from years of kretek cigarettes – one in his mouth now in fact – and sat down in the sheltered part of the yard area and loosely addressed Rob. It was another hot and humid afternoon, and I was sweating profusely from being in the jail yard for most of the day. Aadit began to speak. Most of the talking was done in Bahasa, and we'd rely on an inmate we had befriended who would then translate in parts. Aadit could speak some English, but it just took him too long to say what he wanted, so it was easier for him to talk this way. I think this lack of directly addressing Rob annoyed him greatly, not even making any eye contact when he spoke, and he was even more annoyed about how little time was left on visiting. Aadit told us that he had spoken to the police before coming into the jail, and they said this was a severe case that he was unlikely to bribe his way out of. Therefore, it seemed likely that he should expect to see a length of time in jail, but besides that, we would have to pay a considerable amount to the guy he hit as compensation. He asked for Rob's police issued documents, and then he went off to look for the police again to talk about what the next step was. We both sat there absolutely beaten, processing all the information we'd just heard, feeling we weren't making any progress – in fact, the update from Aadit had taken us back further - at least at the start of the day we had a hope that we might have been able to bribe our way out of this situation. We sat there in silence for twenty minutes on the floor of the jail without saying a word to each other, another particularly low point for us both. I felt so sorry for Rob. It was brutal.

After visiting hours, I went to find Aadit in the police complex for an update on the latest news. He told me much couldn't be done today because last night a police officer was murdered by a subordinate in the very complex we were currently at, so all the police now on duty were involved in that. It was unbelievable—just another day on the other side of the world.

Later that evening, I had a couple of texts from Aadit stating that he wanted, in Euros, 15,000. This was just for his fee and police bribe for a reduced sentence, this didn't even start with the compensation fee. I expected a few grand, but that much? Rob's family contacted Aadit and said that 15,000 was too much, so he said: "Well, what about 10,000?". He was just prepared to wipe five grand off just like that. Our friends and family in England laughed and said no chance we're going with him. I had taken Rimbo's e-mail address from earlier, so made contact, I wrote along the lines of "Is Aadit a joker?" to which the response was along the lines of "Yes he is". After some exchanges were made between myself and those in England, we decided to switch lawyers. Rimbo reckoned he could resolve the whole thing for a tenth of the price, £1500 to be exact. We were ecstatic how much cheaper this new guy said he could do it for.

I met Mel at *McDonald's* that evening for something to eat and told her she was literally the only person in the country outside of the jail that I trusted, amplified now as I felt that Aadit had been trying to take advantage of our situation. The new lawyer Rimbo had done more in half a day than Aadit had done in two, in just terms of showing concern and replying to messages. I will say about the *McDonalds* too; I'd had weeks of eating street food since getting back here from Australia. I find flies on the food sometimes and it can be by a busy road with traffic kicking up all sorts of shit and pollution up. Yet, I've been perfectly fine eating it. I have one *McDonald's*, and the next day I nearly had to cancel the next day's jail trip as I had diarrhoea not seen since that day at the Taj Mahal.

Rob didn't go to the Taser Guy, opting to stay in his cell the whole night.

Friday 21st March 2014

I was to finally meet Rimbo today in person. He said he didn't like I was staying squashed up at my friend's place and would organise a proper hotel for me to stay at. He met me at a nearby *7/11* from where I was staying – two hours late, of course, which to be honest had seemed early for Indonesian timekeeping standards. Because I met him via contacts who are younger than me, I was expecting a guy maybe in his thirties at most, so when this old bloke in his mid-sixties arrived, I was startled. Perhaps it was his old bones or something, but he had a very distinguishable chimp-like walk about him. On the rare occasions that certain species of ape who naturally prefer to stay in trees have to go down to the ground and walk over to pick up a banana they've dropped or whatever, they don't look comfortable walking across the floor with their hunched build and legs considerably shorter than their arms. This guy reminded me very much of that now as he walked across the *7/11* to greet me, but with noticeable thinning hair and a yellow short sleeve shirt and tie. He shook my hand and seemed nice enough, and as I got into his car with him, he sparked up a cigarette, apologising for being late due to the bad traffic. Blimey, could that man smoke, heavy even for Indonesian standards, he smoked ten cigarettes alone on the drive to North Jakarta. Preferring to live up there, he told me it's better for an older person there's less traffic and pollution. I noted it was a long journey from the jail area. He elaborated on his credentials, ash going all over his dashboard as he excessively expressed himself using his hands. He was ex-military, had government connections amongst other impressive things, showing off his awards and badges kept in his glove-box, often reiterating he was part of Indonesia's elite. This was odd, I would never have thought I would have crossed paths with someone like him on my travels, but I guessed the whole situation I was in was odd.

Rimbo dropped me off at a rather plush hotel around the corner from where he lived, on the outskirts of a mall and said he'd sorted me a room to stay at. I saw him on and off all day around the hotel, sorting things out, and I duly obliged when he wanted any information and such. He had even kindly organised my ride to get up to the airport that evening, as Jen had finished her stint in Brisbane and was catching up with me. She had kept abreast of the antics that had been going on and really wasn't that keen on staying in the city all that long. "Welcome to the madness!" I said to her waiting at arrivals, trying to make light of it all. At least it was a Friday night, so we'd be able to get out and have a bit of fun. I was keen to show her it wasn't all bad here. Jeroen was still in the city too. The three of us met Mel at one of the clubs and went for a well-deserved big blow-out on the beers. Sometime into the night, Jeroen went to the bar and got a round of cocktails for us. Still new to all the money, Jen insisted she paid for her drink and pulled out a note with 2000 on it. Going through the same issues I had when I arrived dealing with all the zeros in the currency, she assumed 2000 must have been a lot. It was worth about 10 pence. Jeroen laughed, rolled it up and smoked it in front of her.

Saturday 22nd March 2014

There was no visiting from Friday to Sunday, so again I wasn't able to see Rob. Another day by himself. I thought of my friend stuck in there for three days, but there was nothing I could do. At the very least I was able to give his food to the guards who were able to take it to him, for a fee, of course. The food provided in the jail was borderline lethal, days old rice with flies on it from all accounts, so eating edible food meant inmates often relied on people from the outside.

That evening Rimbo invited Jen and me to his apartment block, a two-minute walk from our hotel, which on the ground floor offered an impressive shared swimming pool area for the residents. A small bridge ran across the pool which glowed different colours from the garden lights around, nearby a small fountain bubbled away. The guy came across like he had a lot of money and took pride in showing off his wealth. He left us to swim, insisting we enjoy the facilities here and came back with a bulging file under his arm shortly after. He asked us to dry off and sit by him, then he was straight down to business.

I was astounded by the information he had managed to dig up in just a couple of days. In the fight, Rob had hit only one guy, the same guy who was pressing charges, and within that file, Rimbo had his photo, his real name and alias, Henry, plus information about his father. Henry was not actually Indonesian but rather a Singaporean on holiday in the country at the time with a group of friends. Furthermore, his father was an influential businessman in Jakarta with apparent links to certain members of the government. During the night of the incident, as Rob was forced on his knees by Henry's mates outside of the club, one of them grabbed Rob's wallet and took a picture of his driver's license. Allowing this would ultimately be Rob's downfall, as whilst we were in Bali, this gave Henry and his father time to organise how they were going to capture Rob, armed with a copy of his identification to work with. There was a strong possibility there had been beefed up charges brought against Rob too, as Rimbo said Henry wasn't put into a coma, like the police had told us, so we could have likely been fed lies by the police. What Rimbo's connections couldn't quite place their finger on was how the police knew we'd be on that particular flight back from Bali, as that was some Interpol level shit to access flight records. Maybe this family was just really connected, or somehow the information leaked from someone I knew in Jakarta? To be fair I had maybe twenty local friends who knew we were coming back that day, maybe there was someone who knew me and Henry's family or friends as well? It was a stretch but still within the realms of possibility. Had this something to do with the weird job offer Rob had on the last night in Bali, which was passed through Kim? As I would learn over time, upsetting someone who's wealthy and connected is bad news in this country, and regardless if you're in the right or wrong, if you've got the connections and money then you're bulletproof – got neither then you're fucked. Rimbo said you can absolutely have someone put into jail here if you've got beef with them. Rob had befriended people in the jail, some of whom insisted they had been set up by rich people. I'm sure some were bullshitting, yet I could definitely see some of them being innocent. The wealthy run the system. In September 2013, a fourteen-year-old took his father's car *with* his father's permission, drove the wrong way down the motorway and ploughed into a people carrier killing all seven people inside the vehicle. The fourteen-year-old survived. Usually, this would be a straightforward case of a crime committed, yet as the father is a rich Indonesian pop star, he had managed to keep him and his son out of trouble. It's a well-known case here, and there has been uproar about it that justice hasn't been served.

What was up for question now was the extent of Henry's injury and how deep his connections ran within the Indonesian government. I sat there, looking at this entire file on Henry, pictures of him, details of his life, and for a second wondered if someone somewhere also had one on me and my involvement in the whole thing. I looked to my side and saw Jen wrapped in a towel, looking shocked at the scope of the problem she was getting involved with. I knew she regretted leaving Australia to come here. Rimbo seemed confident though and said now he was involved, it didn't matter who this Henry guy was, we'd get Rob out. He then got to the payment part, and requested the £1500 he had asked from us earlier and said if we got the money to him by tomorrow, we were told to expect a strong chance of release for Rob on Monday. It could all be ending soon. Me and Jen would still make it to Thailand!

I asked how much from the £1500 was his payment. He told me to wait a second. He got up and left for several minutes and came back with a young girl, wearing a hijab (that's one of those Islamic head-scarfs, you uncultured swine). He introduced the shy girl as his daughter and said,

"I am helping your friend Robert for free. The only thing I ask is that when my daughter starts school in England in December, she has someone to rely on if she ever runs into trouble. I hope that will be you or Robert". I said, of course, it was the least we could do. What a decent guy.

Sunday 23rd March 2014

Due to it being a weekend, the banks here and at home were shut, so the only way we could get the cash to Rimbo was for Rob's family to transfer it to mine and Jen's accounts, and then us withdraw as much as we could from cash machines. Even though we weren't breaking the law, running around in a mall and withdrawing what we needed across multiple cash machines, maxing out our allowance, somehow didn't feel right, plus it *was* all for bribes. It was a hell of a lot of paper in the local currency, stuffing our pockets with millions of it. In Rupiah, we had taken out over 28 million and took it back to our room.

Probably never again seeing this much money in the Indonesian currency again, we spread it out across the bed just to see it. It covered every inch of the mattress even with some notes as high as 100,000 in value. I lay down on it so I could say I'd been on a bed of money. We took it in turns to leave the room for food or a cig, so there was at least one of us guarding the money at all times, just imagining some cleaner turning up for the find of their life. Rimbo came to pick it up in the evening.

Monday 24th March 2014

There was no release on Monday. Rimbo's plan, which involved bribing the police and separately asking the embassy for legal assistance – essentially attacking all fronts – primarily fell on its arse and left us with a need to change tactic. Rimbo insisted the set-back would only take a couple more days. To be honest, I thought it all seemed a little ambitious, but I kept these thoughts from everyone but Jen and Mel. After all the drama the police went through of having him arrested at the airport, and then him just being able to walk out a little over a week later seemed a bit unlikely. I still thought we'd have some luck soon though.

By this point, I had learned to expect the unexpected as every day brought its own special deranged event. Today brought the worst to date: On the way to jail in the passenger seat of Rimbo's car, he asked me to smuggle a phone inside the jail. He just dropped that on me during the ride there like it wasn't a big deal at all, as he grabbed a phone out of the glove box and started getting it out of the packaging. On previous visits, the guards had on most occasions been loose about checking me as I passed through security, and I'd definitely thought to myself how easy it would be getting something through, but still, on the off chance of being caught, smuggling something like a phone in would be a stupid idea. I protested, but Rimbo said it'd be worth it so Rob could help organise things from within the cells. Wracked with anxiety on the drive, I had an idea that as I could still bring my cigarettes into the jail, I could remove the last four cigarettes – which was done by chain-smoking in worry anyway – and slip the phone inside the empty packet. Let me clear this up right now that I think drug smugglers are knobs, but even if I was ever tempted by the lure of the financial reward, I could never be one anyway because I lack the ability to act natural when facing any sort of pressure. Rimbo dropped me off at the gate of the jail and said he had some police officer to meet, leaving me there to get the contraband through. I was sweating anyway due to the humidity, but knowing I had a *Nokia* in my fag packet had the forehead taps on. I fumbled around at the security gate, getting my wallet and keys out like an awkward idiot. If the guards were any good at reading people, then they'd be onto me straight away. I got the bugger through though! Pleased with myself, I handed Rob his new phone as we sat down for visiting. Just as Rimbo said, Rob was able to help organise some of his own business with the embassy and talk to Rimbo directly, plus talk to people back home. It certainly relieved the pressure off me as everybody's go-between. And that is the last time I'm breaking the law here, I told myself!

A young man named Ahmad Imam Al Hafitd had also recently made his way into the jail. He was in there for the murder of his ex-girlfriend aided by his current girlfriend, both of whom were visible around the visiting area. Their story was horrific; They reportedly kidnapped the ex-girlfriend, forced her into a car and stripped her naked so she'd fear embarrassment if she was caught trying to escape, and performed hours of torture on her. They stuffed newspaper down her throat so she couldn't breathe properly, then continually tasered her until she choked to death. These guys love their tasers around here, don't they? They didn't mean to kill her, so they said, but whilst the case was ongoing, they were plastered all over Indonesian news. You could see them on television or other media outlets, and now here they were sat inside the same jail as us. Ahmad saw me passing over the phone to Rob, and curious, came over and introduced himself. He spoke English perfectly and was curious as to what we were doing here. He seemed friendly and polite, and upon shaking his hand, I couldn't help but think this is the same hand that had ended another person's life. Interestingly, as his current girlfriend was in here too, they could actively spend time together here during social hours. Ahmad was overweight with spots around his face, but he must have had something going for him as his girlfriend was pretty attractive. But she was also a killer, so it confused my penis.

Friday 28th March 2014

The end of our first week with Rimbo had arrived and he had yet to deliver on any of his claims. With no one else to turn to, we put our trust into him and gave him a second batch of cash to deal with the latest twist in what those involved at the top wanted. He assured us we didn't have long to go. Suspecting we might be here for the long haul, me and Jen found an apartment with the help of Mel, (a "kosan" if your memory serves), downtown in a little street called Setiabudi V. It was a ten-minute drive from the jail, traffic permitting, and took a complete hour off the journey we were doing from the hotel in North Jakarta. Despite the constant city-wide gridlocked traffic, it's still quite easy to find calm residential areas within the mass urban sprawl. Some would be quiet little roads with tropical foliage around them, absorbing some of the traffic noise from the busy streets surrounding the area, but never quite far enough away to escape the city-wide smog. The real pull of the location was a little shop just on the corner from my place where I was able to get pre-cooked snacks and ice-cold beer on demand, plus the room wasn't bad for the price if you excused the leaky roof and sporadic WiFi connection. It was perfect.

I wanted to move to Jakarta to live and work, and I pretty much had my wish granted – I now had my own place and being Rob's presence outside of the jail required more hours than a full-time job (it was a shame there was no pay involved!). I'd work up to ten hours a day from Monday to Thursday, answering e-mails, translating documents, running around Jakarta on missions to retrieve important paper or to meet people, and then with the weekend mostly free, I'd go out and get drunk with Mel and Jen. I was still never wholly free from the jail visits on the weekends as I was still Rob's chef, bringing him food into jail every day, relying on paying the guards to deliver food. I'd get in after a "shift" totally knackered some days, not to mention poor Jen dragged around Jakarta on the latest errand we'd have to do. Over the weeks, Rob lost weight (not from my cooking!) and grew a big dirty beard, but like his beard, he grew rough and resilient and after getting comfortable in there, well, as much as you can, and was eventually back to his old self cracking jokes and having fun. I was conscious too that as every day myself and Jen remained in Jakarta, it was eating up time of our planned trip this year. There was still hope we'd be able to salvage some of it. At least we still had the weekends for a blast out; it may be corrupt, but there's nowhere to party like Jakarta.

There were many news stories on Indonesian news channels running simultaneously to our case that had a certain notoriety attached to them. The interesting thing was that many of the people who I'd see on the TV or newspaper accused of crimes would end up in the same jail, only for us to then meet in person. Ustad Guntur Bumi, or known by some as UGB, was one of the more high profile cases, a celebrity in Indonesia who, as far as I could work out, was a sort of magician / Muslim cleric combination, and was accused of fraud. He was a quiet character who kept himself to himself and would usually hide around the cells during visiting hours, but expressed he thought Mel was pretty to Rob on the times she came to visit.

UGB was big news, but the most significant case out of our time there had to be the apparent rape case of a small boy at an international school in Jakarta. I'm not particularly keen to bring this one up, but as the case which also made international news, I need to touch on it briefly. Accounts still vary depending on the news source, but for me this is the story that told the extremes of the corruption within Indonesian law. As I initially gathered how the story went, two contract cleaners at the school took a six-year-old boy into a stock room and raped him, leaving him with anal herpes. Worse still, the two men involved were supposedly part of a larger paedophile ring of six people. I had seen the suspected paedophiles in the news arriving at the jail, it was surreal seeing the place I had been going to for the past fortnight on the news whilst eating my morning cereal. Before their arrival at the jail we were told by other inmates they'd be treated harshly, I guess like child molesters would be in jails at home. These guys were moved to A-wing. The shame must have been so much for one of the accused, he took the first opportunity to kill himself by drinking a bottle of bleach. One of the accused was called Neil, the only foreigner, and he was paraded around in the news, locally and internationally, even making newspapers back at home. Rob was outright dismissive of him at first and wouldn't shake his hands when introduced by a guard due to the allegations. Now, if you believed the first news reports to emerge along with the police, this is what you'd generally think, and to be fair, I think me and Rob bought it along with everyone else.

Holes soon began to appear in the story presented to the public. At first, conflicting accounts over details began. Then, the evidence became odd. Perhaps the most outlandish part was the accused pulling magic stones out of the air to seduce the six-year-old boy, putting him into a trance and he was then assaulted. This was *genuine testimony* that was used, and it was enough to convince the judges, who issued a ten-year sentence each to those involved. The young boy was tested for herpes, from several independent laboratories, and the tests came back negative. It appeared to not matter to the courts. The guy who drank bleach in jail? There were then stories in media outlets that he had been beaten up so severely as the police tried to force a confession that he was killed. The whole case stunk. Whilst I am attempting to tread carefully about what I publish under my name here; the press has raised important questions of those behind the accusations including a multi-million-dollar lawsuit against the school. A lot has been published on this case by people far more qualified to talk about it than me. It is well worth a read further into it all. Either way, I am convinced that this is the country's corruption at its absolute worst, with innocent people being incarcerated for horrendous crimes that they did not commit. Rob ended up becoming friends with Neil and some of the accused after realising something wasn't right and offered support for the horrific situation, they had been put in.

Mid 2019, after over five years in prison, Neil was granted clemency, largely thanks to pressure from those fighting for justice. For the others accused, who are all Indonesian nationals lacking foreign government pressure for their release, their prison sentences continue.

Singapore City - Friday 4th April 2014

Like many countries in the world, Indonesia offers tourists a thirty-day visa on arrival. Most tourists on a two-week getaway use no more than half of it before they are back on their way home. My thirty days here were nearly up, and I was weighing up options for a classic trick backpackers use if they want to stay in a country – fly to a neighbouring country and return, which renews your thirty-day count. It's called a *visa run*, and if done right, it can be cheap and done in a single day. Singapore ticked a few boxes - due to its proximity to Jakarta, I could be there and back within a day and the flights cost peanuts. Plus, it was somewhere new to tick off the list. I would have liked to have written about Singapore independently to everything that had been going on in Indonesia, perhaps on a several day's visit seeing the sights. Sadly, it was not to be. Jen and I did plan our flights in a way that gave us six hours free in the city, so we tried to make the most of it. Another bonus was I had kept in contact with Jack from Borneo who was now living and working full time there. He offered to meet us to show us around (that's two I owe him now!).

I couldn't quite believe how clean the city was, not to mention the decent public transport we took. I quickly got into the swing of things in Jakarta, taking ages to get everywhere with traffic on the chaotic roads, throat aching because I've been stood outside in the smog for five minutes. Yet whilst in Singapore, we might as well have left Asia entirely, as it was just so clean and efficient, like nothing else I had experienced on the continent. We could even drink the tap water too, which was a first in Asia for me! As we left Jakarta at 3 AM before the flight, there was a split bin bag near our apartment with rats around it, scampering off as we approached, the pavement it sat on broken off into pieces, leaving massive holes to the underground sewers. As Jen later pointed out, there was none of that here in Singapore, just clean streets, minimal traffic, and level pavement. We did some of the main tourist attractions and finished the day off wandering a huge casino somewhere. This casino was as huge as any I'd seen in Vegas, and yet in the neighbouring country where Rob was holed up, gambling is totally illegal (well, outside of the jail at least!). There was a guy in Rob's cell who was inside for making a $1 bet and was looking at a sentence of up to four years.

Jack was an excellent guide for the day, and Singapore offered a welcome day's break from the trouble in Indonesia. We arrived landed back in the evening, and Jakarta, the city I once loved, was beginning to seriously grate on me.

Saturday 5th April 2014

The foreigners that we were, tied up in an unorganised legal system, were in a constant crash course on Indonesian law and how it all works. Our information sources mostly come from word of mouth from inmates or police, with the added caveat that not everything was to be taken as the truth. Sometimes even Rimbo's explanation of the process didn't make sense, and it was a given that police information couldn't be trusted. Rob's first twenty days were up, and it potentially meant something; We were told people accused of doing a crime stay in here in blocks of twenty days, up to three times. If charges are dropped by the victim of the crime, then the individual leaves jail before the next block of twenty starts. If the victim of the crime intends to pursue, the accused stay in jail until the end of the third block – a total of sixty days – and are then moved from the police jail to a district penitentiary, the conditions of which are notably harsher. There's even more to it than that, if the victim decides to drop the case because both parties have resolved the issue, if it's considered a "pure crime" such as stealing, for example, the authorities can still proceed with the case regardless. Rimbo told us that he had managed to drop it as a "pure crime", we were now just dealing with the victim's family.

We were beginning to hear all sorts of conflicting information from Rimbo, and our trust in him began to wobble. One minute we heard that someone who wasn't Indonesian couldn't report a crime, which was strange because we were told Henry was Singaporean. We then heard that it was Henry's Indonesian uncle who reported the crime – but was later told Indonesians can't report a crime for other foreigners. Whether he was getting wrong information from the police might've made some sense, but then wasn't he this well-connected guy here who had connections above the police? Surely, he'd know how the law works regardless? Even, our own embassy wasn't always clear on the process either, and their list of potential lawyers had been a dud. The whole thing was such a mess. Rimbo again wanted money, for the third time, to pay another round of police and officials off. Between me, Rob and our friends in England, we doubted making yet another payment, but we had already gone this far with him, and as a decision, we thought it was best to keep going. It wasn't lost on us though that these promises from the early days had begun to fall remarkably short. I fished around for lawyers again, but just felt lost with it all, and gave up.

Saturday 5th April 2014

I'm not ashamed to admit that the stress was beginning to get to me a little. Rimbo had me running around Jakarta doing what seemed like pointless little errands eating up my time, sat frustrated in taxis or stood around in offices waiting for documents. Go there, collect this paper, take it to there, sign this, go back here and collect that paper. There never seemed to be any results for all the work. Day after day of it, but I would blindly do anything to help. We could only speculate what was going on behind the scenes between Henry's family, Rimbo and the police. Rimbo kept telling us that the release date was getting close, we just needed to be patient. In the early days, I'd question what it was doing, and it was met with Rimbo rambling on and on in response, so it became more comfortable for me just to go with the flow. I was juggling so much with these long days, among offering support for Rob and his family back home, that it began to take its toll on my health slightly. I often found myself relying on beer and cigarettes in the evening too much to unwind the stress.

I hadn't really seen much of my other friends in the city, other than Jen and Mel. It was still too much for me though, one night I just thought "Fuck it", met a group of local friends and had one of the biggest sessions I've had since leaving the UK. I can't recall ever blacking out for a solid five hours of a night before. I vaguely recall dancing on a bar by myself with a bottle of wine in my hand in front of hundreds of people, then the next thing I know, I'm in a bed with a girl I had never met before in my life. I'd lost Jen, Mel and Jeroen at some point in the night. I must have started to sober up because suddenly realised I was in a bed not knowing where it was, I could have been out of Jakarta for all I knew. I had a call from Rimbo at 9 AM saying he needed me to go into jail to get some papers signed by Rob. Why couldn't he do it? Also, it was a Sunday, this is allocated as pure "me time" mate. There was also no visitors allowed on a Sunday, how vital were these papers? As a complete mess, I arrived into jail with the girl I met the night before, in last night's clothes stinking of booze and swaying. I paid my bribe to the guards for letting me in on a Sunday, got Rob to sign a load of papers, handed them to Rimbo elsewhere in town and then went off to a bar to drink a lot more beers with this new girl – and blacked out again. She was the first outsider I had let into my life since this had all kicked off and she thought I was some sort of crazy guy living a fucked-up life. She met me dancing on a bar off my head from wine and with a light foam around my mouth from dehydration, whilst one of my friends was in jail. Rock' n' Roll.

Thursday 10th April 2014

Jen's limit for Jakarta had reached a breaking point. She was only seeing the shitty side of the country, fed up of being stuck in a corrupt city, only ever making visits behind bars or to drinking bars. I think Jakarta, in general, scared her a bit, adamant her long blonde hair was getting her unwanted attention. "They're just curious people, there's not many foreigners around here" I tried to tell her, but she wasn't buying it, the stares of locals in and out of jail had been unsettling her. Our travel plans around Asia were getting spoiled by the day; *Songkran* and *Full Moon Party* in Thailand had long gone, our flights to Cambodia had passed, and there was still no end in sight. Jen had decided to meet Mo who had left Australia and was doing a stint of travelling around New Zealand. Jen's plan was to wait around there to see if Rob was to get out soon, then if so we'd meet up and resume our trip. I escorted her to the airport, sad to see her go, and then it was back to more of the errands Rimbo had me doing. Today's dogshit errand was to go to the British embassy, pick up a signed letter saying that Rob had no criminal record in his home country, then deliver it to the police. Why Rimbo couldn't have gone himself, I don't know.

The British embassy in Jakarta is in a compound with high walls and lots of security. To my joy once through, I could see British style 3 pin plug sockets were used there and momentarily got a little bit homesick seeing them. I received the letter after finally meeting some of the staff face to face who I'd only spoken to on the phone, then headed straight to see Rob that afternoon to catch the last hour of visiting. I'd been texting him all day, and it was strange for him because he didn't answer once. It turns out during the morning, there was a random search of the jail by Internal Affairs, and the inmates' phones that were found were taken away, including Rob's. Internal Affairs were an enigmatic wing of the government that seemed to come into the jail and always cause some sort of hassle on their visits. On the same visit, Taser Guy's taser was finally found and removed, not only that, Taser Guy had gone with it, moved to a tougher prison more suited to house the deranged nutter more safely.

Friday 11th April 2014

It was a Friday night, and in the evening, I met up with a small group of friends who I hadn't seen since last September. I planned to meet them at a kosan they shared across town, which I got lost finding my way to due to the concrete labyrinth that is Jakarta. I passed through a subway and noticed some graffiti. In the golden age of social media, I thought it was good to see the youth expressing themselves in the more traditional way of spray paint. Amusingly, I spotted *Jalal suck ass* written in giant letters across a large face of concrete, even more impressed they were attempting to use English despite being in Indonesia.

I finally got to the kosan, arms aching from carrying eight litres of beer a fair distance. One of the girls I knew there had a lesbian lover who *Skyped* us not long after I arrived and addressing the room from the computer said she could do tarot readings. After the initial Q&A session from my friends about Rob's case when I arrived, they wanted me to do a tarot reading on behalf of him. To me, tarot reading falls under the same umbrella of bullshit as ghosts, religion, and Ouija boards. And I certainly didn't want to do it right now but was pressured into it by the group around me. The girl through the monitor ran her fingers over the cards, told me to focus mentally on Rob and to say 'stop' when I wanted to select a card. Okay, I sighed, understood.

"Stop!" The first card was lifted and met with a look of shock from the girl.

"Oh, um, you got the Devil". The first card was a bad one she told me, but she likes to put a positive spin on even negative cards, but clearly struggling for the right words that I can't remember exactly, she told me it was something like maybe the devil put Rob in this situation as a bit of mischief. She was sure the next card would be fine. Next card came out– Death. She let out a little shriek this time as her eyes met the card. Again, trying to put a positive spin on it, especially after realising the shriek sounded terrible, she said it could signify the end of something and the beginning of something new. Yeah, but usually death means death, mate. Final card – Fire, which is ambiguous at best, but would usually be interpreted as a negative card. Weirdly though, there was a little boat sailing in the fire in the background picture of the card, and the girl told me that it could indicate that help would come in the form of something unexpected. To be honest, there might have been something in this tarot reading, after all, everything did seem a bit hopeless with no end in sight. The Devil, Death & Fire cards seemed about right. I had shared everything with Rob that was going on outside of the jail but thought I'd best leave this little event out. Certainly one of the more interesting video calls I had ever done.

Monday 22nd April 2014

In an extraordinary use of his social skills, Rob had amassed a group of friends in the jail, and they were a great bunch of lads. Rob mentioned that the guys inside were better than the people on the outside running the law system – most of the inmates were generally honest and open about their crimes, usually ranging from low-level thefts to things we wouldn't get in trouble for in the west, like gambling. In contrast, some jail officers were gambling inside the jail or were receiving bribes for various things. Most in here were criminal Rob told me, the only difference being was whether they wore a uniform or not. Our new inmate chums would go above and beyond, translating documents for us or relaying information to the guards who didn't speak English. There were maybe four or five guys that became close with us, and then perhaps another thirty as part of the extended group. They were all Indonesian men, whilst the female inmates always kept their distance. Some of the guys would take the opportunity to have photographs with us when their families were visiting, I mean, we were still two white guys miles from home, tied up in the Indonesian law system, seeing us was a novelty for most. I noted that many had bothered to have phones smuggled in purposely to do this! Of all we befriended, perhaps the closest Rob came to was a forty-year-old journalist from the island of Sulawesi called Harto. In there accused of fraud, he offered a lot of support through the ordeal. He was a large man but spoke softly and had a good sense of humour. He would usually sit with us throughout visiting.

There was one bloke who stood out head and shoulders above the rest. Senta, an Indonesian of Chinese descent, in his late thirties, was smart enough to speak at least three languages, but it was questionable whether he was all there mentally. He was skinny, his clothes hanging off him as he shuffled around the jail, collecting trash or dispensing drinks. There was something about him, I'm not sure if he was faking how cerebrally challenged he actually was, putting on a show to make others laugh perhaps, or if he was genuinely unhinged. Either way, without a doubt, he helped keep the other inmates' spirits up by giving them entertainment. At the beginning he was a quiet guy, coming over for a handshake and leaving soon after admitting he was a little wary of foreigners. Over time his confidence grew with us, and once he was comfortable, he'd at times sit with us during the whole duration of visiting hours. He asked if we'd like to see a magic trick. These weren't magic tricks in the slightest, but genuine abuse of his body. He sat down and pulled out two sachets filled with a cream-like mosquito repellent and a tablet that people can put in their wardrobe to keep clothes fresh. He opened both packets and crushed the tablet, he then squeezed one of the packets onto his tongue and swallowed it. I could tell from the screwed up facial reaction on his face that it wasn't pleasant. He then took around half of the wardrobe freshener and swallowed that too, grimacing as it touched his tongue.

"Me no die. You do, you die", he said straight after, the group of us consisting of me, Rob, Mel and four other Indonesian inmates chuckling away with that sentence. "David Copperfield would die" he followed with, implying that even a real magician couldn't do this sort of stuff. With that, he picked up the second packet of mosquito repellent that he forgot he opened, put it in his pocket and walked away.

In Senta's head lives a guy called Angel Brother. The way he spoke about him we at first assumed it might have been his actual dead brother or something, but no, nothing as potentially profound like that, it was a 'real angel' who decided to stay around Senta's head and give him free life advice. The problem was, Angel Brother wasn't your classic angel and was apparently a bit of a lad, who enjoyed gambling and eyeing up women. Any critical thinking required for everyday situations, Senta would rely on Angel Brother. As mentioned, gambling is freely done within the jail, including card games, and Senta was on a roll one afternoon, all thanks to Angel Brother's guidance. After a sudden massive loss, Senta told everyone that Angel Brother wasn't around to advise on the last gamble, as he had left to go to the women's wing to have a look at them undressing. It seemed Angel Brother enjoyed the occasional prank too, and told Senta he could stare at the sun if he wanted to, for as long as he liked, without any permanent damage. During visiting we would often catch Senta stood in the courtyard, arms by his side, mouth slightly ajar, looking at the sun without blinking. I think Angel Brother might have been a by-product of ingesting too much of the wardrobe fresheners.

The ever-ominous Internal Affairs made a surprise visit not long after the last batch of phones were swiped. As you might imagine, everyone in jail has to hide their phones as best they can, as leaving the poorly hidden ones puts them at risk of being confiscated, or worse, the owner getting reprimanded. Although never seeing the cells myself, I was told there were some ingenious places to hide phones, in the cracks of bricks, or when Rob was there, being much taller than the other inmates, using his height to put them high out of the way. Usually, the inmates with some standing within the jail would receive a tip-off from a guard before Internal Affairs arrived which they relayed to everyone else, giving them time to hide contraband. Senta was busy in conversation with someone as the notice was passed round, saying he would get round to hiding his phone "in a minute". By the time he got around to doing so, it was too late, and Internal Affairs were already in his cell tearing the room apart, watched over by one of the nicer guards from the jail. In a moment of panic, Senta grabbed his phone and put it into the pocket of the guard on the sly. The guard was clearly pissed off but unable to do anything about it at the time due to not wanting to get in trouble himself. The guard had to escort Internal Affairs around with an inmate's phone in his pocket, which could have rung at any time. When Internal Affairs left, the guard was so pissed off that as an act of humiliation made Senta "roll like a sausage" back and forth across the courtyard, as Rob described it.

Why was Senta in there you ask? Scamming money out of people. With this being Indonesia, however, it can't just be a normal scam and has to be a bit weird and absurd like everything else to do with the law. With a phone that had been smuggled into the jail, Senta would guess at a mobile number and pretend to be someone that the person on the phone knows. "Do you recognise my voice? This is my new number as my old one is lost. Yes, I am your friend/uncle/neighbours' nephew's son", whatever it took to convince them they were talking to someone they knew. It sounds mental, and it is, but people surprisingly fell for this pretty often. They would say "Is this Dave?" or whatever the equivalent common name out here for "Dave" is, and of course, Senta would say "yes". Once the recipient on the phone thought they were talking to "Dave", Senta would then ask them to send money as he was stuck somewhere. Already in jail for committing this crime, he continued unhindered with access to a phone and lots of free time and even arranged someone on the outside to collect the money and bring it into jail for him. This is where it gets really fucked up – One day he obtained a number which only turned out to be someone high up in Jakarta's police force. Instead of panicking like most would and put the phone down, Senta pretended to be another top-level policeman and asked for money. You may think this is all bollocks, but I swear it's true and a prime example of how messed up things are here. The policeman sent the money, then a couple of weeks later asked for the money back from the person he thought he sent it to. Which of course led to "What money?" which had the police tracking the number to Senta, then it led them to the very jail on the same complex they operated at. The officer walked in, up to Senta who was using his phone at the time on another scam –

"Is that your phone?"

"Yes."

"Well, you're arrested then". Brilliant.

One day as Senta was sat there cracking jokes to a group of eight of us, me being the only non-inmate, and only one of two foreigners, sat in a group absolutely howling with laughter. It made me think how far we'd come since our first day here. Originally two foreigners sat in the corner, scared to talk to anyone, now we were getting looks from others in visiting as we sat there laid back having genuine fun with a gang of Indonesian inmates. At times it would be fun enough to temporarily forget our worries. The only thing we needed right now to complete the set up were some beers.

Monday 28th April 2014

Another visa run was looming soon, and I was weighing up my options. I mentioned to Rimbo one afternoon I may have to head to Singapore at some point. He said not to bother and suggested that with his "powerful connections" he could organise an extension for me so I wouldn't have to leave the country. For the extension he told me to meet him early at the airport, I would hand my passport over to the airport staff at the immigration counter, and they would renew the entry stamps for me, saving me any flights. Sounded a bit unlikely, breaking some sort of law no doubt, but if it's doable and saves me a few quid, then let's try it. On my way to the airport to get my stamps early in the morning, he called me and said there had been a change of plan: I had to meet him at an immigration office instead because the airport plan was now going to cost too much. I arrived at the car park to the address where he said, called in Indonesian *Kantor Immigrasi,* and oddly noticed him sat in a police car with a policeman. Rimbo saw me walking over, and fumbled to get out of the car, being so old he struggled with his chimp like body, and managing just about to get out to shake my hand. He introduced me to the policeman, who was apparently one of his good friends who could get him *"anything"*. The policeman, in his late forties perhaps, seemed nice enough, although he spoke no English, so all translating had to be done through Rimbo. The policeman was here because he was going to help me get a visa extension, which I could have for as long as I wanted. Like the airport trick, I thought it seemed rather unusual considering Indonesia's strict immigration rules, but regardless I arbitrarily said I wanted three months. No way I'd need one for so long as Rob would be well out by then, surely, but just in case it would be good to cover me. Standard visa extensions were one month, I read on the internet and again once at the inside the *Kantor Immigrasi,* so it was a little curious how they intended to pull this off. I filled out forms which included Rimbo being my required Indonesian sponsor and chucked my money over. I was to get my passport back with its extension after a few days.

Finished with the visa business and noticing it was entering well into the afternoon, Rimbo took me to a lawyer's office he worked as a fixer for in downtown Jakarta and introduced me to the top lawyer there called Tarik. He was an "Important three-star military general" who was even known by some of the inmates in the jail when we mentioned his name. He was hugely overweight, much like many of the older Indonesians here that appear to be on a good income, and he smoked just as much as Rimbo. Before the introduction, I was told by Rimbo he was a reputable and corrupt-free ex-military lawyer, and he would be someone good to have fighting in our corner. It felt a little bit relieving to have someone else on the team now, as trust and faith in Rimbo had begun to break down in recent days, as he still hadn't delivered on anything. Rob's family back home had begun to lose patience with Rimbo, I was fed up with him to be honest, but I remained civil as I was the one dealing with him daily. All involved had made a collective decision to stick with him, as he appeared to be trying all angles for us, including this introduction to the new lawyer guy. It did say to me that he might have been out of his depth if we were roping this guy in. Problem was, like the police officer earlier, Tarik spoke very little English, so all communication had to be done through Rimbo. It made conversation a little tricky, regardless I was told by Tarik, through Rimbo, that he had done some more digging on the case and it didn't bring any good news. Henry's family had paid a whopping $10,000 USD for Rob to do time, and that was probably peanuts for them being as rich as they were. The company Henry's father worked for is well known out here (we have a branch of it in the UK also) and it was confirmed they had those connections within the government of Indonesia that we'd previously heard about. It seemed like we would have a huge uphill battle, financially and legally, but nonetheless, Tarik assured me he would fight for the case.

The guy who killed his ex-girlfriend with his current girlfriend by tasering her until she choked to death, the pair of shits from the jail whom I mentioned earlier, was found by a guard with a knife under his bed today. He looked like a computer geek, but having a bed in the A-wing with the other murderers and rapists, I wondered if he felt the need to have a weapon handy, ready in case trouble started with some of the more aggressive inmates, or those partial to a spot of impromptu cell rape. After the guards found the weapon, they proceeded to utterly batter him. We didn't see him around visiting for a good week or so after, probably too bruised to get up and walk around. I found my relationship with him so strange, probably even more so for Rob because they would often meet up for a chat outside of visiting. With him, I found he was just such a nice guy to talk to, polite, spoke English well and would go out of his way to say "Hi". Yet underneath all this friendliness lay a killer, a genuine psychopath, and it was unsettling for me. We had heard one or two rumours about the Taser Guy since he left the jail. Funnily enough, Rob had given one of his football shirts of his local English team to another inmate as a leaving gift. This somehow didn't leave the jail and had made its way into the hands of the Taser Guy before he left. It looked odd, an Indonesian Mafia hitman swanning around in a *Crewe Alexandra* shirt. I like the idea that whichever hardcore Indonesian prison he's at now, there's also *Crewe Alexandra* footie shirt still floating around in the system too.

I quickly found myself missing Jen, she had been around me for weeks, a British presence, and a little bit of home I could hang around with and get drunk with. She'd kept me grounded, and now she was gone, at times I felt lonely when I was by myself. Thankfully I was still seeing Mel two or three times a week to hang around with, the only Indonesian I could really trust. I loved spending time with her, even if I was completely friend-zoned.

Thursday 1st May 2014

My passport had been processed and delivered to Rimbo, who I'd met early morning before the jail visit so I could collect it from him. This was his last chance to prove to me he had these connections to do something. I'd asked for a law bending three months extension, and he said at the start of the week he'd be able to get it for me. I instantly flipped through the pages the second I got it, eager to see how long this visa was going to be, all my trust in this man riding on this one moment. Ah, shit. Only the standard month's extension had been issued. He made his excuses, a confusion with my passport at the office, blah blah blah. Rob's faith in him had been wobbled well before this, and he'd been hounding him on some evidence of progress. Rimbo's solution for this was to hand me a document which contained all papers from police, prosecution, lawyers and most importantly a signed copy of all his expenditures, now running into the thousands of pounds. It was a printed out excel sheet with a breakdown of what money had been given to him. As Rimbo handed it to me and before letting go of it, he looked me in the eye and said not to show anyone else this documents and that he was the "only person me and Rob could trust". On the occasions he had met Mel, she would always challenge him as our introductions were done through her work colleague, and a lack of progress was making them look bad. Mel quickly activated her fiery temper with him on the rare occasions they met and he didn't give satisfactory answers. I could tell he didn't like her, probably why he now told me that she wasn't to be trusted. To round of the weird few minutes, he looked me in the eye and said that we couldn't even trust our own British embassy.

On the ride over to the jail, I read over some of the print outs, mainly focusing on the financial side. Some admittedly looked fair, such as "pay for cell", which we knew we had to pay to have half-decent sleeping arrangements. Although others I wasn't so sure on like "Pay for jail TV", the ambiguous entries of "Immigration" and "Court" were running at a few hundred pounds each. I was surprised to see the itemised list was pretty long. "Pay for hotel" was on there too, which underneath explained that the hotel he organised for me in North Jakarta had been paid for by our side. I'm sure he said he would be covering those expenses back when I first met him.

Having his phone taken away the other day, Rob was in need a new one. I smuggled a replacement in my sock, with baggy jeans covering it and wasn't quite as anxious about the situation, especially compared to the first time. I was used to the jail now and was confident with the whole environment. The guards weren't as scary to me anymore, and I understood they accepted bribes to supplement their meagre incomes. Some were in it totally for the money and relished in the tiny bit of power they had, but most were just guys trying to make ends meet. I wandered out into the visiting area, chuffed I'd got the phone through, and was greeted with a "Ahhh Mister Steve" from one of the inmates who went to fetch Rob for me from beyond the cells. I sat down and greeted Rob, who looked agitated. He clearly had something to say and launched right into it. He said it was at this point that he truly thought "Fuck this place"; The news showed an incident last week of a man banging on the doors of the cockpit on a flight from Brisbane to Bali. The plane made an emergency landing, and it was initially treated as terrorist activity. It was nothing more than a drunk

Australian bloke being a prick on a flight, but the story had been followed by the news here. What did the Aussie bloke get for causing a potential terrorist scare? Deportation back to Australia... Whilst Rob had been sat in jail seventy-four days for a bit of a punch up at a bar.

Taking his mind off it, I told him there was a glow party on tonight that some of my friends were hosting. I wasn't going, and I had a date with that girl from the other night, but I wasn't really feeling up for it. He asked why, and I told him aside from the fact I wasn't really into her, it was mainly because I still liked Mel and the glow party seemed like it would be more fun. Rob said what the hell am I doing going on a date with someone I didn't like, and that I should just man up and talk to Mel properly. My feelings for her had been building up for months now in case you've missed me mention it six times already, especially with how she'd been supporting me all through this. I was worried about being good friends for nearly a year now, trying to take it to the next level could be weird, and she might reject me. I'd had that crap attempt earlier in the year, and I felt a bit jilted at the time. On Rob's advice, I decided to cancel the date and go with Mel to the glow party. I handed Rimbo's papers over to him along with the smuggled phone, so he could digest it all over the weekend.

After a night of drawing glow paint on each other and dancing around, generally having massive amounts of fun, I just spilled my feelings towards her and did it properly this time – I just happened to be covered in glow paint. She asked if I wanted to have a talk outside somewhere quiet. We sat down outside the building in a little alleyway, with the booming music and party noise in the background and talked for hours. It went well, and I managed to smooth talk myself into a date for tomorrow. Fuck yeah! It had gone well, and I can't believe I nearly didn't come today!

Sunday 4th May 2014

Over the weekend, Rob had gone through Rimbo's paperwork with some of the English-speaking inmates. A lot of questions had been raised about the expenses; thousands of pounds had gone to various things which didn't make sense to others in the jail. The inmates themselves were so suspicious that they brought the breakdown of expenses to the jail chief, and upon inspection, he said they hadn't received any of the money mentioned on the paperwork. For example, not to shave Rob's hair had a payment of $100 which they never received, the fact they hadn't done it was because he was a foreigner. Also, privileges such as having access to a TV hadn't been paid by Rimbo, but even on the printout, it was still four times the price of what it should have been. Rimbo verbally said for $1000 USD Tarik would represent us throughout Rob's ordeal, whereas this paperwork had written in Indonesian it would help Rob get house release on the run-up to court. Red flags were starting to raise, so we told Rimbo via text to get to the jail first thing on Monday morning so it could be sorted out. We gave him the benefit of the doubt, we just wanted this clearing up.

Tuesday 6th May 2014

Rimbo didn't show on Monday and made promises he would today, but didn't, and in the afternoon made excuses about visiting the embassy on Rob's behalf. Detecting a whiff of bullshit, I rang the embassy with the direct line I now had, and they said he didn't even have an appointment all day. He was outright lying!

In the evening, the chief inmate came up to Rob and said as his cell hadn't been paid for since his arrival, perhaps getting wind of the finances recently from Rimbo's document, he expected him to pay. The title of chief inmate usually goes to the person that has there the longest and is expected to act as a debt collector for inmates' rooms. This includes inmates' fees for the cells, food or anything else. Rob said that it couldn't be right as we'd given Rimbo the money to pay for this sort of stuff. This was beginning to get worrying.

Rimbo called me up that night to say there would definitely be no court for Rob now. Was he making stuff up, trying to cause diversions as we had started to unearth his lies? I sternly told him let's discuss it in person tomorrow at the jail.

Chapter Nine

Talking 'bout the big monkey-man

Wednesday 7th May 2014

Early morning over my cornflakes, I fired out multiple text messages towards Rimbo demanding he come to the jail. By 9 AM he must have had at least fifteen messages from Rob and me combined, and again he promised he would show up today. I arrived as soon as visiting was open, ready for a showdown, and could see Rob already sat down with his inmate friend, Harto, and his visiting brother-in-law, also an Indonesian, called Lorenzo. They were all seemingly ready for Rimbo. Harto had been good support for Rob recently, he was a nice guy anyway but his decent grasp of English helped in doing valuable translations when it came to dealing with the police or inmates. It appeared Rimbo's document bombshell had fired up several of the inmates and it had obviously become big news within the jail. Harto had taken an interest on meeting Rimbo to explain himself, whilst other inmates hovered around us and often asked for updates. I had never met Harto's brother-in-law Lorenzo before, who was as interested as everyone else in what was going on and had even come purposely for it today.

It was another hot and sweaty day, and I was feeling uneasy, sitting on the hard tile floor in the visiting area made it difficult to get comfortable, and I just couldn't sit right today at all. I glanced around the room to have a scout which of the inmates were around. Rob told me "the wizard was in today", a really old man who must have been in some sort of traditional dress from some far-flung corner of Indonesia, with a white pointy hat and robes, and indeed looked like a mad wizard this his big grey beard dangling down. He really stood out amongst the inmates and visitors, giving our group a good chuckle with how oddly he dressed. Huge doubts were being raised by Rimbo now, which only increased as the hours of visiting passed without any updates about where he was. It seemed likely we'd have another no show. Lorenzo was inquisitive about myself and Rob, and asked if I was here on a work visa. I said no, just a standard visitor visa. Then it dawned on me I was on a visa extension that Rimbo had sorted. If he was indeed a liar, then this visa might not be legitimate – I could now be in the country illegally – and I started to worry whether it was worth doing a visa run for a fresh one as soon as possible. We approached an hour left of visiting with still no sign of him. I agreed with Rob I'd make a bolt for the airport now to fly to Singapore, and then on a new visa, we'd take a fresh stab at things tomorrow. As I got up to leave, I was stopped in my tracks – I saw a man with that unmistakeable monkey-like walk coming through into the visiting area. It was him! He'd actually shown up! He clocked Rob and me and gestured with his hands for us to move away from Harto and Lorenzo and to sit on the opposite side of the visiting area. We moved over and happened to sit right next to where the mad wizard was.

Rimbo had presented his new idea to release Rob, it was a letter of apology, but this time written in Bahasa, which Rob had to sign. His ideas were getting old, we must have tried twenty different things to date with no results. Rob wasn't interested in it and laid straight into the money problem, pointing to the breakdown list and asked where it had all gone. We didn't get satisfactory answers, in fact, he kept laughing it off as if this was all a misunderstanding. I *really* wanted it to be a misunderstanding as the thought of him being some sort of scammer now was heart-breaking, but something definitely wasn't adding up. Rob started raising his voice and was losing his temper with the answers, which sounded more like excuses. This massive intense standoff about money started – when suddenly I felt a bony finger prod me, I turned around to see who it was and had a mild fright: The wizard, with his two eyes looking in opposite directions and one of them clouded over slightly, seven brown teeth and grey pubes all over his heavily wrinkled face, wanting my attention. The musky old man smell on him was particularly strong. I said, "Hello mate" smiled and tried to get back into the grilling over Rimbo's expenses, which was picking up the intensity by the second. The finger poked my ribs again. Restraining myself from just telling him outright to fuck off, I turned around to see the wizard grinning from ear to ear. He asked where I was from.

"Manchester mate", I replied rather stroppily. I returned my focus to Rob and Rimbo, trying to make it clear I didn't want to have a conversation. The bony finger prodded me again.

"What religion are you?" For fuck's sake lad. The wizard clearly had no ability to understand someone's body language, and proceeded to ask me questions like if he could have a photo with me and if I wanted to be friends with some guy he knew in America.

"Yeah, okay, write his email down, and I'll email him", hoping it would get him off my back. The wizard took a pen out to write it down but had no paper. He grabbed my arm and started writing an email address and a phone number on my skin, the pen didn't work properly, so he opted to use it as an etching tool, my skin turning red with numbers and letters where the ink had given up. Then the guy from America's home address and phone number. I could see Harto and Lorenzo laughing from the other side of the room with my situation with Gandalf-on-crack writing an essay on my forearm, whilst Rob was engrossed with his conversation with Rimbo.

Unsatisfied by the answers Rimbo had given, Rob got up and bolted for the chief inmate as he had questions he wanted to ask too. As I said earlier, the chief inmate title is usually awarded to the guy who has been here the longest, but this particular guy was a rather menacing looking meat-head covered in tattoos. He was in for arms dealing and was arguably as influential around here as any of the low-level guards. It was apparent Harto and Lorenzo was eager to join and did so as soon as Rob gestured for them to come over. We sat in a semi-circle with Rimbo facing us the five of us, and with all this moving around, I took an opportunity to sit away from the wizard. Rimbo sat there and took on a torrent of questions from our aggravated group, the conversation often flipping into Bahasa when it got serious. Myself and Rob sat there in silence when it did, picking up only the odd word from it all. This whole thing was more trouble for Rob, and we didn't need it; Rob's already tied up in this corrupt system, now the guy we trusted with our money had apparently been scamming us. I sat there watching this drama unfold as the beads of sweat began to form on Rimbo's forehead, watching his mouth flap and not understanding a single word, which was sometimes the case even if he spoke in English. Occasionally I would glance over to Rob, and we'd just stare at each other for a second or two. It was all so fucked up. I kept thinking about the time and effort we'd put in with this man, entire weeks now. It had been such a waste of time.

Other things started to click into place now; when he said he was doing this for free, so his daughter had someone to rely on when they started school in England – He told me she started in December, but, correct me if I'm wrong, doesn't term time begin in September back home? Were these lies we didn't pick up on? I could hear now amongst the jumble of Bahasa that of Rimbo saying other inmates' names, I guessed trying to implicate them somehow. The three months extended visa, bullshit. He had no connections to break the rules and get me three months. This might not even be a real one-month extension! I also clicked that he never went to the embassy to collect papers, it was always me that went, and I found that peculiar at the time. Probably keeping his face hidden from CCTV. We were so desperate to get Rob out, and we just put trust into this man, yet the absolute wanker had seen our desperation and taken advantage of it. He had given us good information on Henry at the start, and that had been enough to hook us in. A lot of it at the time I put the confusion down to translation errors as his English wasn't brilliant, often giving him the benefit of the doubt, but now looking back I was being naive. This was such a blow to us. Not one, but two lawyers now, first Aadit and now Rimbo ready to take advantage. Maybe even he'd started with good intentions, and Henry had got to him somehow? It felt now like a win that we were putting him through the heat currently and seeing his little head sweat, but in the long term it still wasn't getting Rob out. The whole group got up and said they wanted to continue the conversation with an actual police chief now in his office at the back of the jail. Rimbo got up to leave through the exit, Rob was straight up to intercept him. He grabbed Rimbo and said no, he's coming with them. Rimbo genuinely looked scared at this moment.

Lorenzo and I were told to stay back in the visiting area whilst everyone else went off to see the jail chief. I duly sat back down with Lorenzo. We had a conversation to pass the time, and I got to know him a little bit. He was in his mid-thirties, and very chatty. I was surprised to learn that he was a penniless man who'd had his savings recently stolen by a Chinese businessman. He didn't look it poor – he was definitely well-fed, and he wore pretty trendy clothing complete with a big gold chain. He told me he used to work on the *Costa Concordia*, the Italian cruise liner that hit both rocks and then headlines a few years back as undercover security. He was Indonesian, but was that why he had an Italian sounding name, perhaps an alias? He now worked selling jewels, and as a chef and a translator. If to be believed, then it seemed he had a colourful past. He was easy to chat with anyway, and the time soon passed. After around thirty minutes the group all piled out of the chief's office, and it had agreed Rimbo was to pay all the money back to Rob, or the police would press charges. Fantastic news. It was refreshing to have the law on our side, albeit over dodgy circumstances.

Visiting was over, and I walked outside with Rimbo and Lorenzo. Rimbo offered me a lift home. I was apprehensive about getting into a car with him after that ordeal in the jail, but I wanted him to think me and him were still friends until he'd paid the money back, so I reluctantly accepted the offer. I was tired after another fucked up day though and didn't really want to hear his half-hour ramble about Rob making a mistake inside there, by trusting inmates. His temper soon escalated, his built-up frustration from the interrogation now being release towards me.

"They are criminals, they are not to be trusted! Robert is not going to court because of what I do!" he yelled, smashing his hand down on the dashboard, old cigarette ash flying everywhere. I'd never seen him like this, I sat there in silence, it was awkward sitting next to the man whose plans had begun to unfold. Breaking his rant, my phone rang, and I could see it was an incoming call from the British embassy. It was rare for them to call my mobile directly, so I had to take it, Rimbo being there or not. He was trying to listen in as I took the call. Our caseworker told me the case was going to court as they'd had an update from the police earlier in the day. The timing was unbelievable, he'd literally just said there was no court, and I'd had an official update that contradicted him. He could tell the call had revealed some important information as he started squirming a bit. I shouldn't have been the least bit surprised, everything else he said has been lies. I ended the call, I looked at him, finally losing my cool with him and said,

"Do you know who that was then? The embassy. They said the case is going to court now. I thought you said this wasn't going to happen two minutes ago?!" He frowned, his face shrivelling like a cold ball-sack,

"It is okay, we go one court date and get the case thrown out". More lies. I could not be bothered to ride with him anymore, I told him to pull up, and I'd walk the rest of the way. The charade was up from both sides, he knew I'd lost trust in him, and I knew he was a bullshitter, and there was no point in pretending any more. The car pulled up, and I left in silence, and he drove off without saying a word.

Tired from a long day when I finally got home, I met up with Mel. Things had gone from strength to strength since last week. I asked her out "officially", and she said yes. It really had been a batshit crazy day.

Thursday 8th May 2014

This extended visa had worried me greatly. Although the little stamp in my passport looked legitimate, was it? Sure, he had *some* connections, somehow getting us Henry's files a while back. But he had lied so much. Overstaying visas in Indonesia is serious business. In contrast to Thailand for example, as long as you don't overstay *too* long, you can pay a fee at the end when leaving the country, I think it works out at around £10 for every day you've overstayed. From what friends had told me about the rules here, I could be looking at a fine with the possibility of imprisonment, now eight days into Rimbo's extension and well beyond my original visa. And regardless of whether it was legitimate or not, I wanted to remove any potential leverage Rimbo had over me as he had been the sponsor. I made a bolt for the airport in the morning intending to fly to Singapore on a cheap airline and come back in the evening. As I came up to the immigration clearance desk, the fear began to kick in. I handed my passport over, the immigration guy looked at it. For a minute. Just for me, whilst everyone there was going through the regular routine here at immigration, I was there in my own personal panic. I could be getting into trouble any moment here. He looked at me, stamped my passport, and moved me onwards to the gate. Thank God for that! For an Atheist, I found I was thanking made up stuff quite a bit lately! The embassy called me again for an update whilst waiting in departures, without Rimbo around like when I spoke to them yesterday, I could talk more freely and mentioned the amount of money that had been taken from us. They were stunned and told me it was best to keep away from him from now on. They said they would inform Tarik about Rimbo's shenanigans, as Tarik was still our default lawyer, not that I even knew if he could be trusted now either.

I would have loved to have met Jack in Singapore even for just an hour, but I had only time for a quick cigarette outside the terminal before having to return through security. After a visa run totalling eleven hours, on the return taxi home I weirdly received a call from Lorenzo of all people, telling me he wanted to meet me near my place when I arrived. Obviously, a lot had been going on today without me around – Harto had convinced Rob in jail that Lorenzo had police connections and wanted to help us. As plans had turned to shit with Rimbo, Rob thought it least worth me having a meet-up with him to see what he had to say. I was tired after my long day as I arrived at the local shop just outside my place, which at least offered beer and a place to sit. Lorenzo was already there and stood up to greet me, sat me down and leapt right into things. He told me he was actually an undercover police officer who works to expose corruption and had many connections within the police force. He told me he was a poor man yesterday as I wasn't trusted, and everyone is told that at first before revealing more about himself. I was suspicious, more bullshit from an Indonesian I wondered. As well as prising Rob out of the legal system, he said he wanted to catch Rimbo for his crimes and make him suffer.

"We have the power to shoot him dead if you want", he told me, "We make it looks like he run away, then shoot him in heart".

"What the fuck?" I replied, the bluntness coming from being snapped out my tired state by this offer of extreme violence.

"Relax, my friend, you will be fine. You will leave Indonesia before this happens".

We still had Tarik sort of working for us, although Rob's contacts in the UK had made several attempts to call his office, no one there spoke English. Tarik had glowing reviews from others I met, but his credibility had been stretched as the introductions has been done through Rimbo. Lorenzo was here now telling me to drop contact with Tarik and to go with him for Rob's case. I asked to be excused from our table and went around the corner of the shop to call Rob's smuggled phone, out of earshot from Lorenzo, which must have been pushing midnight by this point. Rob was still awake.

"Rob, who is this guy I've met today? I mean, like, who is he *really*? He's telling me all sorts of mad shit about shooting Rimbo in the heart. What do we do? Who do we go with now? Lorenzo or Tarik?"

"I don't know. I think we should go with Lorenzo, he's Harto's friend, and I trust him".

"I appreciate that, but really it's fucked up we've met him through an inmate in jail. What if it's more wasted time or another scam?"

"What other options do we have? I want to go with him. I don't trust anyone who knows Rimbo". It was a tense phone call, we had to make a decision which could affect the case massively. Rob really wanted us to make the switch. I returned back to Lorenzo, who was sat playing with his phone, not looking phased by any of this situation.

"If we go with you", I said, "What are your plans, what are your next steps?"

"First", he said, "We stop Robert's case getting picked up by the prosecution office, but first we need money". Here we go, I thought to myself.

"We don't have money, it's all gone to Rimbo."

"We will work something out, don't worry. You will get your money back from Rimbo too! I will protect you from him now." Bringing in Rimbo was high on his agenda. He told me he'd looked into Rimbo and he was a scam artist. We were the eighth group of people he had scammed in recent months. "He's not even a one-star military man, he had his titles stripped for corruption. I looked into him". He continued with saying the police were closing in on Rimbo, the jail chiefs were now pissed off too, and we could give testimony to help send this guy down. It would be a huge career boost for Lorenzo to bring him in. Things were getting deeper and weirder, and we still weren't making any progress with Rob's case.

I gave him two hours of my time sat outside the shop talking, which I was disappointed about – after my visa run, I was just looking forward to watching the latest episode of *Game of Thrones* in bed with no pants on, eating something nice like a huge bag of paprika crisps. I was weighed down with just being here talking to this man, another dodgy person in this country miles away from home. He said I looked stressed and insisted he gave me a massage. My night ended with him giving me a back massage that I didn't want, in the early hours of the morning, in front of twenty bewildered looking people who were also sat watching us outside the shop. What am I doing with my life?

Friday 9th May 2014

After having a full day to talk about our plan of attack, myself, Rob and everyone back in the UK decided getting our money back was a priority and Lorenzo was the guy to do it. We had the jail's backing now, and if Lorenzo was to be believed, we had the police as well. The jail had been really pushing Rob to file a report, and they had been trying to contact him themselves. That night, we translated this exact message into Indonesian through Mel and sent it to Rimbo through my phone:

"Rimbo, I have been informed to tell you on behalf of the jail and Robert: They are going to make a formal police report on the outstanding money if it is not repaid, in full, by 7 PM tomorrow. As an alternative, they will accept a visit from you on Monday during visiting hours to explain yourself and for them to explain in detail what you owe. I have also been informed by both the embassy and police not to meet you in person without a police presence".

He lost his mind over this message, threatening to effectively destroy Rob and have me deported as I was on his visa (so doing that visa run for a fresh one was worth it!). "I will press new charges for slander!" "I have taken no money from you!" His contradictions started again, calling himself a "professional" in one text, then threatening to have Rob's sentence increased on another. "I will use my connections to make your life difficult", "I will have Mel arrested", one text after another, receiving at least fifty that night. Unknown numbers and voices began calling me, screaming down the phone in Indonesian. Rob started getting threatening calls on his mobile in jail. It rattled us both. I expected some retaliation but nothing like this. I was scared. There's this corrupt ex-military guy here, with supposed connections in a corrupt country making clear and scary threats. Lorenzo wasn't picking up his phone. He said I had his protection yesterday, but really, I didn't trust him either. As a joint decision, myself, Rob, and everyone at home was scared into backing down. We sent a second message saying we will back down and he could keep the money he owed us, just leave us alone from now on. He replied saying he wanted his name cleared as his reputation was destroyed, and would go to the embassy on Monday morning at 10 AM to clarify everything. I barely touched my dinner that night and slept for about two hours. It was a rough night for me, even with the comfort of Mel by my side. I can't imagine what it was like for Rob.

Sunday 11th May 2014

I met up with Lorenzo in the afternoon. I was still in fear from last night, and despite my concerns about who this Lorenzo guy really was, I needed to reach out to someone to try and find genuine protection. He took me to a mall on his motorbike for a coffee and talked over things. I showed him Rimbo's texts and gave him the numbers I was called on.

"Don't worry man, we're the good police. We still bend the rules, but we are the good guys, fight corruption. Relax." Which sounded great until the next sentence when he said, "So we bust into this Rimbo's apartment and plant drugs there. Then we go around the next day, make a bust, and pretend he tried to escape and shoot him in the heart". What the fuck is it with this guy shooting people in the heart? And as if I didn't need to be any more frightened, he said: "Don't tell anyone about this plan or they will come for you".

"Look mate, I don't want to be part of this. I just want to get my friend out of jail. That's all I care about".

"Just show me where Rimbo lives, that is all you need to do". He almost seemed to enjoy the worried state I was in.

"Seriously, don't involve me in any murder". I put my head in my hands and switched off to the rest of what Lorenzo was saying. Only four days ago he's telling me he's this poor guy, now he's this well-connected Mafia-style policeman who plants drugs and shoots people in the heart. He is as much of a maniac as Rimbo had been last night. I shouldn't have with met him, I did not need this today.
On our way out the mall, he outright told me he killed someone doing his job as a policeman.

"I shot him, escaping criminal, he died, and now I pay for his children every day. I will not pay for Rimbo's children, though. They will have to suffer for his death".

"I said already mate, don't involve me in murder. *Do not* murder him!"

"We will see mate. See those girls there? They're looking at us because you're a bule!" his mind could go from murder to girls in a second. I got the feeling he loved having a foreigner with him, walking the long way around to places for maximum exposure, or insisting we made plans for during our free time. "Want to grab a movie later?" he asked. Not at all mate, I thought to myself, I've not even watched that fucking *Game of Thrones* from the other night yet.

Monday 12th May 2014

Money completely gone, I had to take a loan out from my parents to keep me out here. I was under the impression it was worth staying out here as Rob's full sixty days were nearly over. There was a small hope that if he stayed over the sixty days, the embassy would step in because the police would be breaking the law on how long they were supposed to keep him at the jail for. Or maybe the case would get dropped and he would be free. It was wishful thinking, and ultimately a kick in the dick once we found out the prosecution office had picked up the case. It meant the case was going to court and Rob was looking at serious time. I came in for visiting as usual, and Rob presented a pink slip which stated he was being transferred.

"I'm getting moved tomorrow, mate". It was a disaster. Lorenzo came to visiting and told us to relax, and he'd try his best to sort something out, but to us, it just meant the whole situation was stepping up another gear.

Rob's move was to the Cipinang penitentiary, possibly one of the worst prisons in the whole country, in one of the most corrupt countries in the world.

Rimbo didn't show at the embassy, and his contact numbers stopped working.

Tuesday 13th May 2014

Lorenzo was now in charge, the man we'd known for less than a week. I didn't like this at all, but ultimately it was Rob's call. He trusted Harto and by extension his friend Lorenzo, and to be fair they'd only appeared to have helped us so far. Lorenzo's plan was simply to make sure the right officials had been paid to stop the imminent transfer to the penitentiary. There was a slight problem in this plan though – primarily for me – as the link between England and Indonesia, I was going to be responsible for handing over cash that was going to be used for bribes. Not only that, Lorenzo wanted me to meet the officials we would be bribing "as it would help the case". Blindly at the start in my eagerness to help, I agreed to everything, but when I actually had five minutes to sit down and think about what I was doing, alarm bells rang. Okay, in case you've not realised already, bribes within the law here are common, and I would have thought that almost all cases have some money passed around at some level.

The problem was, we were on the wrong end of the results of the bribe – Rob's 'victim' had beat us to it and paid for him to do time in jail. We faced an uphill battle here. And we didn't have the sort of connections Henry had. It appeared people were willing to take our money, but we had more people to pay off to reach the top level, not having direct access ourselves. Not to mention the other issue: I am the foreigner here, and with me standing nearly two metres, and white, I stood out and was very noticeable. A big lanky white guy walking into a foreign prosecution office with a wedge of brown envelopes, ready to pay bribes to people who are supposed enforce the laws of a country, it's just absolutely stupid, isn't it? I had stayed as support for Rob to support him through the jail time, if I could help get him out too, then great. Now the shift of responsibility had gone to involving me in illegal activities, which was further than I was prepared to go. After discussing the situation over a tense *Skype* call with my mum who pleaded with me just to get out of the country, I decided I wasn't going to be involved with any meeting of officials or bribe work but would stay out here a little longer to continue to offer support. Lorenzo said it wasn't ideal, but he could still sort something out.

It was a big day, we had a few hours to try and get the money to the right people to stop his transfer to this terrifying new penitentiary from happening. I was worried about losing my friend deeper within the system, and he needed to fight to keep him where he was. I woke up at 5 AM, showered up, prepared Rob's food and made my way down to the jail. Lorenzo wanted me here first thing in the morning with a lot of money withdrawn from an ATM. I was to pass the bribe money in an envelope to him, which I still wasn't happy about doing – I was already bending the terms I had set for staying out here – but it was a one-off, plus there was no other option to get this money to him on such short notice. I was done with the dodgy dealings after this. Stupidly the night before, I had cooked me and Mel some ridiculously hot chilli beef, which wasn't sitting well this morning. By the time I arrived at the jail, I wasn't walking right as I needed the toilet so badly. Walking through the grounds of the police station, I had to take several minutes to sit down just for the hot slurry inside me to settle. It wasn't going away, I waddled around, desperately looking for a toilet. There was another problem: Most of the complex was closed with it being so early in the morning. After nearly twenty minutes of complete agony, I found some cardboard on the floor I could wipe with, and then sat around the back of a quiet building and forced out runny brown agony in a squatting position, using only the cover of a few boxes. The fear of being caught having an outdoor shit on the police complex was utterly overwhelmed by the relief. Luckily I'd had previous experience squatting for a shit at least.

I got outside the jail after cleaning up as best I could and was met by Lorenzo and his team of men. This included our new Lawyer, a skinny middle-aged chain-smoker called Ipin, our driver for the day (who repeatedly said he wanted to kill Rimbo for me – thanks mate) and some teenager who just sat around playing on his phone that I never figured out the purpose of. They greeted me and shook my hand. None of the new guys really spoke conversational English, so most of the time I sat in silence in the waiting area outside of the jail. Lorenzo seemed rather chipper, sat back with his sunglasses on. I had started to notice his favourite word was "Relax", possibly picking up on my constant anxious state, and he said it to me many times. Relaxing, of course, being the last thing on my mind, I'll relax when I'm back in Koh Phangan with ten pints of *Chang* in my stomach. I could see the transport van was already waiting to collect Rob, a stone's throw from where we were sat, and I was told we had to stop get the right people paid off before the cut-off point at 9 AM. Some of the other people responsible for the transfer had been seen to the night before and agreed to keep Rob here pending money, so it was just this last guy, a big status police man, that needed to get on board. He arrived, me and the new legal team entered the jail after him.

It was strange being at the jail at this time of the day, just after dawn and therefore way outside of visiting hours. It was a pretty calm and quiet environment, and certainly a little cooler than the mid-afternoon's heat subjected us to. There were not many people stirring, maybe a guard on duty and an inmate sweeping up. Rob came from the cells, plus a few other of Rob's friends. We sat in the main corridor and discussed Rob's transfer. It was a tense half-hour. Finally, we had a breakthrough, we were told that Rob could stay at the jail, but we would need a document from the British embassy saying that they wouldn't mind the rules being bent. As I stated earlier, the maximum time someone can be held in jail is sixty days whilst they decide what's happening to the case. If you're kept there past day sixty without moving you to a prosecution jail or releasing you, they are breaking Indonesian law, and the embassy could then intervene. The authorities were concerned they would be liable, so needed assurance from the embassy that they wouldn't do anything if Rob stayed. It seemed fair enough, and then it was all eyes on me to sort it with the direct line to the embassy I had, having been given half an hour to get it sorted. I frantically tried to explain the situation and then passed the phone on to Lorenzo who then reiterated what I said. Time passed, and Rob and I spoke in the yard about what our plans would be if he did end up getting moved. He had memorised my phone number, as well as hid cash around his person. Craftily, he had rolled up the bottom of his shorts with as much money in as he could carry. Other inmates started to come up to Rob and began to hug him, saying things in their broken English like "I will miss you".

Over my time there, I had heard stories of embassies of other nationalities doing all sorts to help their people locked up in Indonesia, I'd even heard tales of bribes being paid in some cases. The straight edge British embassy wasn't budging for us though and needed time to review any letter they would have to send. We had run out of time. Rob was led out of jail with a single guard, the authorities said it was now an issue for the prosecution and it was time for us to move on.

"This is it mate, I'm getting moved". I followed him to the booking room around the corner of the jail ready for transfer. In there was an assortment of what I assumed were plainclothes officers sat outside the room. Lorenzo began talking in Bahasa to the guys there, trying his best to halt the process. He'd said earlier to me that he had plenty of tricks to try, but most of them now appeared to just be begging people to stop the transfer. The police handed me Rob's suitcase, which hadn't been seen since the day we got back from Bali. Most of his stuff was there, aside from his suit, which one of the officers must have stolen.

"We must leave now", said Lorenzo who ran out of the door, so I grabbed Rob's suitcase and sprinted across the car park to follow Lorenzo and our team. It must have been pushing 10 AM by this point, and I'd smoked nearly a full pack of cigarettes with stress.

The next stop for Rob was the prosecution office. Whilst prisoners are transferred between the jail and the penitentiary, their papers are checked over at a stop to make sure everything with the transfer is in order. Lorenzo said we should head there, as it was another chance to get the transfer blocked. The problem we had though, it was likely we needed a substantial amount of money, more than what we would have been required to pay at the jail. I said that there was at least a grand sat in a *Western Union* transfer from a couple of weeks back sent from everyone in the UK – it was due for Rimbo's fourth payment, but it had been sat there untouched since the little monkey man had been rumbled. I mentioned it to Lorenzo and said should I go and get it if it's there.

"No man, relax, now we have breakfast". So we moved on from jail to have breakfast. I didn't want a bloody breakfast. I wanted to stop my mate from getting transferred. If I wasn't so tired, I'd have been furious. I piled into a car with four of these dodgy Indonesians, all near enough strangers and off we went for breakfast. There were brief flashbacks from being in that car with a load of strangers in India last year, I looked at my surroundings, here I am on the other side of the world, sat in this car with four men, driving off to god knows where. I thought to myself, seriously, what the hell has happened to my trip? I had been pretty clear I didn't want to get involved with the bribing, yet here I was with a group of men looking for Indonesian officials to give money to. If I wasn't so desperate to get Rob out, I'd have left right then.

We had breakfast at a street food place about a five-minute drive from the station, and we'd sat there alongside the road for twenty minutes or so. As the commuter traffic whizzed past, the young boy who was part of Lorenzo's entourage tried to muster up some conversation with his limited English, but I wasn't in the mood for it.

"From you, where?"

"I already said to your mate before if you heard, Manchester".

"Oh, wow... *City* or *United*?"

"Wigan mate. Dead good team". Lorenzo's phone rang, and without warning, everyone got up, leaving half of the food, and we piled into the car again. After some time suffering the horrendous traffic, we came to a rather fancy looking Dutch colonial building, which stood in rather stark contrast to the usual style of crumbling buildings in parts of Jakarta. After passing through layers of security, we arrived and met the chief prosecutor for Rob's case in an upstairs office.

Expecting another man, I was surprised to see a burly woman in a headscarf, the first woman I'd seen involved in the law here. She spoke softly although it wasn't in English. After Lorenzo had told her Rob's story, and Rimbo's scam, she had sympathy and said she could move Rob back to the jail. We had all the money that we never handed to anyone at the jail, but it still wasn't enough to match what she wanted. Lorenzo began to get agitated and snappy with her. For a man who told me to relax fifty times a day, it didn't take much for him to get riled up. He told me to get the money at *Western Union*, which I mentioned earlier.

"You must go now, man, LEAVE!!" I didn't have much time to get the cash together, less than an hour perhaps, which annoyed me because I could have gone to a *Western Union* when they had breakfast as I suggested, but, whatever. These people don't listen to me. For *Western Union* transfers, I needed to collect my passport, so I would have to get to my place first, then find a *Western Union* whose cap on withdrawal was higher than what we needed, then back to a prosecution office. It was going to be very tight on time. I ran outside to look for a taxi, whilst unbeknown to me, Rob was sat outside in a parked police van waiting to be moved into the prosecution office. I didn't see him, but he saw me run past frantically. One of the guards in the van let him use a phone to text me, I was hanging off the back of a motorcycle as I got the text. I let him know what was going on and was trying my best to get more money together.

Lorenzo sent a stream of texts. "HURRY MAN WHERE ARE YOU". On top of that, I was getting messages from people back home, wanting an update. Considering it was 5 AM back in England, a lot of people were up at this time, desperate for the transfer to stop. They'd read about the conditions of the penitentiary, and it had worried a lot of people – what little literature was available in English online did not make comfortable reading. It was massively overcrowded, hosted murderers, disease and drugs were rampant. It was filthy and dangerous.

The queue was huge at *Western Union*. It was a bit after midday by the time I got back to Lorenzo, who was waiting for me on the steps outside of the offices, and was clearly unhappy when he realised the extra cash I had brought still wasn't enough. I didn't feel it was fair that he put all that on me though, I mean he was the one that hadn't planned things very well. Even if he had told us all last night to make sure we had some money on standby, then even that would have been better prepared. The prosecution woman was now unhappy we were short and ordered Rob onto his next step of the transfer. We all jumped into the car and moved onwards. I sat in the car as it started to rain, absolutely gutted we weren't making progress and was getting frustrated with not knowing what was entirely going on. Already at it for over seven hours, we still had one last shot, so I was told. Rob was on his way to the courtrooms before his final transfer. Just to really grind in pain today, the traffic was horrendous, it seemed worse than usual for the city. I was getting frustrated wanting to take action on something, but was just stuck in a people carrier with nothing to do. We got to the courtrooms, an even fancier building than the prosecution office, with marbled floors and walls, carp ponds and little tropical trees for decoration. Reality was a little surreal by this point, I was feeling exhausted, and needed a shit again, and it was exacerbated as the legal team and I ran through the halls of courthouse looking for Rob, flying past handcuffed inmates, police and lawyers. We found out he had been transferred yet again, and finally to the penitentiary. We were too late.

We drove for about an hour, crawling in the traffic and pulled up in a car park somewhere. The lawyer was on the phone hopelessly trying to figure out if we could still get Rob out of Cipinang somehow. I had heard bits about the place talking to the inmates here, they spoke about it with a touch of fear in their voices. Often, the worst inmates are sent here, heavily populated with the jail's A-wing types, possibly making Taser Guy look soft in comparison. Food and accommodation were a lot more expensive than the jail, but the cells were still overcrowded and filthy. Worse yet, Lorenzo told me he had no connections or authority there. It was a disaster, all of today had been for nothing. The guys talked in Bahasa for another few minutes, I was only picking up the occasional word, and by this point, it was getting on for 4 PM.
Lorenzo turned to me,
"Okay, now we visit Rob in Cipinang to talk to the prison chiefs. Maybe they can transfer him back". I told them no chance, there was no way I was going to sit another couple of hours in traffic, just to sit in another room and not understand a word, more people seeing my face throughout some attempted bribing process I didn't understand, then get carted around to fuck knows where else afterwards with people I don't know. I felt sick, was tired and just wanted to go home. They called me a taxi, and I left. I felt numb on the drive home—a new worst day of the ordeal.

I spent some time with Mel that night, and it helped me unwind a bit. Around 8 PM, I got a call from a new number I had never seen before. I was reluctant to answer it at first in case Rimbo was raging again. Fortunately, I did, and it was Rob, albeit with an awful signal.

"Rob?! Mate! Are you okay?! It's Cipinang you've gone to, right?"

"Mate, this place is so bad, they've already taken some of my hair off… the conditions are terrible… terrified… need you to come tomorrow, please bring money". Fuck me, did it ever sound bad. I sat back down on my bed, still processing the call and told Mel what I had just heard. Poor lad, I felt so bad for him. I called Lorenzo and said I needed to go there tomorrow. My first time to a penitentiary was coming, I didn't know what to expect, and it scared me.

Wednesday 14 May 2014

I met Lorenzo at 7 AM outside my kosan, leaving Mel still asleep there. Ready for Rob, I bought a big bag of food, collected his leftover money he'd passed me at the jail yesterday, and we headed down on Lorenzo's motorbike to Cipinang. The journey was considerably further, perhaps forty minutes as opposed to the five minutes it took to the jail, but we flew through the congested mid-morning traffic, weaving in and out of the commuters. Lorenzo certainly liked to crank some speeds up, possibly showing off. Arriving outside Cipinang, I could instantly tell it was some sort of high-security building. 10ft high chain link fencing with looped barbed wire across the top surrounded the concrete perimeters, and the interior featured intimidating grey concrete watchtowers (I was unable to tell if they were manned or not, but I could just imagine a man with a rifle up there ready to pop someone's head who was attempting am escape). The whole place had a bad vibe, but the edge was taken off slightly, being bustling with locals sat on mats on the floor selling fruit and vegetables, or tat like fake watches. A staple visual of Asia – loose chickens or other animals – were walking around too. The whole complex was large in size, we must have driven around the perimeters for what felt like a full five minutes before we found the right entrance. Lorenzo told me he had been here for cases he'd worked on in the past.

"Relax man, I know what I'm doing" picking up my terror as we got off his bike – I don't think he did know what he was doing as he had forgotten the required papers for our entry. We needed visiting papers or something. Apparently, we couldn't just wander up like anyone could in jail. Not that it was a huge problem, we paid the guards off, and they let us in.

We weaved through the people and then passed a large steel door in an archway, taking us inside a small claustrophobic room, stained yellow from cigarette smoke. The entry was similar to what we'd done at the jail for weeks. Go to the counter, hand over ID and phones and get a visitor card to retrieve them. The atmosphere was more intimidating than the jail though, for a start there were a lot more guards, all of them, of course, new people to us, and the multiple barred doors seemed a little bit more menacing. My first-day fears of the jail had come flooding back. I had contemplated smuggling a new phone for Rob but wisely decided to assess the place on this first visit – another thing different was they gave me a thorough pat-down and examined everything I brought in, whereas in the jail, over time becoming more friendly with the guards there, they didn't even check my bags of food some days. There were even more steel-bar doors to pass through, clunking behind us as they shut, and finally, we entered into the visiting area. I won't lie, I was taken aback, it was visually a little better than the jail. The jail offered only floor seating with mats over it. Here we had proper wooden benches that you might find in the park. Fair enough they'd made an effort with the seating, but what I did not expect to see though was a rock band setting up to play some tunes around the corner in the small outdoor courtyard. A fucking band!

Lorenzo was as lost as me, if he'd been here before then he'd forgotten it all. We wandered into the large seating area, looking around for what to do next. Families were crammed on benches, women holding their sons or husbands, some crying. The inmates looked like they were all having a rough time here, their faces looking weathered from the harsh prison conditions. Some looked ill from drugs, others sat on the floor coughing. Freighting inmates barged passed, muscle heads with fascial scars, nothing like anyone I'd seen at the jail. It smelled terrible from everyone sweating so badly, it was incredibly humid, and the windows didn't allow much breeze through. It was no news that I was the only foreigner around here once again, absolutely lost in this completely alien setting. I'd never been to a prison in my life, never mind in a developing country's.

A young inmate wearing one of the bright orange prison-issued shirts which hung off his skinny frame came over to us and started to talk to Lorenzo. I guessed he was maybe in his late teens, but he looked like he was into heavy drug use with his hardened face, it was hard to gauge accurately. He said if we wanted to see our inmate, we would have to pay him, and he would go and fetch him from the bowels of the prison. That's how this is done here? Relying on drugged up inmates to run visiting? I honestly don't know how they get things done out here, the lack of structure and rules got me frustrated. Remember when I thought the lack of them was brilliant when I first came back here after Australia? Well, look where it got me and Rob now.

We paid the boy, and he left to fetch Rob. We were sat for twenty minutes before he came up looking an absolute state, the worst I had seen him through this ordeal by miles. He was wearing clothes that weren't his, and didn't fit properly, and was clearly in a bad state mentally. Realising we didn't have any luck stopping the transfer yesterday, he braced himself for the move. Those high-rise barbed wire walls outside were intimidating enough as a visitor, I can't imagine what was going through his head seeing this as he arrived, being transferred by a high-security police van as a prisoner. He was stripped down and searched rigorously but fortunately not having the hidden money found. As part of a small group of other inmates being booked in, the guards forced them to lie down naked on the floor in a press-up position. A guard walked in with a bamboo stick and whilst whacking it around on the walls, started screaming at them in the native tongue – an inmate translated to Rob that the message was basically "Don't mess around during your time here" no phones, no drugs, no dicking about. They were then told to get up and then moved into the general population area. As Rob entered through the door he could see hundreds of inmates already inside. Upon him stepping through into the main cell block, the other inmates started pulling on his clothes, some were getting pushy, and others were begging for money. Terrified, he could hardly move from the surrounding crowd, when an inmate from behind pushed him and led him through to the other side of the room to get him away from it all. The floor of the cellblock was only small but had several levels with cells above it, crammed with inmates with no access to toilets or beds, whilst it was dim through lack of natural light. Rob referred to multiple times as "The snake pit" as he explained it to Lorenzo and me. There was a handful of taps, but water only came out from them three times a day for ten minutes – when the water was on was the only way to tell what time of day it was. It was dirty, but people would push to use it for drinking or cleaning, but often leaving those without who couldn't get to it in time. Worse still was finding out that there was a lot of diseases here, but tuberculosis was rampant. I could hear coughing all the time.

There were stories of people getting stabbed with needles with HIV contaminated blood in it with the mentality of "If I have it, why shouldn't you?". There were murderers, sex offenders, you name it, all mixed into the same area, which at least the jail he had come from offered separation from these creatures at night. This was as about as close to hell on Earth as you could get. I sat there dumbfounded at what I was hearing from Rob whilst Lorenzo looked on, relaxed as ever. It annoyed both me and Rob about his sometimes lack of appreciation for what was going on, having a complete disconnect from the emotions of those around him. He kept telling Rob to relax and not to worry, but even with the supposed best intentions of saying it, it was a stupid thing to say.

Having not seen 'The snake pit' for myself, a band playing was perhaps the most unusual thing about this place for me. I usually like live music, but this wasn't the place for it, and they were too loud, it was hard to hear each other sometimes. The sweaty heat and odour of the inmates were pretty bad, and even with the comfort of the benches, it was uncomfortable just sitting there in the intense body odour soup. I missed how chilled the jail was in comparison. We talked about the plans with Lorenzo. He needed money to get Rob moved back to the jail and to speed the court process up to get him out of the country. The small drugged up boy who had fetched Rob earlier had lingered around as we spoke, listening to our conversation. He told us he also worked in the medical bay, and for a large fee could get Rob moved out of the snake pit and onto a hospital bed. Rob was desperate to get out of the snake pit despite the costs proposed by The Boy, so Lorenzo took The Boy's bank details and said he would transfer the money to him once he knew Rob had been moved.

We left, not before handing a load of money to Rob and I genuinely wished him luck getting through another night. I was pretty confident the BCG vaccinations we had in school covered us for tuberculosis at least but made a mental note to check and said I would let him know when I found out. I was sorry to leave him but thankful to get out.

Thursday 15th May 2014

No visiting in Cipinang today. Knowing I couldn't do anything to help Rob today, and with things progressing well between Mel and me, we made plans for me to meet her parents for the first time. I dressed up in a shirt and tie, trying to make a good impression, but it felt more like I was going to a job interview, looking smart but with those underlying nerves. Her parents lived in South Jakarta. I arrived at a rather affluent residential area and saw Mel and her dad stood at the door waiting for me. He shook my hand and said,

"Welcome, please sit. Mel, please give us some minutes". It became like a real job interview, he asked how long had I been in Indonesia for, what I was doing for work, what my parents did for work. Not wanting to have her parents put off from me straight away by telling them the reason I'm currently in the country, I decided it best to leave out anything to do with Rob. Mel had previously said her father only likes to use air-con when absolutely necessary. If today didn't warrant the use of it then it was probably never used – The home was a sweatbox, and I was already a little too hot with my shirt and tie on. He thanked me for my time and wandered off into another room, leaving me there for a moment. I took the opportunity to dry the sweat off my forehead with my sleeve. Mel came out shortly afterwards, smiling. I passed the interview! I took the tie off and spent the day chilling out having fun at her place with the family, and finally having that "relax" which Lorenzo would have been so proud to witness. Talking of him, I saw my phone ringing, he had been hinting at meeting up for a coffee every day since I'd met him, but I had better things to do with my free time so just left it to keep ringing. This is my day off from all the bollocks, mate.

The celebrity figure of UGB whom I mentioned earlier, Indonesia's famous magician guy, who was accused of fraud, came upon the television after we had finished a family dinner some hours later. There was a report or something on the news about his case, it was all in Bahasa, but I recognised his sad face as soon as I saw it.

"This is a famous case in Indonesia" began one of Mel's family members, completely unprompted and obviously unaware that not only had both Mel and me met him in real life, but UGB had expressed his attraction to her too. I couldn't escape the weirdness, even just having dinner at my girlfriend's house.

Friday 16th May 2014

There were a fewer days in the week allocated to visiting in Cipinang compared to the jail, and today was another, so it seemed surprising that Lorenzo had organised a whole meet up for the new lawyer Ipin, a representative from the British embassy, as well as him and myself. I arrived with him early morning only to wait around the prison for an hour. Within the grounds of the penitentiary was a small seating area that sold coffee– upon arriving at it I realised he'd won one..! He'd got that coffee with me I'd been avoiding! He'd organised to come earlier so we'd spend time outside of Rob's case just so we could sit there and talk. I was fuming with him, annoyed that I could have had another hour in bed. I was stressed and appreciated the free time I had to spend to myself. The last thing I wanted to do was sit in the pollution and heat, at some dusty little shack in the grounds of a scary prison with this man that I wasn't settled near. It annoyed me more I was drinking bad coffee, freeze-dried shite which contained already blended excessive sugar in the packets it came with. If I'd at least had decent coffee, I might have been at least able to tolerate him talking about the extremes of where the best place to buy minerals in Sumatra was, to the worst place on a body to shoot someone. For the record, it's the lower abdomen, it makes the most mess and doesn't always guarantee a kill. Fucking maniac.

Despite Lorenzo's pre-arrangements yesterday, the prison seemingly got cold feet about letting me, him and Ipin in on a non-visiting day and we were nearly denied entry, initially at least, although this was sorted by passing around some of those trusty brown envelopes. Looking back, I think it was usually the way with some of the crooked people in authority here, agree on something illegal in principal, then fabricate an issue which can only be remedied by more money than initially agreed. They ushered the three of us through the main doors that we went through for visiting but bypassed typical security protocol, so I walked in with my phone, money and a wrap of cocaine. Joking! I could have done though, the guys here only followed the rules when it suited them, I realised it would have been a little more effort to get stuff smuggled into here but absolutely achievable.

The guards led us through the multiple iron bar gates, then to an office upstairs, and instructed us to sit. We waited for five minutes or so before Rob was escorted in by a guard – he had just woken up and looked positively startled to see us, as we had no way to contact him about the plans today. He looked miles better for his time in the medical bay, he told us he slept for the entirety of yesterday and most of today. I was impressed to see the embassy representatives followed shortly after him, and we sat down in a large group to talk things through. Fair play to Lorenzo, he had concrete plans for everyone to follow, and it finally felt like something would get done today. Rob had to write a letter saying the conditions were brutal and asked for a transfer back to the jail, also followed by a letter from the embassy asking for the transfer to take place too, which would be delivered to the prosecution office. Lorenzo had more plans, which of course involved bribing officials, but thought it was best to not involve the embassy nor tell them about it. The embassy said their part, mainly directed at Lorenzo to leave the Rimbo thing altogether now; he'd won, let him keep the money, despite Lorenzo's constant persistence during the meeting to hunt him down. There were fears Rimbo might have genuine connections that could cause trouble if we pursued him, plus he knew a lot about Rob's case, which could cause more problems than it was worth. One of the embassy representatives told me that in the years the embassy has worked with cases like Rob's they said they'd never seen anyone stick by their friend in terms of what I'd done, and the length of time I'd done with him. Apparently for foreign prisoners, especially in countries like these, the lack of contact from the outside world gets to them. I just thought it was lucky I was able to stick by him for such a long period of time, plus it's not like I could leave him and carry on travelling, is it?

After everyone was up to speed and a decent plan formed for the way forward, the embassy representatives left to write up their letter, whilst me and Lorenzo went to a *Western Union* to receive the new batch of money that our support network of friends and family had sent over. In the queue, he told me Rimbo was getting a bullet either way, no matter what me and the embassy said. I let out a loud disapproving sigh and didn't reply. We headed onwards to the embassy, collected the letter, armed with that and the money, went to meet what I thought was the chief prosecution judge for Rob's case to deliver it all. It wasn't. The guy we met was actually one of the top judges in the whole of the Jakarta metropolitan area who had significant influence over the prosecution offices, evidently one of Lorenzo's better contacts. He was a large fat man who always had sweat beads on his forehead, all those years of receiving expensive bribes meaning it looked like he was eating very well. It was insane that a guy of such high importance was now involved with the case. He's seen my face now. Brilliant. I wish I'd been told earlier that I was meeting this guy, I might have even been, but trying to understand the important stuff through Lorenzo's waffling was tiring. I'm *sure* the fucker said we were just going to the prosecution office today, not to see this massive fella.

We sat down at a mall in a part of the city I'd never been to before, joined with our new judge mate and some of his friends, and the lawyer Ipin joined shortly afterwards. Over coffee, the whole group conversation took place in Bahasa whilst I sat there and listened. Not speaking the language was beginning to get on my tits a little now, especially when important things like this were being discussed. Then we all got up, and I was told we were moving to another destination. I was feeling like there was no point to having me around here and was tempted to leave them to it. The new destination was another type of office that this judge worked at or some sort of building where judges congregated at least. It felt like it was on the outskirts of Jakarta anyway as it took some time to get to. I didn't realise this was the plan until arriving here: Bribing officials involved with the case, right now, today, with me in tow. Kept out of the loop as usual by Lorenzo, finding out the plan moments before arriving somewhere. I complained a lot when I knew something was going on with bribes, usually "Why do I need to be here for this?", but Lorenzo liked to keep me around and would insist my presence was vital. Sweat Bead and his entourage were in one car, our lawyer with a couple of unknowns in another, then me on the back of Lorenzo's motorbike. We arrived at a large lone building in a car park and waited around the end of the building whilst Sweat Bead went inside with the money we'd sent. I was annoyed with Lorenzo for bringing me here. Was I here as some sort of scapegoat in case they were busted? I'd have left there and then had there been any taxis around. After this was over, I was done with this shit, and I wasn't going to meet up with Lorenzo ever again. It was just wasting my time being here, and surely only putting myself at risk.

We sat around idly for half an hour behind the building, making small talk with a group of people I'd only just met. I couldn't be bothered with it, and Lorenzo annoyed me even more, acting as a small talk enabler for the others with his translation skills. Seven people now sat around with us. Who were all these people? What do they all do for a living? Do they all live off bribes and corruption? Why are they interested in Rob's case so much? Snapping us out the small talk, a guy came around the corner and started shouting in Bahasa, everyone started panicking, got up and began to run. I had no idea what was going on but ran with the others. I could see the guys piling into their cars whilst I mounted Lorenzo's bike with him, and we sped off even before I had a chance to process what was happening. We weaved in and out of the traffic, running red lights in the process whilst I struggled with my helmet. I was terrified.

"Lorenzo, what the fuck's going on?" I shouted,

"The newspaper are chasing us, my friend!"

"What!?" just processing what I had heard, barely hearing him through our helmets,

"Don't worry," he said as we tore through another red light, "they won't be able to catch me. Relax!"

For a country so rife with corruption, a curious thing about the Indonesian press is that despite the risks for the journalists, it sometimes tries to expose the corruption that goes on, especially so in Jakarta. With this in mind, I couldn't quite work out why a big group of us had gone to this prosecution office. Sure, we hid around the back of the building out of the way slightly, but knowing the press is so active around these parts, and with someone as high profile as Sweat Bead walking around with brown envelopes, surely they knew this was a bad idea? Something didn't sit right, and I couldn't quite believe the press would bother chasing us, but to my horror, as I turned around, I could see two guys on a moped following, the guy on the back with a camera, presumably snapping away. This was terrible news for me, what a scoop for them though catching a foreigner at it though, I could see the headline now, "Brits Abroad Bribing!" I really hoped they hadn't snapped any sneaky photos of me in the car park earlier. Typical that I'm dead against corruption and all up for exposing it, but the one time I want to use it to help someone, it turns around on me. Thankfully, Lorenzo had a decent motorbike, and they were only on a farty little moped, so we tore it through the streets of Jakarta and lost them in no time. I've not skydived before, but I imagine the adrenaline kick of being chased in a foreign country on a motorbike can't be far off.

We'd taken a big detour but eventually arrived back at the mall we are started this horrendous excursion from. Lorenzo parked his bike up, and we scurried through the multi-storey car park and into the mall itself. I could see others from the group arrive and making a break for the mall's quieter rear entrance. We took escalators to the bottom floor and entered karaoke booths. All of the rooms were soundproof, I realised it was a smart way to hide away just in case any of the pesky press had found us and were outside trying to listen. Shortly after Sweat Bead came in, waddling in through the door. As he updated the group in Bahasa, it didn't matter I couldn't understand, I could tell by his body language it was all good news. Sweat Bead had secured Rob's transfer back to the jail and out of Cipinang. It was to happen after the weekend "for sure". Despite the win, I really wasn't in the mood to stick around as it had been another long and weird day, but Lorenzo told me that I had to stay as a sort of respectful gesture to Sweat Bead. This stay involved listening to him do karaoke, singing some awful Indonesian pop songs without any real singing talent. The legal team let their hair down and started partying, posing for photos with me shortly after, arms around me with big grins, flashing disco lights going around me in the booth. I could not be fucked with any of it. As I politely sat there, screaming on the inside, I lifted my head and noticed there was a mirror directly pointing in front of me. As I made direct eye contact with my reflection, whilst the corrupt legal team were getting a bit wild with excitement around me, and one of the most prominent judges in a foreign city's legal system crooned for me on karaoke, I thought to myself, how out of hand has my life become, seriously?

Saturday 17th May 2014

I finally caved in and met Lorenzo for a weekend drink outside of Rob's case, thinking I would give him a chance to prove he wasn't a complete spazz. He has drunk off two beers and annoyed me the whole time we were together. He told me he could move the empty bottles of beer with his mind, but didn't want to show off. He had his moments of being okay, but overall, he loved the sound of his own voice, and it was too much of a one-way conversation to be of any fun. I was glad when his wife called asking where he was and said he had to go home. Interesting side note that wives are the bosses of men wherever you are in the world.

CHAPTER NINE

Tuesday 20th May 2014

The weekend had well passed, and it was early morning. Knowing Rob was due his transfer today back to the jail, I made my way to there and dropped off a load of food and water ready for his arrival. All the guards I had not seen for nearly two weeks were there, and they looked puzzled to see me here again.

"No Robert", They said, and I tried to tell them in my limited use of Bahasa that he was due back.

"Robert kembali dekat!" I said to them, but through lack of a common language, I couldn't convey the message across. They still took the bags of stuff though, probably thinking it was a gift for them.

Just as I was leaving Lorenzo called me to say there was terrible news and Rob wouldn't be getting transferred today. I thought, here we are, this is Rimbo all over again, get out hopes up, take our money, and deliver nothing. I made my way across Jakarta to discuss in person what was going on. When I arrived, Lorenzo was sat there with Sweat Bead and said things weren't good. Apparently, earlier in the day, the police had called Sweat Bead to discuss the bribes when he was "in a sensitive area", and someone had overheard the conversation. It seemed farfetched, and I didn't believe a single word, but now apparently news had got to the prosecution office, and it spooked them into doing the transfer. Either way, more money was now needed for the transfer back to jail. I called folks in England to tell them the news, and they said, "It's Rimbo all over again!", which is exactly what I'd said. They weren't asking for a bit more either, but literally thousands. We were told by Lorenzo that we needed a decision today and if we didn't pay more, then the money we had already paid would be lost. I decided I wanted to see Rob so we could discuss options, and it was a visiting day so still had time to get to the penitentiary.

I got back to Cipinang, shuddering to be back here again. I was alarmed to see Rob in a state again. We had paid for him to spend days in the medical bay, but over the weekend the guards just decided to take the money and throw him back into the snake pit. He looked worse than I'd ever seen him. Lorenzo told me to explain the current situation with my better use of English to Rob, and Rob was pissed off. Once again, the seating area was packed with inmates and crying visitors, it was hot and humid, and the band that played too loud were on.

"I thought the move was happening today!" Rob said, trying to be overheard by a guitar solo, "We've paid money for what?!" Directing his anger Lorenzo, who appeared offended by it,

"I am not fucking Rimbo, man, I am here to help you". Rob looked defeated.

"So what do you want from us?" to which Lorenzo replied, saying around the same amount of money that you could by a half-decent car with. His family said they would only send more money if he had been moved today as promised. Lorenzo began clutching at straws.

"Tell your family you have already been transferred, then she will send us the cash" Rob was outraged,

"You want me to lie to my own family?!" We weren't getting anywhere. I have to admit this was one of the lowest times of the whole ordeal so far. Do we lose the money we had already paid or take yet another risk with another potential scam?

Rob told me to call his family outside the prison and beg them to stump the money up. Lorenzo was asking for a lot, but Rob said it would effectively be his money, and therefore his gamble. He was just desperate to get out of there, plain and simple. The family said okay, but couldn't get that much together in such a short time. We had been rinsed out by Rimbo, so no one knew what we were going to do for money. We told Rob we'd try our best to gather all the cash together in a short period of time.

I parted ways from Lorenzo outside Cipinang and sat in a taxi home, not knowing how we'd raise the money, as it started to rain hard. I looked through the steamy window of the taxi whilst it crawled in traffic, watching the rain bounce off the ground and everything seemed absolutely hopeless.

A few hours later, Lorenzo rang and said that he was so confident that the transfer back to the jail would happen if he got the cash together, he decided to take a loan out himself, and we could pay him back. Well, I couldn't argue with that. Fair enough!

Wednesday 21th May 2014

That evening the money cleared and was in the correct corrupt hands. Rob was "definitely getting moved tomorrow" we kept getting told. Rob rang me from a smuggled prison phone that evening and said couldn't take any more of it in there, and this needed to work. We were told 10 AM was the time the transfer out of Cipinang would take place, myself and those at home crossed our fingers.

Thursday 22nd May 2014

10 AM came and went. Nothing. 1 PM, no news. I headed to the jail to drop more supplies for Rob off as Lorenzo instructed. As I was walking through the car park, coming towards me, I was horrified to spot the guy who was interrupting me when we were grilling Rimbo a few weeks back, the horrible old smelly piss-wizard. I was not in the mood to talk to him in the slightest, the last thing I wanted right now was to talk about fingering his American mate in a hot car park. Pre-empting the arising situation, I reached for my phone and pretended to speak on it, so when I actually came face to face, I would be able just to smile and walk past. The plan worked fine until metres from him, the phone rang in my hand as I was pretending to talk down it. I must have looked stupid, and it still didn't stop the wizard trying to fire up a conversation. It was Mel asking what I wanted to do for dinner tonight.

Around 3 PM, Lorenzo called, and I could tell he was excited.

"Good news, Rob has left Cipinang and is going back to the jail right now". I couldn't believe it. Everyone back home was ecstatic. We finally had a win.

Friday 23rd May 2014

I literally couldn't wait to see Rob back in the jail on Monday morning, nor the interior of it for that matter. Cipinang had put everything into context about how bad it could be here. The jail was still hot, dirty and unpleasant to look around, but it was all round a better vibe with both guards and inmates, and it wasn't worse than some of the bars I'd been since leaving England. I was looking forward to things to return "to normal". One of the conditions to Rob's return is that he had to shave his head completely. They'd had a bit of a go of it in Cipinang, but it all had to come off now. This included his beard, which was two and a half months old now and very gruff, but also his hair, which must have been pushing a foot long by now. Rob came out of the cells, and I couldn't believe it, he looked like a baby bird with his bald head. It was good seeing him smiling again, though. Many of Rob's inmate friends had left, but some were still there and treated him like a minor celebrity when he re-entered the building. Senta was still there, although preparing to move to Cipinang himself. He was no better than Rimbo I suppose, a little shithouse scamming others out of money, but I couldn't help liking him, and felt sorry knowing what was in store for him at Cipinang.

Wednesday 28th May 2014

Some days passed without any major news on our case, but people's lives who we had encountered were continuing on with their own stories. We'd sadly heard Senta was having a rough time in Cipinang. UGB hadn't been transferred anywhere, and he was still in Rob's cell. Whilst inmates around the world struggle to adjust with their time being incarcerated, for someone who's fallen from the greater height of fame and fortune like UGB, it would be an understandable shock. Despite sharing no common language, Rob took some pity on him and sparked up an unusual friendship which at one point involved UGB phoning his wife who spoke English – she was a famous Indonesian pop star – and gave Rob the phone, so they could talk. Rob also wrote him a letter of support whilst he was at his lowest, getting one of his friends to translate for him, which UGB absolutely loved. Of all the wild stuff me and Rob had been through since March, befriending an Indonesian celebrity and his pop star wife as just another day here.

Friday 13th June 2014

Lorenzo came into jail during visiting hours one day and sat down to talk, giving us our first proper plan in a while. The plan was to do the court dates without Henry realising, who was still being spun by the bribed officials as the victim, effectively just forwarding the court dates, so the "victim" didn't have time to prepare or testify against Rob. I thought that there mustn't be any chance of a fair trial here then as surely any court would see that punches were thrown by both sides that night, and this is a million-dollar nightclub, *surely* there was

CCTV around there? Luckily there were a few time-stamped photos of us at the airport on the flight before Bali, a couple of pictures of Rob's black eye back when this was all funny. We were told there were three court dates that we had a to slide under the radar and before Henry and his cronies had any chance to do anything about it. We were hoping to have the case done and resolved by the end of May, but the dates kept getting pushed further and further back which Lorenzo said was out of his control. The most important thing was though, was that we did them earlier than the originally scheduled dates. I loved the idea of Henry turning up at the courts just to find out Rob was already back in England. Also, the British embassy commented during a phone call in all their years operating in Indonesia that they had never heard of someone getting transferred back to the jail from Cipinang.

"It's usually a one-way street", a representative told me, "You must truly know incredibly connected people to get this done". I guess Lorenzo wasn't a total bullshitter after all, so his plan for the courts looked promising.

I met up with some of my local friends for a pool party with Mel. I hadn't seen most of them in over a month, busy with all this ongoing situation. They were all really keen to talk about the case, and I had to tell them to drop it. There was no escaping it, even in my free time. Compounding my low feeling, I was running really low on money again, my cash had been getting jumbled up with what was getting sent over from the UK into my account, then going into brown envelopes, plus everything that I was spending on taxis and to an extent Rob's food, even with a lot of financial support from his family, it had begun to mount up. My finances were a mess.

Monday 16th June 2014

A genuine court day had arrived. I was just as anxious as Rob. We met in jail first thing in visiting and ran Rob through the plans. Lorenzo told Rob to be ready for 10 AM, we should have known this wasn't going to happen on time, no one is on time in Indonesia, no one more so than Ipin the lawyer, who missed the flight from East Java to be here. This wasn't a big problem though, we were told, Rob was just going to have his charges read to him then he would be sent back to the jail. Myself and Lorenzo left on his bike, whilst Rob was transferred in the jail's security van.

I recognised the building we arrived at, we had been here briefly on the day we tried to stop Rob getting moved to Cipinang. It was the big posh building at the front, with the courtrooms beyond the entrance, and deeper into that which I hadn't seen on my first visit, the holding areas, huge black bars across the cells. There were four separate cells, most of which were crammed with inmates, all of which appeared ready for their own court hearings today. I felt sorry looking at the inmates, whether or not they were guilty or not, seeing other people in such poor conditions, still trying their best to look half decent for their moment in court, fighting a system that would not work in their favour if they didn't have money. Some of the guys looked really poor too and couldn't even afford a white shirt, one guy stood there with scruffy hair, in a t-shirt and flip-flops, arms resting through the bars. Adjacent to the cells ran a seating area where visitors could wait around. Outside was a TV displaying the prisoner's names and what time they were due up in court. Interestingly, Rob's name wasn't on any of the TVs.

"I have organised this" beamed Lorenzo, "Everybody works, so Rob's case is under the radar, Henry's family does not know Rob is in court today". Nice touch with the TV there! The atmosphere was surprisingly calm. Rob stood at the bars with a white shirt, trousers and shoes on. He was genuinely buzzing, I think mainly because his case was finally moving along after over three months of being sat in a cell. He was doing little dances, and we were cracking jokes. After maybe a couple of hours of us waiting around, he was escorted to one of the courtrooms and remained in a seat at the back whilst other prisoners moved around. Lorenzo and I had to hang back in the waiting area for a bit.

Sat on a bench, anxiousness increasing waiting for Rob's court session to begin, Lorenzo came bounding back after going to the toilet.

"Man, do you know what the victim looks like", clearly anxious. Yeah, I did, I had seen a couple of photos of Henry back at Rimbo's place in that big file a couple of months ago, but would I recognise his face now? I offered to go and look for him "Okay, well go to reception and see if it is him", Lorenzo continued. No way he could be here now, could he? After all that big talk from Lorenzo? I walked in the direction that he pointed me towards, passing a group of people in the process. One of them absolutely looked like Henry. "Henry" glanced at me, we made eye contact, and he stared at me for a split second, and he turned away. It was a look almost like he recognised me. I looped my way back through the court's corridors as not to make it obvious and then back to Lorenzo, and told him I was pretty sure it was him. He couldn't believe it.

"Are you sure man? You need to be sure" I wasn't 100% but was pretty confident. I looked over and could see the same group of people had arrived outside the room Rob was in. The guy that looked like Henry began making a punching gesture towards his face as if explaining something to the four men in suits, I presumed which of who were lawyers.

"It has to be him" I whispered to Lorenzo "He's making punching gestures to his face!" as if he was explaining something to the suited-up men. Somehow they had found out the court date had been moved up. It wasn't news to us these guys were connected, so in hindsight, we shouldn't have been the least bit surprised that they had found out about the court date. One thing I noticed though looking at the little gimp for the first time, we'd told from the police he'd been in a coma and left permanently blind. If that was true, he must have made a miraculous recovery as he stood there looking as fit as a fiddle. I could see with my own eye for definitive proof that we had been lied to about the severity of this case the whole time.

We were ushered into the courtroom, myself and Lorenzo sat behind Rob. The room set-up was similar to one found in England, with a large wooden bench where the judge sits, a prosecution member to the right on lower seating and then the regular benches at the rear for everyone involved with the case, as well as the public and in some cases the press. It was a lot smaller than ones at home though, almost a bit claustrophobic, although this was probably just my nerves getting to me. I told Rob that it looked like Henry had turned up, he pondered it for a second, then said,

"Fuck them, let's give them a fight". That's the spirit mate! I looked to my left and could see Henry and his suited up legal team, joined now by what looked like his father and girlfriend, all dressed smart, looking relaxed and laughing. On our side, we had Rob's team: Fat Lorenzo and me, both looking sweaty and worried. Herny turning up had really wobbled Lorenzo's confidence, and it had started to wobble mine too.

Rob was called up to sit in a chair, stationed centre of the courtroom with a translator next to him. I was so nervous I felt unwell, it might as well have been me sat in that chair. Rob's charges were read to him, and he either had to agree or disagree with the version of events on the night of the altercation which

Henry had presented to the police. He of course objected. The court was surprised no lawyer had shown up on Rob's behalf who was still elsewhere in Java. It was embarrassing. I wasn't able to really hear much of what was being said, but it was mainly Rob confirming his identity and the outline of the case. It was over in thirty minutes. Lorenzo said the coming sessions were due to get more intense, though. We had a few minutes with Rob outside the courtroom and arranged to meet tomorrow to discuss plans. Other prisoners from the cells recognised Rob, some were from Cipinang or the jail and were shouting hello to him, his minor celebrity status in the prison system here clear to see.

Chapter Ten

Overactive adrenal gland
in a foreign land

Tuesday 17th June 2014

There wasn't really much that had gone on while visiting Rob in jail other than discussing the events of yesterday at the court. I wanted to know more about what I couldn't hear at the time, but it appeared I hadn't missed much. Lorenzo didn't show for visiting, but he called my phone late evening to tell me about everything that had gone on behind the scenes today; which corrupt people had been bribed, which police were involved, the net closing in around Rimbo and what gun he was going to use on his heart, the usual stuff that went over my head. Mel and I were in my kosan, lying in bed together, listening to him talk on my phone's loudspeaker. During the call, I noticed there was a strange echo on the line. I told him I could hear this echo, and he quickly shouted something in Bahasa.

"Do you know what he just said then?" Mel whispered to me,

"What do you think?" I replied sarcastically.

"He's just shouted whoever's tracing the call needs to stop, he knows who's listening in on the call". The echo subsided for a minute as soon as he'd said it, and then came back after about a minute or two. Then he put the phone down abruptly. Someone was tracing the call? Who? Who the fuck was listening? Police? Henry's family? The press? Rimbo? No question my brain was scrambled from three months of dodgy dealings with dodgy characters, relying too much upon alcohol to switch off, mixed with a constant lack of sleep and pressure to do everything I could to help– I was paranoid. But let us get this straight: Why *wouldn't* someone be onto me? Christ knows I'd been involved with plenty of dodgy shenanigans over the past few months here, like they even needed valid evidence to bust me for them. I was meddling with powerful people here, corrupt ex-military generals, corrupt top-level judges, corrupt police and well-connected individuals that knew what fucking flight from Bali we were on. Or perhaps someone was closing the net on Lorenzo's dodgy dealings, and I was getting caught up with it? To have whoever it was monitoring my calls now was the tipping point. I made a panicked decision to leave the country as soon as possible, after a quick visit to Rob in the morning to give him what I could for money and food. Other than Mel, I told no one, not Rob nor anyone back home that I had plans to leave just in case I was being monitored. The remainder of the night I just spent holding Mel, the pair of us heartbroken, occasionally in tears, that it was coming to an end so abruptly.

Wednesday 18th June 2014

At 3 AM, I decided to book my flights. If anyone was tracing my activity, then I wanted to give them as little time as possible to prepare to get me. The small shop near my place was open 24 hours a day had excellent WiFi – paranoid my internet was being traced at my kosan I made my way there. Mel grabbed us a couple of drinks from the counter whilst I sat on my laptop, looking for the cheapest, quickest flight out of the city. One way to Singapore for $30, leaving in twelve hours. Bingo. As the time came to pay for my flights, I noticed the transaction wouldn't process, and then to my horror, I realised my debit card had been frozen. I rang my bank to ask what was going on. They informed me that I had used my card in a dodgy machine somewhere in the city and it was at risk of being cloned, so as a pre-emptive measure they cancelled it and posted a new card my address in England. I'd used my card all across Jakarta withdrawing massive amounts of money, so it was likely I'd used it somewhere questionable at some point. Whilst the foresight of my bank is marvellous, they didn't think to contact me about the cancellation, which was moronic seeing as every transaction I've made over the past year has been out of England – how am I supposed to access my money now? I was effectively locked here in the country. I had about 100,000 in Rupiah on me in cash, around £5. Mel's debit card was at her parents', miles away. After some time on hold, my bank said they would lift the block for half an hour which they kept reiterating to me that it's rare for them to do it. It gave me enough time to book the flight and to withdrawn the last I had available in my account, enough for spends for taxis and food, and the remainder for Rob to cover him until his family got out here. My bank account was now depleted.

I didn't sleep. I sat on my bed chain-smoking for the rest of the night, waiting for the clock to count down, expecting the door to be kicked in by the police or someone. My head was so fried that as I stared at the walls, they would move around slightly like I'd eaten magic mushrooms. As soon as I could leave the room, I stocked up on water and food and prepared to visit Rob for the last time at the jail. Rob had requested his phone back since he got back to the jail. It had since been sat in my kosan, but he needed it now more than ever if I was going to leave him here by himself. I put some credit on and hid it in my sock ready for my definite last time ever of smuggling something into a foreign jail. The guards on shift today, by sod's law, were almost all a new set of men I had never seen before. At first, they wouldn't accept my driver's license as ID, despite me using it every time before now.

"You passport?" one shouted at me, as I nervously tried to give them the driver's license again.

"Aku menunjungi lalu! Tidak masalah!" I fumbled for the little Indonesian I'd picked up. Whether it made sense, or they didn't want to spend any more time dealing with the agitated foreigner, I don't know, either way, the driver's license was now good enough. They then instructed me to empty the contents of my pockets into a tray, this being your declaration you don't have anything else on you before you pass into the jail, and had been a standard process on previous visits. My wallet, phone and keys left in the tray, I proceeded to walk through, but for the first time ever they stopped me, instructing me to wait and then began giving me a physical search. What the hell is this? I couldn't believe it, there was both a phone and a charger in my sock. I'm definitely going to get caught here! What are my options, will these guys accept a bribe as well when they find it on me? They stopped the pat-down just above the knees, inches away from the contraband.

I needed a minute to compose myself before pressing through to visiting after that close scrape. I sat underneath the camera in visiting again so I could pass the phone and money to Rob without getting caught. Our last visiting time together was half an hour of anguish. I told Rob I was leaving today as someone had been monitoring mine and Lorenzo's call last night. He was sad but understood why I was leaving and that I'd done more than my fair share of work here. I handed the smuggled phone and notes of cash discreetly when the guard was looking away. It wasn't a lot, it would barely last a fortnight, but it would be enough to tide him over until his family got out here to take over. Sat next to us was a woman hugging an inmate, and she was positively bawling her eyes out, which set the tone for us really. This was emotional. I had initially vowed to stay with Rob until this was over, but three months in with no end in sight and financially drained, I had to leave and get someone else to take over for my own health and sanity. I saw him walking into the cells, and that was the last time I saw him in Indonesia.

I needed to get out of here now, to that airport and onto my freedom. As a one last "Fuck you" from the city, I rushed into a shop to buy some water, and I accidentally pushed the glass door at the entrance instead of pulling. It cracked the door right across and gave me a deep cut in my hand. With blood dripping on the floor, the shop owners wouldn't let me go until the door was paid for. This was a little shop, two minutes' walk from my kosan, and I considered just running away. Losing them in the nest of alleyways and roads would have been easy if they followed, but I decided it was too risky, the last thing I needed now was any trouble. They agreed to follow me to my place to meet Mel, relying on her to translate for me. She pleaded that I was a poor backpacker on a budget and they should have some sympathy. The settled with what little money I had on me shy of enough for the taxi to the airport. I hugged Mel for the last time and got into the taxi. I didn't know when I would see her again, she had been my constant support throughout this. I was leaving her now without the proper goodbye I wanted, as the tears started for us both, this moment ruined by urgently needing to leave the country.

Singapore City – 18th June 2014

Before my flight, I had messaged Jack telling him I was leaving Indonesia in a hurry. I asked if I could stay at his apartment for a few days whilst I worked out my plans, apologising for the short notice. I had no idea what he would say nor what if I turned up and said "no". From my visit with Jen a few months back I knew the city could be expensive and with what I had on me it wouldn't be enough to be able to buy a meal, never mind a room for the night. Singapore is on par with prices back home. It was only a mere shipping port in a region of developing countries, then in the 1960s decided to transform itself, embarking on a modernisation programme. The decision paid off as it's now one of the biggest economies in the world for its size (it's only a small island), with living standards head and shoulders above its regional neighbours. In hindsight, it was probably a poor choice coming to this place with less than a tenner in my pocket.

Once I landed, I logged on to airport's WiFi, anxiously waiting for a response. I should have had no doubt about Jack's generosity, he had been great in Borneo, and now I received: "No problem. Stay as long as you like". I took a taxi to his place, my mind feeling like it was stuffed with cotton wool, numb from tiredness and stress. It was nice to see a new skyline as the taxi carted me across the city, feeling some relief thinking I was somewhere new and out of the mess. The taxi driver, a man in his late sixties who looked youthful for his age, asked where I was from and what was I doing in the city.

"Leaving problems", I said semi-joking as I clocked the taximeter numbers speeding up, well past the money I had available. Jack had kindly lent me the money to pay for the taxi when I arrived outside his apartment. It was good to see Jack again, a familiar face I was able to count on.

I needed to eat something decent, a proper meal for the first time in days was well overdue. Luckily, residential areas in Singapore have brilliant little food courts conveniently located within them, which offer cheap and tasty food, and there was one across the road from Jack's place. Sat down eating Chinese style duck and noodles, I told him what had happened since the last time we'd seen each other back in April with Jen. Meeting other friends over my time in Jakarta I didn't want to talk about it but being free from the country and being away from it all now, I couldn't stop talking about it. I wondered if Jack thought I was making some of the past three months up, as repeating it did sound a bit mad. He had his own drama going on at the minute, although mild in comparison. Putting the hours in, staying back late in the office one night, he'd caught two of his managers at work shagging in a quiet room and was worried if they would deploy tactics against him to keep him quiet. Everyone's problems are relative, I guess, and I thought that was quite an amusing situation he was in there. Although my friend was still in jail, my personal problems seemed to evaporate. I slept for hours that night in Jack's spare room, comforted by the lack of threat that police could barge through my door, nor having Lorenzo pestering at all hours. It was so peaceful and safe, yet ironically in Henry's home country, and I feel asleep seconds after my head hit the pillow.

Over the next few days, I stayed around Singapore, figuring out what my next steps were, mainly resting and eating, enjoying all the free time that had opened up. I was able to go for a leisurely run which I hadn't done since Australia, and I ran for hours, getting all of the pent up frustration out. All that smoking as a means to unwind had done a number on my lungs, up to forty a day when things were really kicking off. I sat on a curb, coughing up phlegm after a few minutes. I did what I could to help with the case in the meantime, still passing occasional messages from the embassy, England and Lorenzo, but it was a fraction of the time compared to what I had been doing in Indonesia. It took Lorenzo a few days to realise I was in Singapore, which I kind of liked, for all the crap he had been telling me it was nice to keep him in the dark on something for once. My mum had sent me another loan out, enabling me to get a few plans together on my last few days on the continent. I'd booked flights – home of course – but with a detour of a final few days in Koh Phangan for Mel and me. There was no chance I was just going straight home after everything that I'd been through. I deserved some sort of break. I wanted to go to the place that I started this trip on, with the most important person I'd met on my time out here, to get that proper goodbye I wanted.

On the ferry heading towards the island a few days later, I could faintly see it on the horizon through the haze, and it reminded me of leaving here fourteen months ago, nervous and heading away by myself having just left Liggy. I had changed in such a relatively short space of time, physically and mentally, here now with my new partner, too. No one could have predicted how much of a wild ride this trip this ended up being, or the impact it would have on my life.

I wouldn't say the story had a particularly happy ending for Rob, but an ending, nonetheless. The court had initially based their case on Henry's testimony claiming Rob had assaulted him and ran off, showing no remorse. Rob was able to discredit this and prove the events that had happened that night. As a witness, bar staff were also able to confirm that Rob had been hit (because a time-stamped photo of him with a black eye we managed to obtain wasn't enough!), and both bar staff and the night club security, who were there when the events spilled outside into the car park, confirmed that Rob was apologetic, and the vulnerable one. Despite proving all this in court, he was still looking at a five-year sentence at first. Whether it was down to bribes, sympathy, or a combination of both, the judges gave him eight months. Whilst Lorenzo did deliver a result eventually for the case after I left, the absurd situations as a Westerner dealing with the Indonesian judicial system continued. They are from this point, however, not my story to tell.

I returned home in July, entering a mild depression for the first few months. I couldn't adjust to life being so normal at first. I had left Rob and Mel behind in Asia and come home to financial debt. My arrival back in England, having not seen most of my friends and family in almost a year and a half was somewhat anticlimactic, I had planned a big return party but had cancelled it as it didn't feel right without Rob there. I had taken a fair bit from the experience though, the naivety of how myself and everyone back home dealt with the situation initially, to fully come to realising out there that anything goes. I couldn't believe there were people like Rimbo in the world. He looked old and walked like a chimp, yet had a crafty, evil mind, that was able to take advantage of people in a vulnerable position. I realised too that whilst not perfect, British law is still pretty good in comparison, and isn't to be taken for granted. It's something that had never even crossed my mind before this, it's just a given coming from

England you have a working and relatively efficient law system. Of course, there is some corruption here, but as far as I know, you can't pay for someone to do time, and you can generally expect a fair sentence for a crime. Likewise, a big lesson for me was if you're tied up in the law in a foreign country, being British doesn't matter, but sometimes being rich does. Had it put me off Asia, or more specifically, Indonesia? Absolutely not. In fact, I want to emphasise here that you should travel there at least once in your life time. It's a brilliant country, the people there are still the friendliest in the world, and the countryside is second to none. Likewise, I don't want to leave the impression that everyone working in authoritative positions are corrupt, we met honest police and others higher ups, most trying their best to help us in their small ways. I have since spent many months at a time there, having initially dared to return a year later. I just have a deeper understanding of how Indonesian law somehow functions.

Time went on, I got back into work, Rob came home, and everyone started moving on with their lives again. Mel and I sustained a long-distance relationship, her moving even further away to Australia for some time until she permanently moved to England. We got married in May 2016, exactly two years to the day I asked her out.

Despite everything that had happened, it hadn't put me off getting back out there to see more of the world. After getting my shit back in order, I was back on the road, but this time joined with my new wife. Some would argue that at least Rob's ball and chain had a time limit on it.

Printed in Great Britain
by Amazon

71117358R00129